The records left by the ceramic art have furnished keys to many a secret which would otherwise remain locked. They reflect manners, customs, taste of the times to which they belong and by their help we may not only therefore study the present but if we choose enter a wide gateway to the past . . . .

from LIPPINCOTT'S MAGAZINE,

1876

Official White House China

1789 TO THE PRESENT

Margaret Brown Klapthor

SMITHSONIAN INSTITUTION PRESS

CITY OF WASHINGTON

1975

Smithsonian Institution Press Publication Number 4826

Printed by the Imprimeries Réunies S.A. Lausanne, Switzerland
A Helvetica Press Production

Distributed in the United States and Canada by George Braziller, Inc.
Distributed throughout the rest of the world by Feffer and Simons, Inc.

Support for the publication of this volume was provided
by The Barra Foundation

Designed by Stephen Kraft
First edition

Frontispiece: *Wall cupboard in the Smithsonian Institution's First Ladies
Hall displaying pieces of the banquet service purchased by President
Washington from Comte de Moustier*

Library of Congress Cataloging in Publication Data

Klapthor, Margaret Brown.
   Official White House china: 1789 to the present.
   Includes bibliographical references.
   1. Porcelain—Washington, D.C. 2. Washington,
D.C. White House. I. Title.
NK4427.W3K55   738'.074'0153   74-6171
ISBN 0-87474-135-1

*Unless otherwise credited, all pieces of china illustrated are in
the collections of the Smithsonian Institution's National Museum of
History and Technology.*

Contents

Foreword

My interest in beautiful tableware began in childhood. I can remember my grandmother's lovely Haviland china, which she used on formal occasions. My mother's well-appointed table was a source of pride to her and a pleasure to her family.

When the General and I came to live in the White House in 1953, it was an experience that gave me no time to think about the things one usually is concerned with in a new home. That came later.

I soon learned to love the President's House. I wanted to make it not only a home for our family, but a source of pride and an example of gracious living for everyone in the United States as well as for visitors from abroad. So I began to think of what I could do to add to the enjoyment of those who might pass through it.

I soon found that many presidential wives had ordered chinaware for the president's table. Remains of these were retained in the White House, but they had never been studied, cataloged, or exhibited.

A collection had been started in the 1890s by Mrs. Benjamin Harrison—who herself painted china—but it lacked pieces representing five administrations, for no official state china had been purchased by Presidents Andrew Jackson, William Howard Taft, Warren G. Harding, Calvin Coolidge, or Herbert Hoover. It seemed sad that these names were missing in the White House collection; but since several other presidents were represented by their personal china, I felt that the collection would be enhanced by the addition of china owned by these presidential families.

It was my privilege to arrange for this to be done, so that examples could be seen and enjoyed by visitors in the pine-paneled room prepared for such purposes when the White House was renovated in 1952. When this was finally accomplished in 1959, it gave me tremendous satisfaction to see the collection completed.

As you now see it, the china exhibit at the White House recalls the history of the United States from its beginning as a Nation. Today, the White House has pieces used by every president from George Washington through Richard M. Nixon.

Shortly after I had decided on this project, I realized that professional advice was needed to assure proper identification. I then learned of the research on presidential china already being done at the Smithsonian Institution, and it was from that Institution that the author of this book came into the picture. From the day that I first met her, Mrs. Margaret Klapthor, curator at the Smithsonian's National Museum of History and Technology, has given willingly of her time and knowledge to assist us, and through this collaboration the china collections of both the White House and the Smithsonian have been vastly improved. The Smithsonian lent to the White House some pieces not represented in our collection, and we in turn sent them pieces needed to fill out the collection exhibited there. This arrangement has been so satisfactory that, I am happy to say, it has continued to the present day.

In the 1950s our efforts at the White House had been handicapped by a lack of an authoritative reference work on presidential china. This book by Margaret Klapthor answers the questions we then asked. It is not only a basic reference and a definitive study, but a labor of love—the happy result of this cooperation over the years. It will, I am sure, be a boon to historians and collectors alike.

I am most pleased to be associated with her book on this particular subject.

Mamie Doud Eisenhower

March 28, 1974

Introduction

The house in which the president of the United State lives has always had a great fascination for the people of this country. This interest is prompted by the psychological climate of a democracy which makes every American citizen feel that he has a personal ownership of the house.

The style in which the president is permitted to live, however, used to be determined by the money appropriated in Congress for this purpose. This appropriation comes from public funds which the people have provided by taxes. Small wonder that the citizens have considered the President's House their own and have taken such a great interest in its furnishings beginning with the administration of President George Washington. It is only within the last decade that gifts of furnishings to the mansion have influenced the style in which the president lives.

Through the years this public interest has created a climate in which every expenditure for the President's House made from public funds has been examined with care, debated at length in the Congress, and extravagantly praised or vigorously denounced depending on either the politics of the speaker or his own personal taste or both. The written record can be found in the newspapers of the period, in the records of the debates in Congress, and in the acts of Congress. It is also found it the wry comments left in diaries and letters in the presidential papers. Gossips and social historians give us a glimpse of the intense interest that the people of the City of Washington and the rest of the country took in the way the house was furnished. Beginning with the day John Adams first moved into the President's House at 1600 Pennsylvania Avenue, invitations to it were coveted and the fortunate person who went there was expected to share his impressions with family, friends, and neighbors back home. Because hospitality is so bound up in ceremonial eating and drinking, these accounts usually included some description, even if meager, of the type of food which was served and the manner and ware in which it was served. This interest in food and the dishes of the Executive Mansion has a very real expression in the collections of White House china which began to be assembled in the last half of the nineteenth century and continues to be collected today.

The collections have come about because Congress from the very beginning until into the twentieth century had made possible a way for the public to acquire articles used in the President's House. The act of March 3, 1797, granting John Adams funds for furnishing his house also gave him permission to sell things that were worn out, out of style, or unusable—quaintly styled "decayed furniture"—with the privilege of adding any such money acquired to the so-called "furniture fund." The authorization for sale, often at public auction, gave the people a chance to buy the furnishings which public funds had provided for the president's household.

By the middle of the nineteenth century, china was most sought after at these periodic auctions and then cherished by the persons who acquired it. Often the purchaser had only a sketchy idea of the administration in which the piece had been used in the President's House, but the fact that it had been used there was indisputable and reason enough for the piece to become a rare family possession. The lack of mobility of nineteenth-century Americana has resulted in a heavy concentration of these early collections in the Washington area.

In 1876, for the first time, presidential china which had been privately collected from White House sales was included in an auction sale of the "Governor Caleb Lyon Collection of Oriental and Occidental Ceramics" held at the gallery of Henry D. Miner in New York City. The printed catalog list of the pieces offered for sale is headed "Presidential Porcelain" followed by an explanation that "the following porcelain has been used by the different Presidents and includes specimens from all the sets purchased by Congress at various times to refurnish the White House; some of the Presidents provided their own china or used that which was left by their predecessors in office." The list from that sale, from numbers 823 to 858, describes the china in such detail that it is easy to recognize the known presidential services even though many are attributed to the wrong administrations.[1]

The next indications in print of the growing interest of the general public in the subject of presidential china are two articles written for *The Ladies Home Journal* in 1889 by Theodore R. Davis, the artist who designed the state china for the administration of President Rutherford B. Hayes.[2]

The White House staff and the presidential families who lived there apparently did not feel that they should preserve pieces of various china services as a White House collection because of their historical importance. Probably the money acquired by the sale of the china was more important then than the china itself. It is known that the china was personally collected at the auctions by members of the staff, and pieces of presidential china turn up with great frequency in the presidential house museums scattered throughout the country.

Mrs. Benjamin Harrison was the first presidential wife who was particularly interested in the china still to be found in the storerooms of the White House when the Harrisons moved there in 1889. Her interest was a personal one. She was one of the growing number of American women who painted china as a hobby. She also had a love of American history which had been strengthened by the great wave of patriotic fervor produced by the celebration of the centennial of the United States in 1876. Her interest in American history was also politically expedient as her husband had come into office on a platform of "America first," advocating high tariff to protect American industry while publicizing the superiority of America's products.

Mrs. Harrison channeled her interest in the history of the United States into an involvement with the objects which are the three-dimensional expression of this history. In her years in the White House, she made a persistent search for furniture, accessories, and other articles associated with the house and succeeded in doing a great deal toward their preservation. One of her cherished ambitions was to save for posterity some specimens of the presidential china and plate still in the house. It was her plan to have a cabinet built in the state dining room to

display the china, but she was unable to do so because of her illness and death during the last year of her husband's administration. Though Mrs. Harrison was not able to complete her plan, public interest in the china had been awakened.

The book *China Collecting in America* by Alice Morse Earle which was published in 1892 contains a chapter on George and Martha Washington's china and one on presidential china. The chapter on presidential china, per se, is the first time that the subject was treated in a book. It repeats much of what Theodore Davis wrote in the magazine articles in 1889; however, it is useful for the information it gives on the market value of the china at that date, and the names of persons who then owned examples of the china.[3]

In 1900 Theodore A. Bingham became the commissioner of public buildings and grounds, and in this capacity he had responsibility for the care and repair of the President's House and its furniture including the preparation of a periodic inventory of all public property in and belonging to the mansion. He found in making the inventory that there was comparatively little china left in the house which had been used in previous administrations. Before his appointment as superintendent, Colonel Bingham had served as military aide in the American embassies in Berlin and Rome. While at these posts, he was impressed with the care and veneration given to royal palaces and their furnishings and felt this care was lacking at the President's House in the United States.

Colonel Bingham expressed his feelings to Mrs. Abby Gunn Baker at a chance meeting during the summer of 1901. Mrs. Baker was a journalist who specialized in articles on historical subjects. He suggested her doing a story about the presidential china in the White House in the hope that the interest engendered would lead to its preservation. According to Mrs. Baker, he said that "if somebody does not do that pretty soon, there won't be any left to preserve." [4]

Mrs. Baker was delighted with the opportunity and told him that before such an article could be written, she would have to make a thorough study of the ware that was and had been in the house and also of the records concerning it. Colonel Bingham got the necessary permission from Mrs. McKinley. It was arranged that Mrs. Baker should come to the White House that summer, while the family was away, to make whatever study was necessary. She spent the next four months working not only in the White House on the surviving china, but also in the files of the Treasury Department and other government agencies where pertinent records were kept.

Like all later researchers in this same subject, Mrs. Baker was handicapped by the meager details given in the official records. The president's assassination at the end of that summer put an end to Mrs. Baker's research, but fortunately she had already gathered enough material to do the first definitive article ever written on the subject. It appeared in *Munsey's Magazine* in December 1903.[5]

By this time, Col. Thomas W. Symons had succeeded Colonel Bingham as commissioner of public buildings and grounds. Colonel Symons showed the Baker article to Mrs. Theodore Roosevelt and "The White House China Collection" was launched. Mrs. Roosevelt, who, like Mrs. Harrison, had always taken a great interest in American history and felt the obligation of being First Lady keenly, ordered two cabinets to be made in the lower east corridor of the mansion where they could be seen by visitors. She then had Colonel Symons ask Mrs. Baker to come to the White House to choose the pieces of china to be displayed in the cabinets.

Mrs. Baker chose examples of Mrs. Roosevelt's new dinner service, a few miscellaneous pieces belonging to the McKinley and Cleveland administrations, pieces of the handsome state china designed by Mrs. Harrison, miscellaneous pieces from the Arthur administration, nine pieces of the Hayes service including the turkey platter, pieces of the Grant state china, and six pieces of the Lincoln china.

Soon after the china was placed in the cabinets, President Theodore Roosevelt stopped to admire the pieces. He was so enthusiastic about it that he directed Colonel Symons and Mrs. Baker to continue to add to the collection until it contained some ware representative of every presidential administration.

This began Mrs. Baker's association with the collection which was to last until her death in 1923. She publicized the search in the public press, descendants of the presidents were contacted, and contributions were sought openly. Nothing was to be bought, for Mrs. Roosevelt's instructions were that pieces must be either given or loaned. In an effort to form a collection representing every administration, Mrs. Baker and Mrs. Roosevelt accepted china that was privately owned by the earlier presidents as well as that purchased with government funds. Mrs. Roosevelt had the collection made official government property and placed with other White House furnishings under the care of the commissioner of public buildings and grounds to insure that it would be a permanent feature at the White House. This was the beginning of the collection displayed in the China Room at the White House today.

There is a glimpse about White House china in a letter Archie Butt, personal military aide to President Theodore Roosevelt, wrote to his sister-in-law, Clara Butt, on December 11, 1908.

I had a rather interesting time the last few days looking over the china at the White House with a view to destroying all that is chipped or broken in any way. Mrs. Roosevelt does not want it sold at auction, for she thinks this method cheapens the White House. I took the matter up with Bromwell [commissioner of public buildings and grounds] who really has it on his papers and is responsible for it, and he thought it ought to be sold and that it should be sold by private bids to cabinet officers and others who are connected with the White House in some way. In former years, it was regarded as the property of the mistress of the White House, who would give it away as she desired but Mrs. R. thinks it should never be given away—and it should not in my opinion for it is government property just the same as the furniture. If it were sold by private bids it would create an awful howl in the press should it become known and so I convinced all concerned that it should be broken up and scattered in the river, which will be done. When I think how I should value even one piece of it, it hurts to smash it, but I am sure it is the only right thing to do. . . .

I ran across one plate in a pawnshop the other day which, if I am rightly informed was one of the Grant set. The owner wanted fifty dollars for it. Sloan, the auctioneer tells me that he would be able to get from ten to fifty dollars for every plate which the White House would sell and badly broken pieces would bring something.[6]

The last paragraph of the letter expressed Captain Butt's idea of the involvement of the Smithsonian Institution in the collection being made at the White House.

Mrs. Roosevelt has collected nearly all the china of past administrations which is now in cabinets in the White House. She has had some pieces donated to her and others she has purchased at very high prices. Of course, she paid for them out of the contingent expenses of the White House and they belong to the Government, but if she had not interested herself in collecting what remained of the china of former administrations it is doubtful if it would ever have been done. In order to insure the continuance of their care she has donated them to the Smithsonian Institution, but to be kept in the White House crypt as long as it is desired to have them there. This means that the Smithsonian Institution is responsible for them and takes stock of the collection at regular intervals.

There is no record of the Smithsonian being offered the collection or the responsibility for it.

The collection was displayed in the downstairs corridor until the second Mrs. Woodrow Wilson decided it was endangered by the heavy traffic. She selected the room on the lower floor across from the foot of the stairway and had it equipped with built-in cabinets and glass doors.

Following the custom begun in the administration of President Theodore Roosevelt, all broken or defaced china had to be condemned, removed from the yearly inventory, and then destroyed. Mrs. Elizabeth Jaffray, housekeeper from the time of the Taft administration to that of President Coolidge, describes accumulated tubs of nicked and broken china, glass, and crystal which were smashed and dumped into the Potomac River so that no pieces would fall into the hands of collectors and souvenir hunters. She states that "every year when the inventory has been taken, the broken china and glassware have been destroyed."

Pieces of the state services ordered by Presidents Wilson, Franklin D. Roosevelt, and Harry Truman were added to the White House China Collection as soon as they were received at the White House. Following the renovation of the White House in the spring of 1952, the china-ware of the presidents was reinstalled in new cabinets in the same China Room.

Early in 1956, President and Mrs. Dwight D. Eisenhower selected a set of handsome service plates with a wide gold rim which could be used with any of the other state dinner services. It was the addition of these plates to the china collection and Mrs. Eisenhower's own love of beautiful china which prompted her great interest in the collection. With the assistance of a staff member of the Smithsonian Institution all of the pieces in the White House China Collection were carefully examined in 1957, and many of them were relabeled on the basis of research done by the Smithsonian staff.

Because the state china services used during the administrations of Presidents Andrew Johnson, Taft, Harding, Coolidge, and Hoover were purchased during earlier administrations and were more closely identified with other presidents, Mrs. Eisenhower subsequently added to the collection various pieces of personal china used by these presidents.

The interest of the Smithsonian Institution in presidential china began with pieces of china acquired in collections of presidential memorabilia. In 1955 this china was for the first time exhibited as a collection in the then newly renovated First Ladies Hall in the Smithsonian Institution's Arts and Industries Building. To classify the pieces and label them for the new exhibit, research was necessary. It soon became obvious that there was a great deal to be learned about the subject by using modern techniques and facilities available today. The information gathered was invaluable when Mrs. Eisenhower wished to improve the exhibition of the china collection at the White House. At her request, this writer spent several weeks at the White House helping the staff to identify and arrange the pieces in the collection. In return, the White House agreed to send to the Smithsonian Institution pieces of state services not then represented in the museum collection. As the China Room at the White House is not open to the general public and as the White House did not have the facilities or staff to answer the numerous public inquiries on the subject of White House china, it was agreed that the Smithsonian Institution could contribute significantly by acting as the public service agency in the area of the White House history.

When Mrs. John F. Kennedy became First Lady in 1961, her concern for the house and its furnishings prompted her to establish the position of curator of the White House and to appoint a Fine Arts Advisory Committee to assist her in her plans to restore the furnishings of the White House. In recognition of the fact that in years past there had been a continual loss of pieces of furniture, fixtures, and decorative objects associated with the White House through public auction, private sale and/or the generosity of the people who have lived in the House, Public Law 87-286 was passed at the request of Mrs. Kennedy and her committee. The law, approved September 22, 1961, provides in Section 2 that:

Articles of furniture, fixtures and decorative objects of the White House when declared by the President to be of historic or artistic interest, together with such similar articles, fixtures and objects as are acquired by the White House in the future when similarly so declared shall thereafter be considered to be inalienable and the property of the White House. Any such article, fixture or object when not in use or on display in the White House shall be transferred by direction of the President as a loan to the Smithsonian Institution for its care, study and storage or exhibition and such articles, fixtures and objects shall be returned to the White House from the Smithsonian on notice by the President.

Under the terms of the law, the president alone has the power to lend items to the Smithsonian Institution or to order their return to the White House.

With the establishment of the Office of the Curator of the White House during the administration of President Kennedy the public-service aspect of the relationship with the White House has understandably decreased, but the research done at the Smithsonian Institution continues to contribute materially to the work done in that office. Such a study as the one presented here was possible because of the co-operation of each of the curators of the White House and the members of their staff. Matching the china to the written record has proved to be a challenging task. What success has been achieved is due to the constant and continued examination of the surviving china as new records are found and evaluated.

This study began by encompassing the whole range of presidential china, both the china owned personally by the presidents and that which was purchased with government funds. Since the days of Alice Morse Earle and Abby Gunn Baker, it had been the generally held opinion that our earlier presidents had brought their own china to the President's House for official as well as personal use so that the china still to be found in family possession and presidential house museums could be considered White House china. The issue had been further confused, because Mrs. Baker—acting for Mrs. Roosevelt—had accepted such privately owned china for inclusion in the White House China Collection. The records being searched began to show the quantity of china purchased for the house with government funds for each administration beginning with President George Washington. It began to appear that there was very little reason to suppose that any of our presidents had used their own china while in office. President Washington who used his salary as an expense account did so. He felt that he personally owned anything purchased during his eight years in office. Others who might have used their personal china were those who had lived in rented residences in Washington during long careers of public service and who moved directly from such a residence to the President's House. There was also evidence of private purchases made by presidents in office for china to be taken home on their return to private life.

In an effort to clarify these confusing issues, *it seemed advisable to confine the scope of this study to china purchased for the President's House with public funds.* There are only a few instances where there is reference to privately owned presidential china, and these are well-documented private services—each of which has a particular reason for being included. Once the china purchased with public funds has been identified, it will then be possible to move into the broad area of all presidential china with greater understanding.

The limitation of scope to the recorded purchases has a second advantage. The vouchers are concrete evidence of many different facets of history. The places of purchase, the types of china being used, the pieces which make up a dinner service and its design, tell much about the material culture and the social customs of our country. The White House was buying the kind of china being purchased for other elegant homes in the United States, and the vouchers which had to be submitted to the Treasury Department offer an excellent opportunity to study a pattern of buying from the end of the eighteenth century to the present day and the changes of taste during the same period.

For the earlier administrations both the miscellaneous china purchased for general household use and the formal services are listed in some detail in this study, but as soon as the pattern of purchase becomes clear, repetitious details are no longer included. The term "state china" is used to refer to a banquet service purchased for use on state occasions such as the formal dinners given for members of Congress, foreign diplomats, and heads of states, and any other occasion which calls for a formal meal served in courses.

In addition to a state service, the First Lady often purchased less elegant china out of public funds for everyday use. Sometimes the only clue to distinguish between the state china and the less formal china is the number of pieces listed and the price paid for the china.

The term "china," used throughout this book, can be defined as both porcelain and earthenware used for table services at the Executive Mansion. The term acquired this meaning as early as 1889 when Theodore R. Davis wrote his first articles on "White House China" for *The Ladies Home Journal,* and it was continued by Abby Gunn Baker and the other writers of the early twentieth century. It is still in use today at the White House where the terms "China Room" and "The White House China Collection" include both porcelain and earthenware used on presidential tables from 1789 to the present.

It should be noted that over the years, the residence of the presidents has had various titles. The term "President's House" changed in the mid-nineteenth century when it began to be referred to as the "Executive Mansion." While this title is still used, the popular term "White House" became the legal name by an executive order of Theodore Roosevelt at the turn of the century.

Sources of Information

This study is primarily an exploration of the written records of the china purchased for the residence of the president and is an attempt to reconcile this written record with the surviving pieces of china. On the basis of those records, an attempt has been made to identify china which has an association with the President's House. The records are preserved in the National Archives, the official repository of all government records, but they are not to be found in any one single record group.

The money spent for china used in the President's House came from the so-called "furniture fund." This fund was always appropriated by an act of Congress when the administrations changed, but a special appropriation could be requested to meet any particular need which might arise while the president was in office. The act of Congress providing the money authorized expenditures from the fund by the president personally, but the president could delegate this authority to some member of his official household or to the government official whose job it was to take care of the public buildings and grounds in the City of Washington.

The procedure for spending the appropriated funds was to issue the money in treasury warrants to an authorized purchasing agent who had to account to the Treasury Department for the warrants he had received by submitting bills or vouchers certifying each expenditure. It is in these itemized vouchers that information can be found about the specific china bought during each administration.

The other source of information about the china used in the President's House is the surviving White House inventories. An inventory of the furniture and furnishings purchased with public funds was supposed to be taken at the end of each presidential administration so that the incoming president could identify and accept responsibility for the things in the house when he arrived. The records indicate that the inventories were taken as required, but only a few have survived in the public records. As the list went to the outgoing president, the incoming president, and the person in charge of the house, some of the missing inventories may still be located.

The absence of itemized bills and vouchers for expending the fund for the first fifteen years of the President's House is due in part to the fact that the Treasury Department was slow in setting up procedures to account for money spent from the public funds. George Washington's decision to use his salary as an expense account meant that he was purchasing household furnishings with his own money, so he did not have to submit any vouchers for purchases made during his administration. He did, however, delegate the expenditure of his money to his secretary so that in the account books kept by Tobias Lear some references are found to the china purchased for the president's household.

John Adams, himself, signed the warrants for the money in the furniture fund from 1797 to 1801, but no vouchers can be found for his expenditures. The inventory taken at the end of his administration, however, gives us an insight into the china he purchased.

Thomas Claxton, doorkeeper of the House of Representatives from 1794, was the first authorized agent for expenditures from the president's furniture fund. He was appointed in 1800 to supervise the move of the household furnishings from Philadelphia to Washington, and he acted as purchasing agent for President Adams from that date and continued on until the end of the Jefferson administration. James Madison gave the authority to spend the fund to Benjamin H. Latrobe, superintendent of the City of Washington, in 1809. From that period on, the person in charge of the public buildings in the City of Washington was the one who dealt with Congress in procuring funds for the upkeep of the President's House and for furnishing it. From 1817 until 1849, the commissioner of public buildings was directly under the supervisory and appelate powers of the president.[7] In 1849 the Department of Interior was created, and the Office of the Commissioner of Public Buildings was placed under the secretary of the interior until 1867.[8]

All of the treasury accounts pertaining to furnishing the President's House from 1800 to 1867 are to be found in a group of records called Miscellaneous Treasury Accounts for the President's House, Record Group 217. In order to identify the accounts in the group, it is necessary to determine who had the authority to expend the furniture fund for each president and then search for all the accounts submitted by that individual.

Accounts for the period 1800–1867 are found under the names of the following men who served as commissioners of public buildings from 1816 to 1867.

Samuel Lane	*April 1816*
Joseph Elgar	*May 1822*
William Noland	*February 1834*
Andrew Beaumont	*November 1846 (temporary appointment)*
Charles Douglas	*March 1847*
Ignatius Mudd	*April 1849 (permanent appointment effective July 1850)*
William Easby	*March 1851*
Benjamin B. French	*June 1853 (permanent appointment effective January 1854)*
John B. Blake	*June 1855 (permanent appointment effective December 1855)*
William S. Wood	*May 1861 (temporary appointment); (temporary appointment renewed August 1861)*
Benjamin B. French	*September 1861 (temporary appointment effective January 1862); (permanent appointment continued until 1867).*

It is also necessary to check for accounts which were submitted by the members of the president's household who had been delegated the authority to expend the furniture fund. This requires enough knowledge of presidential history to be able to recognize names of individuals close enough to each president to be appointed his agent. In this group are found accounts for:

Thomas Claxton	1800–1809
Benjamin Latrobe	1809–1811
Louis Deblois	1813
George Boyd	1817
Seth Hyatt	1843
W. W. Corcoran	1846–1849

W. W. Bliss	1849–1850
Sidney Webster	1853–1857

Occasionally, accounts were submitted directly under the name of the person or firm which supplied furnishings or services such as those under the names of:

Joseph Russell	1818
William King	1827
Hugh Smith & Company	1841
Edwin Green	1841
William H. Carryl	1861
A. S. Zimaudy	1861
Alex T. Stewart	1861

In 1867 Congress abolished the Office of the Commissioner of Public Buildings and transferred its functions to the chief of engineers, War Department, where it was known as the Office of Public Buildings and Grounds.[9]

The duties of the officer in charge of public buildings and grounds under the War Department were specifically mentioned in the act passed in 1867. Along with other duties, he had charge of the care and repair of the mansion and its furniture, the preparation of periodic or annual inventories of public property within, and the supervision of additions to the house and its furnishings.

Correspondence relating to purchases for the Executive Mansion after 1867 are filed with the papers of the Office of Public Buildings and Grounds in Record Group 42. The basic information about the money expended is found in the accounts themselves in the Treasury Department. With the account, found by number and name of the purchasing agent, are filed vouchers relating to the purchases in the time period covered by the account.

Accounts for the period 1867 to 1901 are in the following names.

Maj. Nathaniel Mitchler	1867
Maj. Orville E. Babcock	1871
Col. Thomas L. Casey	1878
Col. Almon F. Rockwell	1881
Lt. Col. John M. Wilson	1885
Maj. Oswald H. Ernst	1891

Lt. Col. John M. Wilson   1893
Col. Theodore A. Bingham   1897

It should be noted that the military ranks given above are the official ones. Some received brevet promotions.

The National Archives has no accounts for White House purchases from Theodore Roosevelt's administration to the present; the records of china purchases from 1900 on have to be requested through the Office of the Curator of the White House.

All the functions of the Office of Public Buildings and Grounds were, by the act of February 26, 1925, transferred to the Office of Public Buildings and Public Parks of the National Capital.[10] This office was abolished in 1935 when its functions were transferred to the Office of National Capital Parks under the Department of the Interior's Park Service.

The Office of Curator of the White House was created in 1961 by Mrs. John F. Kennedy and legally established by Executive Order in 1964. The staff of this office is a major source of information on every phase of the history of White House furnishings.

Even after carefully searching all of these records, it is possible that there may be additional information in some series of records not yet suspected of pertaining to the story. As government records are periodically reexamined and reinterpreted, the history of the china purchased with government funds is one that is unending. Supplemental material is also to be found in the presidential papers and presidential house museums, and this body of information will continue to grow. The account presented in this book should be read with the understanding that it is the most complete information available at the present time, but that it is by no means the final story. The author hopes this study will be the basis for new information and new pieces of presidential china coming to light as a result of it.

I

The Period of French Influence, 1789–1845

The decorative arts of the early Republic reflect the close ties of our founding fathers to the French due to the assistance provided by France during the American Revolution. As the leaders of the new Nation journeyed to France to arrange that alliance and to work out the details of its operation, they had ample opportunity to see and admire the way the French people furnished their homes and ordered their lives. The baggage of these men returning home contained things to enhance their homes in the same fashion. Next came the commissions from friends and neighbors at home to Americans still in France to purchase similar furnishings for them. Nowhere is this delight in French taste more evident than in elegant furnishings for the dinner table, especially in the porcelains ordered for the use of the president of the United States. In this early period, the ware chosen for formal use as the state banquet service were of neoclassic design and typical of the large dinner services made in the Paris factories early in the nineteenth century. Even the eagle used on the state china of the Monroe and Jackson administrations was Napoleonic rather than the American bald eagle.

During this same period, the ware chosen for less formal use in the President's House was English earthenware of the type made in the factories in Staffordshire, England. This was the kind of tableware most readily available at the retail stores in the area.

George Washington

AT PHILADELPHIA: *June 6—I had the honor of an interview with the President of the United States to whom I was introduced by Mr. Dandridge, his Secretary. He received me very politely and after reading my letters, I was asked to breakfast. . . .*

Mrs. Washington herself, made tea and coffee for us. On the table were two small plates of sliced tongue, dry toast, bread and butter etc., but no broiled fish, as is the general custom. . . . There was but little appearance of form: one servant only attended, who had no livery; a silver urn for hot water, was the only article of expense on the table.

Excerpt from Henry Wansey's *Excursion to the United States in 1794* quoted in *Washington after the Revolution 1784–1799* by W. S. Baker (Philadelphia: Lippincott Co., 1898), pages 277–278.

From the administration of our first president, funds were spent by the government to properly house the chief executive of the country, and the first tableware purchased for the President's House with government funds can be found in the lists of these expenditures.

The seat of government of the United States under the Constitution of the United States, which went into effect in 1789, was to be the city of New York. The Congress which began to assemble in March of that year soon acted to arrange suitable housing for newly elected President Washington. On April 15, only a few weeks before the arrival of the president, Congress requested Samuel Osgood, proprietor of a house at Cherry and Queen streets which had been occupied recently by the president of the Congress, "to put the same and the furnishings thereof in proper condition for the residence and use of the President of the United States." [12]

William Duer—treasurer of the Congress under the Articles of Confederation and son-in-law of Washington's Revolutionary War general and personal friend, Lord Stirling—was assisted by Osgood in spending the money which Congress had appropriated for the purpose.

A contemporary letter from Sarah Robinson, Osgood's niece, to Kitty F. Wister credits most of the furnishing arrangements to the wives. The "house on Cherry Street was taken for him and every room furnished in the most elegant manner. Aunt Osgood and Lady Kitty Duer had the whole management of it. I went the morning before the General's arrival to look at it. The best furniture in every room and the greatest quantity of plate and china I ever saw. . . ." [13]

The young lady does not seem to have exaggerated very much. The list of the furnishings purchased for the house has survived in the Samuel Osgood papers in The New-York Historical Society. It is headed "Abstract of Accounts of Sundry persons for Goods furnished and Repairs done to the house occupied by the President of the United States." The abstract is dated from the auditor's office, December 29, 1789, and signed by George Nixon, clerk. [14] The same list can be found in government records preserved in the National Archives in Washington, D.C., in the records of the Office of the Register of the Treasury. Both of these lists record the first china to be purchased for the use of the president of the United States with public funds and give the names of the dealers from whom china was purchased and the cost.

4 sets of Breakfast china—J. & N. Roosevelt— £ 14/0/0 [15]
Looking Glass, china & etc.—Samuel Dunlap— £ 18/4/0 [16]
Glass and Queen's Ware—James Christie— £ 281/0/3 [17]

The four breakfast sets were probably the blue and white Chinese export porcelain which was readily available on the New York market and was the porcelain in common use in colonial America. The china purchased from Samuel Dunlap at the same time as the looking glass might have been ornamental vases or figurines for decorating the house. The "Queen's Ware" from Christie's probably was intended for use as the formal dinner service. The purchase of it as the elegant china service reflects the dominance of English ware on the American market after the Revolution. It was being used in many affluent homes in this country at this same period. Besides, it was practical for it could be purchased from local dealers and additional

Chinese export porcelain dinner service decorated with the emblem of the Society of the Cincinnati purchased for George Washington by Col. Henry Lee of New York City in 1786. Washington was the first president of the society.

1. A Washington plate with a border in underglaze-blue Fitzhugh pattern. The center decoration is the angel of fame blowing a trumpet in one hand; from the other hand is suspended the badge of the Society of the Cincinnati. There is no mark on the reverse. Diameter, 9⅝ inches.

French porcelain banquet service purchased by
President Washington from the Comte de Moustier
in New York in 1790 and used as the state china
during his presidential administration.

2. *White porcelain soup plate with narrow gold rim. Obverse and reverse views of identical soup plates showing the mark of the Angoulême factory. Diameter, 9¾ inches.*

3. *White porcelain dinner plate with narrow gold rim notched on the inside edge. Obverse and reverse views of identical dinner plates showing the mark of the Sèvres factory. Diameter, 9½ inches.*

4. *Mark of the Nast factory found on a tapered cylindrical cup. The diameter tapers from 3 to 2 inches; height, 2⅝ inches. The cup is of white porcelain with a narrow gold rim.*

2

3

4

pieces could be added when necessary.

Queen's Ware was the name given to the cream-colored earthenware perfected by Josiah Wedgwood about 1762. It was called that in honor of Queen Charlotte after Wedgwood made a tea service for her in 1765. It varied in color from pale cream to almost deep straw or yellow and had a clearness of tone which made it a good background for decoration. After the Revolutionary War, an ever-increasing amount of creamware or queensware was imported into this country from England.

This first purchase of china for the President's House inaugurated a practice that was to be followed in administration after administration in selecting china for official use. It was almost always a ware in general use, and it was also the ware that could be procured on the local market or that a local merchant could order from abroad. Unfortunately for the collector of presidential china, none of this first ware purchased with government funds can be identified today.

President Washington considered only the china found in the house on Cherry Street when he arrived in 1789 to have been purchased with public funds. He had decided to use his $25,000 a year salary as an expense account, so any additional china purchased by him while he was president was paid for from his salary and actually was owned by him personally. The household accounts of Washington during his first term as president were kept by his private secretary, Tobias Lear, in a series of cash memorandum books and ledgers, the manuscripts of which are still privately owned and are not available for examination. An explanation of how the accounts were kept and a random selection of purchases made in the period from 1789 to 1793 may be found in *Private Affairs of George Washington, from the records and accounts of Tobias Lear, Esquire, His Secretary* by Stephen Decatur, Jr.[18] Lear kept a ledger with accounts for specific expenses entered under various headings. One of these headings was for "House Expenses." There were separate entries "to the President's private account" for expenses incurred for the estate at Mount Vernon. The heading which is most interesting to this study is "To Contingent Expenses" which supposedly took care of all expenses not covered by the other more specific categories designated by Lear. Any purchases of a permanent nature for the household were charged "To Contingent Expenses" rather than "House Expenses." The ledgers that covered the years in New York were kept in New York currency.[19] Those for Philadelphia began in Philadelphia currency and also in dollars; before the end, the entries were simply in dollars.

It is in this New York ledger under "Contingent Expenses" that the following entry, dated March 8, 1790, appears: "By Cont'g Exp Pd Mons Le Prince for furniture and china bot of the Ct. de Moustier as per bill £ 665/15/6." President Washington had found the Cherry Street residence too small for his official family, so in February 1790, he moved to a house at 39 Broadway which was being vacated by the French minister to the United States, Count de Moustier, who was returning to France. This house was a great deal larger than the one on Cherry Street, so Washington purchased out of his salary some of the furnishings which the count did not wish to take home with him. Among the purchases was a quantity of Sèvres porcelain. As Washington himself put it, the move "enlarged my table and of course my guests" as the new dining room would seat up to twenty guests whereas fourteen was the limit of the house on Cherry Street.

The original list shows the following pieces acquired for the sum of £ 136/3/0.[20]

2 Iceries compleat	36 Ice pots
1 Porringer & Cover	23 Platters
2 Sallad dishes	21 Egg dishes
4 square stew dishes	8 Pocottes
4 shells	20 small pots
15 Round dishes	12 chocolate cups and saucers
4 Saucers	15 coffee cups & saucers
4 butter boats	17 tea cups & saucers
4 Confection dishes	3 sugar dishes
4 mustard pots	2 cream pots
4 sugar dishes	2 flower pots
12 Ice plates	7½ dozen plates

The china purchased from the Comte de Moustier was plain white with a narrow gilded trim. Much of it survives in the collections of Mount Vernon and the Smithsonian Institution, and in the possession of Custis heirs. The variety of the dated factory marks on the china suggests that the count had been assembling the table service over a long period of time. In addition to the Sèvres, there must also have been pieces of porcelain made at the factories at "Angoulême" and "Nast" in the original purchase in 1790. There is no record in Washington's letter or accounts of additional purchases of table china to match the banquet service, and there is gold and white porcelain from Mount Vernon with all three marks. The china from all three factories was so similar in body and decoration that a table could be set without the guests being aware of the diversity of manufacture. This china is at Mount Vernon, the Smithsonian Institution, the White House, and in private collections.

President Washington used the gold and white French service as the state dinner service from the time of its purchase in New York to the end of his administration and then took it home with him to Mount Vernon.

During the session of Congress in the summer of 1790 it was decided that the City of Washington, the permanent capital of the United States, was to be built on the Potomac River and that until it was ready for occupancy the temporary capital would be moved to Philadelphia. When Washington and his family left New York in August to have a brief rest at Mount Vernon, he left behind Tobias Lear, to oversee the transfer of his household goods from New York to Philadelphia.

On their way home, the Washingtons stopped in Philadelphia and the president visited the house that had been rented for his use at 190 High Street. As a result of the visit, he wrote Lear a series of letters containing detailed instructions for the move from New York to Philadelphia. One letter specified that "there is a small room adjoining the kitchen (by the Pump) that might, if it is not essential for other purposes, be appropriated for the Images, the save [Sèvres] china and other things of this

sort, which are not in common use."[21] The images referred to here are small porcelain figures used on a plateau to decorate the table.

Lear, at about the same time, was advising the president about John Hyde, the steward of the household who would move to Philadelphia with them, "so far as relates to the furniture, linen, china, etc. under his care, he seems to have been very careful of it and on a late inspection everything appears to be in good order and much less china and glass destroyed than one could expect in so large a quantity and the pieces of those broken are all produced."[22]

The market in New York was so devalued by the exodus of all the people attached to the seat of government that nothing was sold there, and all the furnishings in the house on Broadway were put on board a ship bound for Philadelphia.

By October 24, Lear was writing from Philadelphia that "we have not yet opened the Save [Sèvres] and Cincinnati China as the closets in which they are to be put have been lately painted and are not yet dry; but the common china [probably the blue and white export porcelain] which we have unpacked is preserved beyond expectation, not a single piece is broken."[23]

Because the gold and white china was moved to Philadelphia and was used on state occasions at the Executive Mansion, it is included in this study even though Washington purchased it from his salary rather than with public funds.

This letter of Tobias Lear is also documentation for the use of the Cincinnati china in the President's House. China decorated with the insignia of the Society of the Cincinnati was purchased by George Washington in 1786. Col. Henry Lee wrote to President Washington from New York stating that he could buy for him a set of Chinese export porcelain with the Cincinnati eagle for approximately $150. Washington records payment for the china on August 23, 1786, as "32 Guineas + ¼ of Mordore [a Portuguese gold coin] sent of Colo. Henry Lee at New York, by Col. Humphreys to pay for a set of China bot. for me there £ 45.5.0." A receipted bill in Lee's name shows the service was intended for breakfast and teatime use and numbered 302 pieces. The Washington service is distinguished by the fact that the insignia of the Society of the Cincinnati is suspended from the figure of Fame who is blowing a trumpet. This service of porcelain is probably the best known of the Mount Vernon tableware. In her will, Mrs. Washington bequeathed it to her grandson George Washington Parke Custis as the "set of Cincinnati tea and Table China."[24] There are miscellaneous pieces of the Cincinnati china at Mount Vernon, in the Smithsonian Institution, in the White House and State Department collections, and other museum and private collections. By far the greatest number and variety of pieces are to be found in the collections of The Henry Francis du Pont Winterthur Museum in Delaware, where they were acquired from the descendants of George Washington Parke Custis.

After the move to Philadelphia, there are several more entries for miscellaneous china in Lear's account books.[25]

May 20, 1791—By Cont'g Exp^s for 2 doz^n cups & saucers, 12 bowls, 24 teaspoons and 24 tablespoons for Serv^{nts} 4/70

June 13, 1791—By Cont'g Exp^s for doz. of soup plates 2/

Nov. 10, 1792—By Cont'g Exp^s p^d Gallagher for Glass China 34/66.

At the end of his second term in Philadelphia in 1797, just preceding his return to Mount Vernon as a private citizen, George Washington made out his *List of Articles, Public and Private, 1797*.[26] No china is listed. There is, however, a note at the bottom which states that "nothing herein has been said relatively to the Table Linnen, Sheeting, China and Glassware which was furnished at the expense of the United States because they have been worn out, broken, stolen and replaced (at private expense) over and over again."

When it came time for President Washington to return to Mount Vernon, Tobias Lear again handled the details of the move. The public furniture, that which had been bought for the house on Cherry Street, was carefully listed and much of it can be identified on the list of purchases made by Samuel Osgood in 1789. From the furniture and things purchased by Washington personally and listed in his accounts as "Contingent Expenses" the president selected some things to be returned to Mount Vernon and the rest was to be sold.

On March 15, 1798, Tobias Lear reported to President Washington:

The House is now preparing for the President [meaning Adams], and he proposes to come in on Monday next when I presume everything will be in as good order as it can be put.

The furniture of the Green Drawing Room and other articles sold at auction went off very low indeed. The number attending the auction was considerable; but they were disappointed in an expectation that they had formed that the paintings, prints, etc. were to have been sold—The Lustures, Stoves and other fixtures in the House will be taken by the President at cost or a fair evaluation. There is nothing to be sold of the public furniture.[27]

John Adams

At the same time, we are giving John Adams
FOURTEEN THOUSAND DOLLARS *to buy furniture*
for his house. The latter motion went through
the Representatives by sixty-three votes against
twenty-seven. It is impossible to withstand the
pathos of Mr. Samuel Sitgreaves, when describing
the crazy bedsteads, the broken chairs, the ragged
linen, the moth-eaten curtains, the rusty saucepans,
and the fractured waterpots, that General Washing-
ton was to leave behind him in Market Street.

Excerpt from *The History of the United States for*
1796: including a variety of Interesting Particulars
relative to the Federal Government previous to
that period. Philadelphia, 1797.

Even before the count of the ballots on February 8, 1797, affirmed the election of John Adams as the second president of the United States, he had begun to worry about expenses of maintaining the presidential household. On February 4, 1797, in a letter to his wife Abigail, he wrote:

House rent at twenty-seven hundred dollars a year, fifteen hundred for a carriage, one thousand for one pair of horses, all the glass, ornaments, kitchen furniture, the best china, settees, plateaus etc. all to purchase, all the china, delph or wedgewood, glass and crockery of every sort to purchase and not a farthing probably will the House of Representatives allow though the Senate have voted a small addition. All the linens besides.[28]

The "china, delph" mentioned by the president-elect was probably "delftware," a term which is applied to a ware which was coated with a lead glaze containing oxide of tin which turned it opaque white. This glaze could then be painted before firing with cobalt blue, manganese purple, copper green, antimony yellow, and an orange. It was made in England and should not be confused with Delft with a capital D which was a similar ware actually made in Holland. It was the most popular ware shipped to America in the mid-eighteen century, but was going out of style to be superseded by creamware after 1765.

Despite the forebodings of John Adams, the Congress of the United States did take the accom-

modation for the new president under advisement. "The Report of Joint Committee [of the two houses of Congress] on accommodations for President of the U.S. after 3d March next," made on February 14, 1797, recommended the following.

The committee of the two Houses appointed to consider whether any and if any what measures ought to be adopted for the further accommodation of the President of the United States for the term commencing on the 4th of March next.
Report that they have unanimously agreed to the following resolution as proper to be adopted.
Resolved that the President of the United States after the third day of March be authorized to cause to be sold such parts of the furniture and equipage belonging to his household as may be decayed and out of repair and that a sum not exceeding of 11,000 dollars together with the proceeds of such sales be appropriated for the accommodation of the household of the President of the United States and to be laid out at his discretion and agreeably to his directions.[29]

The original $11,000 suggested in the committee report was raised to $14,000 in the act of March 2, 1797, largely due to a speech made by one of the congressmen in which he described the poor condition of the public furniture which Mr. Adams was inheriting from the Washington administration.

As Tobias Lear reported to President Washington, "there is nothing to be sold of the public furniture,"[30] President Adams evidently did not choose to take advantage of the permission granted him to sell the "decayed furniture." The permission granted in this appropriation was to have a long-lasting effect on the history of the furnishings of the President's House including the china purchased with public funds.

It was from sales held under this kind of authorization, repeated in every appropriation bill thereafter, that remnants of presidential china came into private hands throughout the nineteenth century. Fortunately, some of the china acquired at these sales survived because of the respect and reverence which people of the United States have for the office of the presidency and the material objects associated with it. But for many of the administrations, the only thing that remains is the written record.

John Adams wrote to his wife on March 17, 1797: "I hope to get into my house Monday next but shall purchase no nice furniture till you come." Mrs. Adams arrived in Philadelphia on May 9, and a dinner service was probably one of the first of her purchases. She was soon entertaining thirty or forty guests for dinner— the senators on one occasion, the members of the House in groups, and department heads, diplomats, and other dignitaries.

John Adams took personal charge of the expenditures for the first three years of his term of office. There are no account numbers or vouchers surviving for these expenditures in the Miscellaneous Treasury Accounts, so that any purchases of china during those years are unknown. The submission of vouchers for such expenditures began after the president delegated this authority to an agent. During the years in which he took personal responsibility, the records of the Office of the Register show simply that President Adams spent $8,300 from the furniture fund in 1797; $1,000 in 1798; and $3,595 in 1799 for which he personally drew warrants from the Treasury Department.

At the time the seat of government was moved from Philadelphia to Washington, D.C., in 1800, Thomas Claxton, doorkeeper of the House of Representatives, was appointed to serve as agent for procuring new furnishings for the President's House in Washington. Claxton also had the responsibility of moving the contents of the President's House in Philadelphia to the house being built in Washington. For this purpose, Claxton spent $5,593.95 which he states was used to purchase "carpeting, cabinet work and other Articles of Furniture including Freight, porterage and his own expenses to and from Philadelphia." [31]

The money expended has little relationship to the obvious physical drain and mental

suffering endured by Claxton. In a letter to John Adams dated November 3, 1800, he tells of some of the problems he was facing and apologizes for the condition of the house in Washington. He complained that he had been persuaded to accept the responsibility for the move only "six or seven weeks ago"; that he was confronted with a house in "unfurnished condition" and that "the season of the year— unfortunately was prior to the arrival of new importations, and after the old were nearly exhausted." Even the most "trifling articles" had to be brought from a great distance. He advised the president that it was only by working his crew "by day at the President's House and by night in the Capitol" that "a degree of satisfaction will be experienced with both places." He ends his letter: "Sincerely wishing, Sir, that you may enjoy comfort in your new abode." [32]

The lack of comfort in the new abode was reflected in Abigail's letters written from Washington after her arrival later that month. In a letter to her daughter, she reveals that "many things were stolen, many more broken by the removal; amongst the number, my tea china is more than half missing. Georgetown affords nothing." [33] Tea china is specifically mentioned in the inventory of the public furniture taken at the end of the administration of President John Adams, so it is possible that Mrs. Adams is speaking here of the china which belonged to her in her official capacity rather than to her personal possessions. This seems to be a valid assumption because William Shaw, nephew and secretary of the president, in February 1801 said specifically that all the furniture in the house was public property.

Because the written record does not specify the kinds of china purchased by the Adams's with public funds, reference is made to the letter of John Adams to his wife before he took office in which he specifically mentions "delph or wedgewood." [34] Mrs. Adams fondness for blue china is legendary at The Adams Mansion in Quincy, Massachusetts. On two occasions, November 13, 1780, and March 17–25, 1782, Abigail reminded John—who was then in Europe—of the blue dishes she wished him to purchase. Blue and white china—either delft or Chinese export porcelain—was readily available in the Philadelphia shops, and Abigail most certainly purchased it. In a letter to Maria Mallan Brooks from her husband, David Brooks, a member of Congress, he writes of having dinner at the President's House. It was one of those dinners given in June 1797 soon after Abigail arrived in Philadelphia. He describes the dinner in detail to her and of the table, he comments that "the utensils were only common blue china plates." [35]

Blue and white Chinese export porcelain, imported through England, was the most common table china in use in colonial America. After the Revolution it was imported in even greater quantity, only now it came directly from Canton to America on American ships. In recent years, archeological research indicates that much of this china was blue and white porcelain decorated with stylized landscape scenes or foliate motifs. The pieces were decorated in underglaze blue, but were of reasonably good quality. The term "common" used by David Brooks pertained to the quantity of the china available on the market rather than its quality.

Soon after President John Adams learned of the election of Thomas Jefferson to the presidency, he requested directions for turning over to his successor the public property in his hands. A joint committee of Congress was appointed for this purpose.

In a letter from William Shaw to Wilson Cary Nicholas, the chairman of the committee, Shaw stated that $1,102 of the appropriation of $14,000 made in 1797 for furnishing the President's House during Adams's tenure was still unexpended. He also stated that all the furniture in the mansion at the time he was writing was public property, and that the President's House was open to inspection by the congressional committee or anyone it chose to authorize.

Thomas Claxton, the purchasing agent who had supervised the move to Washington, was appointed to take the inventory. In a letter addressed to committee chairman Nicholas, dated "City of Washington Feb. 26, 1801," Claxton stated: [36]

Sir: Agreeably to your directions, I have taken an Inventory of the furniture and other property in the possession of the President, belonging to the United States. In performing this service, I have given a general view of the Household furniture, omitting in some cases a compleat detail, the time allowed not being sufficient to enumerate and describe such a variety of small objects as compose a part.

In this inventory, Claxton reported on the china and "Queen's Ware." Under a heading of "China," he listed "3 Table Setts complete" and "Tea China, a considerable quantity." Under "Queen's Ware" was listed "Dishes and plates, a large quantity."

Claxton advised the committee that "having been informed that the President intends leaving this city early in the morning of the 4th of March, I have thought it my duty to suggest to you the propriety of naming some person to lodge in the House on the night of the 3d with authority to receive the Keys the next morning. This arrangement appears necessary as all his confidential servants are going with him." [37] Concerning the inventory, it should be noted that at this time "china" usually meant porcelain and may be so interpreted here, because Claxton put the "Queen's Ware" in a separate category. The three table sets were probably the "common blue china" that David Brooks reported seeing in 1797. The amount of china listed in the inventory makes it seem unlikely that the Adams's had any personal china at the President's House in Washington. There was enough to take care of public entertaining; and with the problem of transportation to Washington, even if some private china had been in use in Philadelphia, it would probably have gone from there back to Quincy, Massachusetts, rather than being brought to Washington for three month's use.

None of the china bought with public funds during the Adams administration has been identified.

Thomas Jefferson

At his usual dinner parties the company seldom or ever exceeded fourteen, including himself and his secretary . . . his guests were generally selected in reference to their tastes, habits and suitability in all respects, which attention had a wonderful effect in making his parties more agreeable, than dinner parties usually are. . . .

One circumstance, though minute in itself had certainly a great influence on the conversational powers of Mr. Jefferson's guests. Instead of being arrayed in strait [sic] parallel lines, where they could not see the countenances of those who sat on the same side, they encircled a round or oval table where all could see each others faces and feel the animating influence of looks as well as of works.

A description of President Thomas Jefferson's dinner parties by Mrs. Samuel Harrison Smith, wife of the publisher of the National Intelligencer, excerpted from Margaret Bayard Smith's *The First Forty Years of Washington Society* (New York: Charles Scribner's Sons, 1906), pages 388 and 391.

Thomas Jefferson came into a house only partially furnished, but with enough basic necessities for him to take up his residence there on the day of his inauguration. To finish the job which had only begun, the Congress passed an Appropriation Act on April 24, 1800, authorizing him to spend $15,000 to complete the furnishing of the house.

President Jefferson was evidently satisfied with the way in which Thomas Claxton had been handling his job as "Agent for procuring furniture for the President's House," because he continued to act in that capacity during Jefferson's two administrations. Eventually the total congressional appropriations for furnishings for the house during those eight years equaled $29,000.

In the fall of 1801, Claxton submitted a statement for carpeting and cabinet work to the Treasury Department. This is recorded in the National Archives as Miscellaneous Treasury Account 12737 covering the period from January 20 to October 3, 1801. The next account for the period from October 22, 1801, to April 28, 1802, lists his expenditures for "Cabinet Work, Upholstery, China and Crockery Ware, grates and kitchen furniture and cost of a clock." No vouchers accompany this order, so there is no clue as to where the china and crockery ware were purchased or how much they cost. It is known that the total amount came to $1,714.90 [38] and as freight and cartage were included, the purchases could have been made in Philadelphia rather than in the Washington area.

In the account covering the period from March 3 to November 1, 1802,[39] Claxton again lists "China ware" among his purchases. None of these purchases can be identified today, but it can be assumed again that the term "China" was being used to refer to porcelain.

The accounts of Thomas Claxton were submitted each year for the furnishings purchased within the time limit specified at the beginning of the individual accounts. Time gaps pointed to missing accounts in the set of records called the Miscellaneous Treasury Accounts, but they were found later in the books of the first auditor of the Treasury Department. Account 17199 is found in the auditor's record, and it lists "Mahogany furniture, Cabinet Work, Upholster's Work, Plated Ware, China and Glass Ware, Carpetting, Bed furniture, table linen, etc. including the cost of a clock and Polygraph"—all purchased for $8,479.90.[40] This sum includes Claxton's compensation for his own service.

Account 19357 covering the period November 15, 1806, to March 21, 1807, again included "China and Crockery Ware," and "Crockery Ware" [41] was bought again in the period from June 18, 1807, to April 30, 1808.[42]

Thomas Claxton's last account for the Jefferson administration is account 21304 for expenditures from October 13, 1808, to January 27, 1809.[43] This is the first account and the only Jefferson account which has the vouchers attached, so it provides a clue to the other expenditures made during his administration. The first voucher in this account is for Claxton's services as agent for which he charged $250. The personal payment is marked "App'd" and signed "Thos.

Jefferson." All the other vouchers are receipted by either Claxton himself or by Stephen LeMaire, steward of the president's household. The purchase of "China" is found in a voucher submitted by Thompson and Moxley on a hand-written statement without any letterhead. As no freight or cartage charges were included in the account, it seems certain that Thompson and Moxley were merchants in the Washington area.

The following purchases are listed.

July 15, 1808

4	pudding dishes	6.00
11	china dishes	10.00
2	pitchers	2.50

Oct. 4

2 doz	small china plates	6.00
1	china soup tureen	8.00
2	china dishes	5.00
2	pudding dishes	3.00

Oct. 6

2	china dishes	@ 2½	5.00

Nov. 15

4	china dishes	@ $3	12.00
1	large china soup tureen		8.00

These seem to be miscellaneous pieces which were purchased as needed. From the inventory taken at the end of the Jefferson administration, the pieces were probably listed on the inventories as "blue china" under the term "Common China."

On February 19, 1809, Jefferson wrote to Claxton and returned an inventory of the furniture Claxton had made shortly before Jefferson's administration ended. In the letter, he advises Claxton that he had added kitchen furniture purchased by Mr. LeMaire and some articles of plate "lately obtained" by himself. The letter closes with Jefferson's compliments on the satisfactory manner in which Claxton had conducted himself in purchasing furniture for the house.[44] The letter is accompanied by a copy of the inventory which included the list of tableware.

China

2 large Punch bowls or Terrines for soup
16 Dishes different sizes 3 do round pudding
52 Plates—16 do for soup 3 do Dessert
18 Coffe cups and saucers
18 Tea cups do 2 small cream Terrines
2 sauce bowls 24 saucers
3 gilt teapots—4 blue gilt bowls for preserves
6 different sizes slop
8 dishes for apples—compote dishes

Common China

8 Tea cups and saucers
33 Blue china Terrines
34 Blue china dishes
74 blue china soup plates
76 flat plates—blue china
78 blue china dessert plates
76 blue china smaller plates
18 blue china custard cups
5 blue china sauce terrines
5 oval sauce bowls
4 round Pudding Dishes
9 Chamber Pots
8 Water pitchers and Basons

Earthen Ware

9 Chamber Pots
12 Common Plates
7 Deep Pudding Dishes
42 Common Plates
30 Common smaller
10 Wash Basons [45]

President Jefferson preferred small dinner parties, so it seems again that the administration had adequate china purchased from the public funds appropriated to take care of the President's needs which justifies some doubt that he had any personal china in the Executive Mansion. None of the china listed on this inventory can be identified today.

It is interesting to note that the heading "Queen's Ware" which was used by Claxton when he inventoried the President's House in 1801 was not in his inventory of 1809. Instead, he uses the term "earthenware," and the only tableware included are plates. This is probably transfer-printed English earthenware of the type produced in Staffordshire. The major tableware in the 1809 inventory is divided into "China" and "Common China." The "Common China" should probably continue to be identified as the cheaper grade of blue and white Chinese export porcelain, and the term "China" may be either a fine Chinese export porcelain or perhaps elegant French china of the kind being used by President Jefferson and his contemporaries in their own homes.

James Madison

The dinner was certainly very fine, but still I was rather surprised as it did not surpass some I have eaten in the Carolinas. There were French dishes and exquisite, I presume, by the praises bestowed on them. . . . Ice Creams, macaroons, preserves and various cakes are placed on the table which are removed for almonds, raisons, pecan-nuts, apples, pears, etc. Candles were introduced before the ladies left the table and the gentlemen continued a half-an-hour longer to drink a social glass.

Excerpt from a letter of Sarah Seaton's (wife of William Seaton publisher of the *National Intelligencer*) quoted in [Josephine Seaton] *William Winston Seaton of the National Intelligencer: A Biographical Sketch* (Boston, James R. Osgood and Company, 1871).

Because of the inventory Thomas Claxton took at the end of the Jefferson administration, the public record shows how much china the President and Mrs. Madison found when they moved into the White House. Previous to that, President Madison had designated Benjamin H. Latrobe, an English architect, who had been superintendent of public buildings during the administration of Thomas Jefferson, as the agent for expending the furniture fund. Latrobe was a personal friend of the Madisons. As he wrote to his brother, Christian, in England, shortly after the election: "I have for many years been on an intimate footing with him. Mary [Latrobe's wife] has known his very excellent and amiable wife from a child." [46]

It was a good thing that Latrobe admired Dolley Madison for the president directed Latrobe to take his instructions from Dolley and to present his accounts to her.

On March 2, 1809, Congress had passed an appropriation act providing $14,000 for the furniture fund, and it also authorized the customary sale of the "decayed furniture and equipage."

Early vouchers attached to Latrobe's accounts in the National Archives are for miscellaneous pieces of china. These were bought singly or a few dozen at a time. Because of the quantity of china left in the house by Jefferson, these purchases probably were to replace breakage which occurred during Madison's administration.

All this china was purchased in the area and was the kind of ware that could be bought from merchants in Alexandria, Georgetown, and the City of Washington. On October 10, 1809, Latrobe purchased the following from Hugh Smith of Alexandria, Virginia. [47]

2 cc Soup tureens stands & ladles	@12		1/4/0
12 dishes assorted			1/10/6
4 setts Fluted cups & saucers	@3/6		/14/
2 Sets Teapots, sugars & creams			/16/
4 Slop bowls	1/12 qt Bowls		/13
6 cc 2 qt Pitchers		2/6	1/0/3
6 doz cc Plates		4/6	1/7
			7/4/9
equalling			$24.12½¢

The "cc" used to describe the pieces stands for "cream color" and was the common designation for English creamware in bills and inventories of the period. This identification is strengthened by the price being recorded in British currency. As this was long after the decimal system had been adopted for this country, the use of the British pound in the bill can be considered proof of purchase of English china.

Perhaps the most interesting entry in the miscellaneous Treasury account 28634 is a voucher for the first auction of "decayed furniture" from the President's House for which there is a public record. [48] *The Independent American*, a newspaper published in Georgetown, advertised the sale in 1810. *"On Monday, the 22nd of October next at 12 o'clock, at Jones and Andrew's auction store, Pennsylvania Avenue* Sundry articles of furniture from the president's house. . . ."* [49]

Some of the china inherited from Jefferson was sold at the auction. The voucher lists:

5 doz and 10 plates at 1.62½ a half doz to Long & Dixon [50]	18.95
2 doz and one sm. plate at 1.60 pr ½ doz. to Long & Dixon	6.67
a sett of china dishes to Dixon	26.50

The total money realized on the auction, $475.67, went into the furniture fund to be spent for

Dinner and dessert service of French porcelain purchased for James Madison in France in 1806 when he was secretary of state. This service was probably used as the state service after the President's House was burned by the British in 1814.

5. *Dinner plate of white porcelain bordered in orange decorated with a geometric design in black and gold and edged with gold.*

6. *Reverse view of the plate showing the mark of the Nast factory.*

5

6

7. *Shell serving dish, 8⅞ inches at widest.*

8. *Reverse view of the serving dish showing a variation of the factory mark.*

7

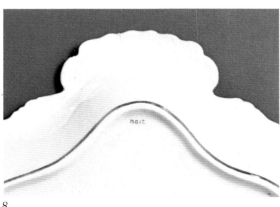

8

more furnishings, and for the first time some of the china purchased out of public funds returned to the public which had originally provided the money to buy it for the President's House.

The accounts for spending the money appropriated during the Madison administration are very difficult to follow in the records in the National Archives as Benjamin Latrobe served as agent until September 1811 and in that year Congress did not appropriate money to continue his job of surveyor or superintendent of public buildings. Latrobe then left the city having authorized that the unpaid balance in the fund be given to Lewis Deblois, who was his attorney, his assistant, and his friend. The money was intended to settle accounts outstanding, but Deblois continued to make purchases of miscellaneous furnishings as agent in his own right. A few pieces of china continue to be purchased every few months and again these would seem to be replacements for pieces broken in daily use. All of this china came from merchants in the Washington area. During Madison's administration, there are separate accounts for china purchased from Charles Moxley and from John Thompson who must have dissolved their firm of Thompson and Moxley which had been patronized by Thomas Claxton during the Jefferson administration. The largest purchases coincide with preparations for the major receptions of the president's social calendar—Christmas, the New Year's reception, and the celebration of Washington's birthday on February 22. They also show a direct relationship to the series of dinners traditionally given by the president for members of Congress during the period that Congress was in session.[51]

The items listed for purchase are too meagerly described for positive identification, but "edged plates" are mentioned several times. This could be the feather-edged creamware or pearl ware. The "red" and "blue printed" teapots and the "blue printed" cups listed were probably Staffordshire. Enormous quantities of printed earthenware were coming into this country from England by this time. Liverpool was one of the major English ports serving the American market and wares made in the Liverpool factories enjoyed great popularity in this country. On February 11, 1811, John Thompson sent to the President's House two dozen Liverpool china plates, but they must not have met with Dolley's approval for they were returned for full credit on February 23.

The largest single expenditure was for "1 sett of Blue and White Dining China" which Deblois bought on November 26, 1813, at the auction of George Beale for $230 and "2 doz. Blue and White Desert Plates" for $5 which were probably needed for the social season during the congressional session of 1813–1814.[52] The acquisition of a whole set of china may explain why no small purchases of china were made during the remainder of the winter.

During the War of 1812 (1812–1815), the President's House was burned by the British in August 1814. China is not included on the list Dolley Madison made of things she saved from the house, so it must be assumed that all the china then in the house was destroyed by the fire. This would include not only the things purchased during the Madison administration, but also those which had been inherited from both the Adams and Jefferson administrations.

There are no expenditures from public funds during the winter following the fire when the Madisons lived at Octagon House, which was rented for them from September 1814 until March 1815. The elegant furnishings already in Octagon House would have been adequate for most occasions, but there is a possibility that this is the period when the Madisons used their own personal china. Their service of orange, black, and white French china has acquired the history of being the state china of the Madison administration and it is thought to have been used as the state banquet service at Octagon House.

This handsome table service of French porcelain had been purchased for them in Paris by their personal friend and fellow Virginian, Fulwar Skipwith, in 1806 and was used by them in their home in Washington during the time James Madison was secretary of state.[53] The fact that this china remained in the hands of the family seems to indicate that it had not been taken to the President's House where it would not have survived the fire when the British burned the city.

The china has an orange border which is decorated in a geometric pinwheel pattern of black with white tracery. On the back appears the stamp of the manufacturer "Nast à Paris." Skipwith, in a letter to President Madison in 1806, wrote that "Mr. Nast, the china manufacturer, has at last executed the order which I gave him on my arrival here for your Table and Dessert sets of china....of the celebrated manufactory of Sêve [Sèvres] and is just 40% cheaper."

Specimens of this china are in the collections of the Smithsonian Institution, the White House, in other museum collections, and in private collections. Individual pieces still turn up in private hands or at public auction. All the known pieces have come from individuals who had a connection with the Madison family, and they have consistently been identified as the "state china" used during the Madison administration.

A new purchasing agent for the president's furniture fund was appointed when Congress in November 1814 appropriated additional money to take care of the president's household after the fire. George Boyd's expenditures began on April 4, 1815, and lasted until the end of the administration.[54] Probably because the owners of Octagon House wished to return to their home, another residence was rented for the Madisons. Rent for the corner house—one in a group known as The Seven Buildings—at Pennsylvania Avenue and Nineteenth Street, N.W., began on March 4, 1815, and ended on March 4, 1817. This house was rented unfurnished, so Boyd had to purchase all of the furniture and furnishings.

It is during this period and in Boyd's account that a peculiar phenomenon of Washington society is vividly illustrated. Because the society of the city was so fluid with continual arrivals and departures of diplomats and United States government officials, there were major sales of household goods at public auction and at private sales during the entire first half of the nineteenth century. Diplomats who came to this country with household furnishings could dispose of them at great profit when they were ordered home. Government officials who were maintaining either full or part-time houses in Washington usually sold their Washington furnishings when they moved to another government job overseas or returned home to private life. The constant mobility of furniture and household furnishings traveling from one household to another in Washington is a study in itself. Sometimes things were sold simply because the seller was acquiring something new, and there was no stigma attached to this traffic in secondhand furniture. These were people on the same social and economic level buying and selling from each other. To understand this completely, it is well to remember that less than fifty years prior to this time these same people were dependent on acquiring their household goods, sight unseen, from purchases made by an agent overseas. At least under the current arrangement, they could see what they were buying. And there was no waiting for furniture to be made by a cabinetmaker or for china to come by ship from Europe.

Thus, most of George Boyd's purchases were secondhand furniture and furnishings. He bought a "sett of Breakfast china" from F.D. Lear for $20. Frances Dandridge Lear was the niece of the late Mrs. George Washington and the widow of the general's secretary and trusted personal friend, Col. Tobias Lear.[55] He bought a "sett of dining china and a sett of waiters" from Harriet Campbell[56] for $183.00, and a "sett of tea china" from J. Doyne for $50.40.[57] He bought from Samuel McKinney of Georgetown "6 Canton China Dishes @ $2¼ $13.50 and 2 doz Blue print Custards @ $3 6.00".[58] Unfortunately, none of these purchases can be identified today.

The miscellaneous china, both elegant and cheap, bought over the next two years came from a dealer named Alexander L. Joncherez who had a shop in Georgetown and was supplying china to all the best families in the city. Joncherez's name, the wave of anti-British sentiment which

9. *Urn-shaped ice pail with liner. The lid is missing. Height, 12⅝ inches; width, 8¼ inches (with handles). For a similar piece, see* English Porcelain 1745-1850, *edited by R. J. Charleston (London: Ernest Benn Limited, University of Toronto Press, 1965), plate 3, illustrating an ice pail with liner and cover, 12½ inches in height, of about 1800.*

swept the town after it was burned by the British, and the fact that Joncherez was chosen to appraise President Monroe's French china seems to indicate that some of the merchandise stocked by him and sold to the President's House was French china.[59]

George Boyd did not purchase anything after December 1816, and there was $209.12 unexpended from the furniture fund when President Madison retired from office on March 4, 1817.

James Monroe

We had the most stylish dinner I have been at. The table was wider than we have and in the middle was a large, perhaps silver, waiter with images like some Aunt Silsbee has, only more of them. Vases filled with flowers made a very showy appearance as the candles were lighted when we went to the table. The dishes were silver and set around this waiter. The plates were handsome china, the forks silver and so heavy you could call them clumsy things.

Description of a dinner party at the President's House by Mrs. Smith Thompson, wife of President James Monroe's secretary of the navy, quoted in Ona Griffin Jeffries's *In and Out of the White House* (New York: Wilfred Funk, Inc., 1960), page 74. Reprinted by permission of McIntosh and Otis, Inc.

Reconstruction of the President's House began soon after it was burned in 1814, but at the time of the inauguration of James Monroe in 1817 it had not been sufficiently completed to allow the family to move into it. Until warm weather permitted them to go to their country home, Oak Hill, in Loudon County, Virginia, the Monroes stayed in a house in which they had previously lived on I (Eye) Street, N.W., when Monroe was secretary of war and later secretary of state.[60] As custom and the absence of Congress from the city decreed no large state receptions during the summer months, there was no immediate need for the Executive Mansion to be made habitable; by autumn, however, Monroe wished to be in residence and entertaining.

On March 3, 1817, Congress had passed an act appropriating $20,000 for a furniture fund, and President Monroe designated Samuel Lane, commissioner of public buildings, to take charge of the fund and control its disbursement. He also asked his old friend, William Lee, to digest the plan he had made for furnishing the house and to contract for the furnishings listed in the plan.

The new president was anxious to have the house furnished in a manner appropriate to the architectural dignity of the structure. Because of his familiarity with France, acquired on two diplomatic missions to that country, the presi-

dent wrote to the firm of Russell and Lafarge at Le Havre asking them to act as his agents to procure the things needed. Joseph Russell of the firm was an American from Boston and was personally known to the president as he had been consul at Le Havre when Monroe was minister to France. Included in Monroe's letter to the firm was a list of objects and a request that the intended price not be mentioned. Among the things listed to come from France were a dinner service of china and a dessert service.[61]

William Lee was also experienced in dealing with the sources of furniture and house furnishings in France as he had been American consul in Bordeaux. In 1817 Lee was in Washington serving as second auditor of the Treasury Department, so he would have been on hand to take care of receiving and arranging the furnishings from France and ordering supplemental pieces in this country.

The first thing Lee did was to make a survey of the public furniture which had been in President Madison's temporary residence at the time his term expired. Of the china he found there, he stated: "There was no recourse in the remnants of glass, earthenware, china, linen etc. of which scarcely an article would serve indeed we may say there remained none of these articles fit for use." [62]

As it was unlikely that the things ordered from France would arrive in time for the fall social season, Monroe volunteered to sell to the government his own household furnishings from the house on I (Eye) Street, N.W. The price was to be arrived at by "two persons of respectability" aided by persons in the trade who were knowledgeable about current prices.[63] The listing of items owned by the president and sold to the government included the following.

1 table set of French china, white and gold:

13 3/12 doz. plates	159	pieces
12 oval dishes assorted sizes	12	"
13 round dishes	13	"
2 soup tureens	6	pieces
4 fruit baskets	4	pieces
3 sauce boats	6	"
2 bowls	2	pieces

2 sugar dishes	4	”	
4 butter boats	8	”	
4 stands	4	”	
16 fruit dishes	16	”	
20 custard cups	40	”	
12 oval fruit dishes	12	”	
	286 pieces		600.00

The list also included:

1 set white and gold tea china, broken	20.00
20 cups and saucers, teapot, sugar dish and cream pot, best French china	60.00

Alexander Joncherez, the Washington dealer in glassware and chinaware was one of the experts who advised the appraisers on the value of the china.

Early in the autumn, Messrs. Russell and Lafarge notified the president that they were sending his order to the United States on the ship *Resolution* which sailed on September 17, 1817. The ship arrived in Alexandria the following November 11. Accompanying the bill was a letter in French from Russell and Lafarge describing the items on board.[64] The china received was listed as:

Un service de table, en porcelaine dorée pour trente personnes composé comme suis:

2 soupières rondes et plateau		200
32 plats ovales, diverses grandeurs		824
8 plats carrés en couvercle		280
3 douzaines assiettes creuses [and]		
12 ” ” plates	@ 108 la douz^e	1620
4 Plateaux de saucière		40
4 Saucière		80
36 Pots à crème		180
4 Guéridon		96
4 Saladieres octogonales		160
4 Moutardiers		48
36 Coquetiers		108
		3636

Also on board the ship was:

Un service de Dessert en porcelaine pour Trente personnes Bordure Amaranthe avec Cinq Vignettes, representant la Force, l'Agriculture, le Commerce, les Arts & les Sciences & les armes des Etats-Unis dans le fond de l'assiette composé comme suit:

3 Douz^{es} assiettes creuses [and]		
7 ” ” plates	@ 120	1200
24 Compotiers diverses forme	@ 18	432
4 Jattes à fromage	@ 20	80
4 ” à pieds·élevé	@ 30	120
2 Marronniers	@ 24	48
4 Sucriers de table	@ 36	144
4 Glaciers	@ 60	240
4 Corbeilles	@ 40	160
		2424
		6060
Escompte 10 pour %		606
		5454

The above lists are translated in note 64.

In a letter justifying the amount of their bill written eight months later by Russell and Lafarge in an effort to collect the money, the dessert service is mentioned specifically: "The dessert set of Porcelain has been manufactured by Dagoty. All the manufacturers competed for this and Mr. Nast would not make it for less than 50 per cent more and instead of four vignettes they have made five." Settlement was being asked because the partnership was being dissolved and Joseph Russell wished to return to Boston.[65]

Because the Monroe dessert service is so well described in the original order, it can easily be identified as the service which was purchased for the President's House. The amaranth—a reddish purple color—border and the five vignettes are recognizable on pieces of the service in the collections of The Henry Francis du Pont Winterthur Museum in Winterthur, Delaware. There are also pieces in the White House collection, the Smithsonian Institution, and various private collections. The Winterthur collection, which has 64 pieces including most of the plates and the compotes listed, has a history of being acquired from James C. McGuire who had an auction house in the City of Washington in the middle of the nineteenth century. McGuire had stored the china, packed on a top shelf in his auction room, until it was purchased privately about 1880. Many of the pieces of the

French porcelain dessert service ordered by President Monroe from France in 1817.

10. Dinner plate of white porcelain with amaranth border. The vignettes on the border represent Strength, Agriculture, Commerce, Art, and Science. The center decoration is the Arms of the United States in color.

11. *Pieces from the Monroe dessert service at*
The Henry Francis du Pont Winterthur Museum,
Winterthur, Delaware. (Courtesy, The Henry Francis
du Pont Winterthur Museum.)

12. *Mark on the reverse of the Monroe service in*
reddish orange: "M^{ture} de Madame/ Duchesse
d'Angoulême/ P. L. Dagoty   E. Honoré/ à Paris."
(Courtesy, The Henry Francis du Pont
Winterthur Museum.)

11

12

surviving china bear the mark on the reverse "M^{ture} de Madame/Duchesse d'Angoulême /P.L. Dagoty. E. Honoré/à Paris." [66]

Dagoty was only one of the factories which had sprung up in Paris or its surroundings at the end of the eighteenth and early nineteenth centuries. The major production of these factories was large table services of hard-paste porcelain which were used throughout the European continent and also exported abroad.

The design of the Monroe dessert service was typical of the period in which it was produced. In the opinion of one expert on early nineteenth-century French porcelain, the French porcelain artist of the Empire period was already overshadowed by the scientist. He was no longer inspired by the material in which he worked, but was "concerned only to achieve a heroic grandeur and to cover it with gilding or marbeling or with minutely executed pictures in the manner of oil painting."

The five vignettes set into the dark red border of the Monroe dessert service represented Strength, Agriculture, Commerce, Arts, and Science and were transfer printed, with enamels over the transfer printing. In the vignette dedicated to Science or Learning, the inscriptions on the book and the manuscript are mirror images; the manuscript is marked "Homer" in reverse,[67] indicating that the transfers came from another source.

The handsome eagle in sepia in the center of the plate is designated on the shipping list as the "arms of the United States." He bears a red, white, and blue shield on which is superimposed a banner with the motto "E Pluribus Unum." In this case, the printing is not a mirror image, suggesting that the transfer of the center design was actually made for use on the porcelain.

An exhaustive search has been made without success to find a source for the depiction of the eagle used on this china. A search of diplomatic papers, ships' papers, revenue stamps, military buttons, and coins has failed to locate an exact design. The similarity to the eagle with the shield on its breast used on the fifty-cent piece first coined in the United States in 1807 and the portable nature of a coin suggest that it may have

been the inspiration for the design.

More than likely, Russell and Lafarge shared with the china manufacturer the design of the Arms of the United States sent to them for the rug for the Oval Room as they describe the rug as having "in the centre the arms of the United States of America, colored according to the design sent us." [68]

There is a letter from France written by James Brown to James Monroe in June 1817 concerning the things being procured from Russell and Lafarge. "He [Lafarge] informed me that he had directed the Eagle to be placed on the chair and some other parts of the furniture but that bird being in bad repute at Court the workmen were ordered to desist and told that a special permission must be obtained to enable them to execute the work. For this purpose Mr. Russell's partner sets out for Paris next week. I presume upon giving proper assurances that this bird of evil omen will speedily take his flight to America, he may be permitted to work upon the furniture of the Government house." [69] Certainly the eagle on the china is more like a Napoleonic eagle than an American bald eagle, and the spirited position of the wings in flight suggests that he is indeed fleeing to America.

There is an eagle of similar design in bas relief on the base of an ormolu clock made in France about 1815. The clock is surmounted by a bust of Gen. George Washington and the legend "First in War, First in Peace and First in the Hearts of his Countrymen." [70] The difficulty of determining the exact year of the clock and the similarity of the depiction of the eagle to the one on the china pose a question as to which one came first. It was used many times thereafter suggesting that is was greatly admired by contemporaries both in France and in America. This depiction of the eagle can be found on a French engraving designed by A. Maurin entitled "Les Presidents Des Etats—Unis" which was made in 1825 and used for toile de Jouy produced for the American market the same year. John Quincy Adams so admired this representation of the eagle that he had a similar one engraved for the skippet of the diplomatic seal which he authorized soon after he became president in 1825.

The importance of a dessert service on the tables during the eighteenth and nineteenth centuries is little understood by the average person today. The brilliant "dressing out of a dessert" was an art of importance from ancient times. Dessert services were the most elegant part of the tableware of the household. Numerous baskets and compotes were needed for fruits, sweetmeats, jellies, syllabubs, cheese, nuts, ices, and dragées. The sweetmeats were tarts, candied fruits, or sweet biscuits. Liquid sweetmeats were stewed fruit. Syllabubs were concoctions of cream and wine. Ices and ice creams became part of the dessert course in the sixteenth century, and coolers were added to the china needed for dessert. The most important part of the dessert course were the fruits of all kinds. In fact, the all-inclusive term "fruit" is used synonymously for "dessert."[71] Hence, the elegant baskets found for the dessert service. The plates, both flat and deep, were the same size as those used in the dinner service.

It is evident that there was much competition in the matter of presenting an elegant dessert. It seemed to be the ultimate status symbol and early nineteenth-century cookbooks are full of ideas for the ambitious hostess on how to make her desserts the envy of her rivals. Mrs. Basil Hall, a British writer, who traveled in America in 1827 wrote that the American custom of having various kinds of fruit together in one dish "not only has a prettier effect but prevents the necessity of pulling about the dishes over the table."[72]

Every elegant state dinner service ordered for the President's House from the Monroe administration to and including the one ordered by President Hayes in 1879 included a dessert service which was decorated to be the most beautiful part of the service.

The gilded porcelain dinner service received in 1817 by President Monroe, at the same time as the Dagoty dessert service, lost its identity before it disappeared from presidential inventories and has never been identified.

A reference to the list of pieces received in the dinner and dessert services shows that no cups and saucers were included in the original order received from France. This may account for William Lee ordering from H. Bertrand in Baltimore, Maryland, "Two sets of china of 24 cups and saucers and 16 plates each @ $38" for a total of $76.[73]

The bill bears a note signed by Mr. J. S. Skinner, postmaster in Baltimore, dated November 6, 1821, certifying that he paid Bertrand from a draft on William Lee on December 29, 1817, but that he was unable to get Bertrand to confirm this because Bertrand had gone to France.[74] Bertrand also could have been a china decorator, commissioned to paint plain gold-edged white cups to match the new china, rather than a merchant. This is suggested by the date of purchase so soon after the French china arrived in November 1817, and the fact that other miscellaneous china purchases were made in Alexandria, Georgetown, and the City of Washington during this same year.

When President Monroe volunteered to sell his own household furnishings to the government in 1817, he indicated that he would not expect immediate payment for them. The order from France used up all of the original appropriation and more, so that it was necessary to ask for a supplemental appropriation of $30,000. The president now volunteered to repossess his own furniture if the supplemental appropriation was not adequate for both purposes.

When Monroe's purchasing agent, Samuel Lane, died unexpectedly in 1822, it was found that he had an unaccounted for $20,000 of public money. It was rumored that the president's furniture fund was involved in the shortage. To clear his name, President Monroe in January 1825 sent an extraordinary request to the House of Representatives addressed to both the House and the Senate asking that all matters of accounts and claims between himself and his country be examined by Congress with a view to the settlement of differences. A select committee was appointed by the House of Representatives to receive from Monroe any evidence and explanation the president thought proper to present. The report of this committee contains the complete story of the refurnishing of the President's House.[75] The multitudinous documents submitted by the president showed that he had received only the money authorized by the appraisers. Again, he volunteered to take back the furniture and repay the money. The House of Representatives simply tabled the committee report, so President Monroe left the furniture he had sold to the government in the President's House and kept the money.[76]

The unpleasant situation that had developed with the death of Samuel Lane obscures the purchases made out of federal funds for the rest of the Monroe administration. An account was submitted in 1824 at the end of his presidential term which contained purchases subsequent to December 31, 1821. Included were two vouchers for china. One was a bill from D. Butler and Company of Washington for miscellaneous china described as "blue printed" and "blue edged." The other was for purchase of miscellaneous crockery from the local store of A. B. Waller.[77]

In 1828, three years after James Monroe left office, the Treasury Department directed the administrator of the estate of Samuel Lane to pay the ex-president $1,301.33 for articles of furniture which Monroe had paid for personally and for which vouchers had not been submitted by Lane.[78]

John Quincy Adams

[WASHINGTON] Decr. (20, I believe) 1828.

. . . You ask how the administration folks look since their defeat. They all with one consent, do what I think dignity and self respect requires,— appear cheerful and good humoured, mix freely and frankly with the triumphant party and in Congress all is harmony I am told. Mr. and Mrs. Adams have gone a little too far in this assumed gaiety at the last drawing room they laid aside the manners which until now they have always worn and came out in a brilliant masquerade dress of social, gay, frank, cordial manners. What a change from the silent, repulsive, haughty reserve by which they have hitherto been distinguished. The great audience chamber, never before opened, and now not finished was thrown open for dancing, a thing unheard of before at a drawingroom! The band of musick increased the hilarity of the scene. All the folks attached to the administration made a point of being there. The ladies of the Cabinet in their best bibs and tuckers. Most of them in new dresses just arrived from Paris. Every thing in fact was done to conceal the natural feelings excited by disappointment and to assume the appearance not only of indifference, but of satisfaction. As one of the opposition members observed, "The Administration mean to march out with flying colours and all the honors of war." Well, I think I would do so too, only not carry it so far as to betray affectation. In private and social intercourse, among themselves, where no false assumption is necessary, I have, I must say, seen the same good humour. They treat their defeat as one of the chances of war, which happen to the most brave and skilful, as well as the weak and ignorant.

Excerpt from *The First Forty Years of Washington Society* by Margaret Bayard Smith (New York: Charles Scribner's Sons, 1906), pages 248–249.

The congressional investigation of the expenditure of the furniture fund appropriated for the administration of President Monroe made a deep impression on John Quincy Adams preceding his election in 1824. In 1824 President Monroe had shown Adams, then his secretary of state, the explanation he had prepared to submit to Congress explaining the expenditure of the fund. After reading it, John Quincy Adams commented in his diary for April 11, 1824:

"It enters into details of a very humiliating character and which ought never to have been or to be required of him. . . ." As a respecter of presidential dignity, Adams lamented that the exposure of personal domestic and household concerns was "almost as incongruous to the station of a President of the United States as it would be to a blooming virgin to exhibit herself naked before a multitude."[79] President Adams did not wish to be placed in such an embarrassing position himself. On March 8, 1825, he recorded in his diary his resolution to avoid any complications.

The usual appropriation of fourteen thousand dollars for refurnishing the President's house was made by an Act of Congress at the close of the session. There were during Mr. Monroe's administration fifty thousand dollars appropriated for furnishing the house. He had placed the fund under the management of Col. Lane who two or three years since, died insolvent, with twenty thousand dollars of public moneys unaccounted for, which has given rise to much obloquy upon Mr. Monroe. I have determined, therefore to charge myself with the amount of the new appropriation and to be myself accountable to the Treasury for its expenditures.[80]

The Adams family was not able to move into the President's House immediately, because an illness of Mrs. Monroe delayed the Monroes departure. The official inventory of the public furniture, made just before the new president moved in, was taken on March 25, 1825. It is a very complete accounting of the furniture purchased by the government from Mr. Monroe plus the items imported from France and the miscellaneous additions made in the years between 1818 and 1825.[81] Under the heading "China Closet," this inventory lists the china then in the house.

French China First Service [This is the previously unidentified gilt service listed in the invoice sent by Russell and Lafarge from France.]

2	large soup tureens
4	large dishes
4 2d	" "

8   3d   ”   ”
7   4th   ”   ”
12 5th   ”   ”
8   vegetable dishes
4   celery   ”   one broken
2   sauce boats
4   mustard pots one broken
12 doz and 6 plates   150 pieces some injured
4   stands for custards
27 custard cups not complete
32 egg cups
2   tureens stands
_____

270 pieces

Crimson and Gilt China—Second service dessert
[This refers to the Dagoty dessert service with the
amaranth border and five vignettes also purchased from
France which are now at The Henry Francis du Pont
Winterthur Museum, The White House, the Smith-
sonian Institution, and in various private collections.]

4   large elegant Ice Cream Urns
28 stands for preserves
4   fruit baskets
6   shells, one broken
4   sauce boats or sugar stands
9   doz and 3 plates
_____

157 pieces

[A white and gilt china service is listed next. The
white and gilt china was listed in the private household
furnishings of President Monroe which he sold to the
government in 1817, but is not identifiable today.]

2   large soup tureens
3   large dishes
2   2d size ”
6   3d size ”
2   4th size ”
5   5th do
1   large round dish
14 fruit dishes
2   oval do 8 oval do
4   oval dishes
3   stands for custards
16 custard cups
7   sauce boats
2   sugar boats
4   fruit baskets
2   shells

2   bowls
10 small round dishes 1 broken
11 doz and 4 plates   136 pieces
_____

232 pieces

White and Gilt French Tea Service—China

22 tea plates
1   tea pot
2   doz & 9 tea saucers   33 pieces
4   doz and 1 coffee ”   49 ”
1   doz & 3 tea cups   15 pieces
3   doz coffee cups   36 ”
_____

156 pieces

Blue China Dining Service [This must be the china
purchased during the Madison administration from
Joncherez or one of the blue sets acquired by the
Madisons from private individuals after the fire.]

1   soup tureen and stand
1   large dish
3   2d size
2   3d size
1   4th ”
20 plates
16 small dessert plates
1   bowl
13 saucers
8   cups
_____

66 pieces

With the amount of china listed, it seems as
though there would have been little necessity
for any additional china to be purchased immediately. Mrs. John Quincy Adams, however,
was "a lady proverbial for her correct and refined
taste," [82] and there is a record of a purchase on
March 28, 1825, of a blue-printed dinner set
and two dozen blue-printed coffees, bought at
the local store of A. B. Waller on Pennsylvania
Avenue. More "blue coffees" and two dozen
blue plates were purchased in April.[83] The blue-
printed dinner set probably was transfer-printed
earthenware to be used by the servants, for it
cost only $35.00 and the additional plates were
$1.50 a dozen.

Mrs. Adams's name is also on the bill for a

"Canton China" dinner set (Chinese export porcelain) which was purchased in Philadelphia on November 3, 1825, from the firm of Read and Gray.[84] The beginning of the winter social season must have prompted this purchase as the service was large as well as expensive. The pieces are listed as:

19 dishes—4 of 8" size	
4 of 10" "	
2 of 12" "	
4 of 14" "	
2 of 18" "	
2 of 20" "	
1 of 22" "	$30.50
2 Steak Dishes with hot water pans	7.00
4 Covered Vegetable dishes	9.00
1 Fish Dish and drainer	3.50
2 Soup Tureens & Stands	8.00
4 Sauce "	5.00
9 doz dining flat plates @ 2.00	18.00
4 doz soup plates @ 2.00	8.00
4 doz flat dessert plates @ 2.00	8.00

The Canton dinner set cost Mrs. Adams $97. This set is not identifiable today.

John Quincy Adams had delegated the work of contracting for goods and paying the bills to his son John Adams, Jr., who lived at the White House with his parents. John Adams, Jr., sent a report of the expenditures he had made in that first year to the Committee on the Expenditures on the Public Buildings with a letter, dated February 8, 1826, in which he stated that "expenditures have all been made with an eye to strict economy. Scarcely an Article has been purchased which was not indispensably necessary; everything has been procured when possible, in this City or District, in order to avoid the expenses of transportation; and it is believed that not one cent has been paid on account of Commission or Agency to any individual whomever."[85]

The account was probably submitted to the committee, because in that first year a sizable portion of the $14,000 had been spent; and it was obvious that the committee would have to ask Congress for more money to tide the president

through the rest of the term of office. Accordingly, the committee asked the House of Representatives to pass another appropriation of $25,000 "for finishing the large room in the President's House, for the purchase of furniture and for repairs of the house." This request prompted bitter debate on the House floor criticizing the large amount of money being requested. Congressmen complained about the extravagant manner in which the house was being furnished and about the way in which the previous appropriation had been spent. The debate seemed to follow party lines with those of Mr. Adams's party in favor of the appropriation bill and those of the opposition against it. The argument reflected the dissatisfaction of many of the congressmen with the French purchases made during the Monroe administration, an opinion being openly expressed in contemporary newspapers. In the words of the *New England Palladium and Commercial Advertiser:* "We hope she [meaning Mrs. Adams] will study to adorn her residence with articles made solely by American Manufacturers. . . . . . . we hope the inside of the President's House, during the administration of Mr. Adams, may assume a national aspect. We have no doubt our mechanicks and manufacturers would make it vie in splendour with any in Europe."[86]

The act appropriating the $25,000 was passed, and a bill also was enacted "that all furniture purchased for the use of the President's House shall be as far as practicable of American or domestic manufacture."[87] Either accidentally or deliberately, the bill neglected to authorize anyone to expend the money so the president was not able to spend a penny of it.

The directive to purchase American-made products was treated very seriously by Congress, but was not applied to the purchase of china for another century. The excuse used was that no china produced in this country could compete with the imported china. The words "as far as practicable" in the act gave Adams and future presidents the loophole they needed to continue the purchase of china of foreign manufacture.

President and Mrs. Adams went to Massachusetts in July 1826, called there by the death of the president's father, John Adams. Before they left Massachusetts in October 1826, an order was placed with the Boston firm of J. & T. H. Perkins & Sons for "2 Dining setts of half stone china." These were large services which contained 157 pieces each listed as:

36 flat plates			36
12 soup "			12
24 flat "	2nd size		24
24 flat "	3rd		24
12 custard cups & cover			24
1 soup tureens, stand & cover			3
2 sauce " " "			6
3 butter boats & stands			4
1 sallad bowl			1
2 veg. dishes & c.			4
19 dishes 1-18"; 1-16"; 1-14"; 4-12"			
6-10" and 6-8"			

These sets cost $40 each for a total of $80.[88]

The discovery of the new body called stoneware took place early in the nineteenth century. It was essentially a utility ware because of the strength of the body, but the best of the so-called "ironstone" china came to be used in the massive dinner services which were in daily use. It was dear to the hearts and to the pockets of mid-century America, because it was relatively cheap and well-nigh indestructible.

On their return to Washington from Quincy, Massachusetts, the president and his family stopped in New York City where he purchased more china at the firm of Samuel Grace at 31 Maiden Lane. This service is described as a dinner service of French china containing: [89]

2 soup tureens & stands	
4 sauce tureens	
22 dishes asst	
4 covered dishes	
4 octagon dishes	
8 shells	
10 dz. dinner plates	
4 dz soups	
8 dz dessert (4-6"; 4-8")	340.00
2 dz rich gilt cups & saucers	35.00
2 boxes	2.00
	377.00

This is further evidence of the French china available from merchants in the more affluent cities after 1820.

By March 9, 1827, President Adams presented to the Treasury Department the receipted bills for $1,386.43 of the $14,000 granted to him two years before, and on July 25, 1827, he paid $123.57 which was still due to the Treasury.[90]

In the meantime, the Committee on the Expenditures on the Public Buildings reported to the House of Representatives on February 7, 1827, that the president had been given no authorization to spend the $25,000 so kindly appropriated for him the previous year. They recommended that the appropriation be made subject to the disposition of the president and that the president be authorized to spend from that amount $1,826 for furnishing the large (east) room of the President's House plus $6,000 for purchase of other furniture and the repairs of the house. In justification, the chairman said that the committee had deducted from the amount of money originally requested enough to take care of items already purchased or contracted for as well as enough to cover expenses of maintaining the house in proper condition. The authorization to spend the revised amount was given in an act of Congress on March 2, 1827.[91]

The large services of china purchased in 1825 and 1826 seem to have been adequate for the rest of the administration. The only supplemental china purchased were "8 doz plates" purchased from the Washington dealer, A. B. Waller, in January 1828, and "5 doz blue plates" on September 14 of that same year.[92] On September 13, "2 doz blue plates" were bought from M. Shantz, another Washington dealer.[93]

As the end of his administration approached, the president wrote in his diary on February 23, 1829, that "Mr. Ringgold the Marshal called this morning—I desired him to come in the course of the week and with Mr. Elgar to take an inventory of the furniture in the House belonging to the Public and to be delivered up. . . . " Again on February 29, the President's entry states: "Mr. Ringgold called twice this morning first to enquire when the Inventory should be taken of the furniture of this house to be delivered over, which I told him could not be done till after the third of March all my servants being till then constantly occupied with the removal of my own." [94]

This inventory has not yet been located in National Archives or in The Adams Papers, though it certainly appears to have been made. It is, of course, possible that because of the breakage of china and glass by the mobs who swarmed to the house after the inauguration of President Jackson on March 4, 1829, that the marshall and the commissioner decided that such a document, if taken or recorded after March 4, would embarrass both the outgoing and the incoming president.

Andrew Jackson

I have the beautiful recollection of the whole stately house adorned and ready for company—the great wood fires in every room, the immense number of wax-lights softly burning, the stands of camellias and laurestina banked row upon row; after going through all this silent waiting fairyland we were taken to the state dining room where was the gorgeous supper table shaped like a horseshoe, and covered with every good and glittering thing French skill could devise, and at either end was a monster salmon in waves of meat jelly.

Excerpt from *Souvenirs of My Times* by Jesse Benton Frémont (Boston: D. Lathrop and Company, 1887), page 95.

Probably the most unrestrained White House reception in history followed the inauguration of Andrew Jackson as president of the United States. He was the "People's Choice" and the people had their day. The mansion was thrown open to the immense throng of visitors who had come to Washington to see their hero sworn into office. The dignity of the occasion disappeared under the pressure of the rabble, a mob "scrabbling, fighting, romping." It was said that damage amounting to several thousand dollars was done to the glass and china in the crush to reach the refreshments. It finally became necessary to carry out the punch and the food in tubs and buckets to supply the crowd estimated at 20,000 persons.

Fortunately for President Jackson, an Executive Order of March 3, 1829, gave him the usual amount of $14,000 for refurnishing the President's House. He delegated the responsibility of overseeing the expenditures to his good friend, Maj. William B. Lewis, who had accompanied him from Tennessee.

As usual, the first purchases were for miscellaneous household china which Antonio Guista,[95] the president's steward, bought as needed from the local store of Michael Shantz. Guista had a running account there from January 1830 to January 1831 during which he paid $44.25 for plates, bowls, cups, and saucers. Most of them were called "c. c." (cream color) and a few were called "B. E." (blue edged).[96]

By May 20, 1831, it became necessary to purchase a complete dining service which was bought from Robinson Tyndale of Philadelphia.[97] The following pieces are listed on the voucher.

One dining set, viz:				
4 doz. plates	48	4 covered dishes	8
2 doz. soups	24	2 sallad bowls	2
4 " twiffling	48	4 pickles	4
4 doz. muffins	48	2 doz. custard	24
18 dishes	18	4 bakes	4
2 soup tureens	6		
4 sauce "	16	A total of	258
4 boats & stands	8	pieces which cost	$50.00

This was paid out of a supplemental appropriation bill passed on March 2, 1831, which provided President Jackson with an additional $5,000 for his furniture fund.

The price of this service and the pieces listed would suggest that it was inexpensive English earthenware such as that made at Rockingham. Perhaps the piece of earthenware at the Daughters of the American Revolution Museum in Washington, D.C., and those in private collections which are marked "Brameld" are from this service. These pieces came from the collection of William Crump, the White House steward during the administrations of Presidents Grant, Hayes, and Arthur. Crump thought the china of this set belonged to President Jefferson, but it is now known that none of the china that he used in the President's House survived the fire of 1814.

Guista continued to buy miscellaneous household china from the Shantz store and in the period from March 3 to October 1831, Shantz received $49 for items described as "blue china," "green sprig china," and "stone china." The most elegant purchase listed on this voucher were two dozen gilt cups and saucers which cost $9. Voucher 62, also submitted by Shantz, is much like the miscellaneous china described in the $49 bill.[98]

Just before President Jackson's second term commenced, another $20,000 was appropriated by an act of Congress passed on March 3, 1833, to spend for furnishing the President's House "in addition to the proceeds of such decayed furniture as he may direct to be sold." The need for this additional large appropriation was supported by a list of estimates for services and furnishings drawn up by L. Veron and Company of Philadelphia which is attached to Miscellaneous Treasury Account 61369. President Jackson wished to finish furnishing the house in the style begun by President Monroe. The East Room had not yet been completed and things purchased in 1817 already needed replacing. The estimate prepared states specifically that "upon examination of the china I find it is very broken up and what does remain is very defaced, but it will and can be used for ordinary purposes in the house and save the expense of purchase for everyday use." An estimate was then made for purchase of a "Dinner Service for China for 50 persons $1,500.00 and Dessert Service of China for 50 persons $1,000." [99] The state china was evidently ordered from L. Veron and Company as soon as the appropriation bill was passed. That the porcelain was made to order in France is confirmed in a letter dated July 26, 1833, from George W. South of that firm to Major Lewis at the President's House: "News from france that the china had be [sic] made and was painting." [100] It is interesting to compare this service for fifty with the state service of the Monroe administration which was for only thirty persons.

In November 1833, the following list of china was billed to the President's House.

1 sett French China for dinner, with the American eagle containing:

14	dishes, round	14½" each
10	" "	11½"
8	" "	12½"
12	" oval	13"
12	" "	14"
4	" "	16"
4	" "	18"
6	doz soup plates	
20	doz flat "	
2	long fish dishes—24-inch	
2	" " " 26-inch	
12	vegetable dishes and covers	
4	sugar covers and plates round	

4	" " " oblong
6	pickle shells	
6	olive boats	
4	octagon sallad bowls	
	440 pieces, made to order	$1,500.00

One dessert set, blue and gold, with eagle:

6	stands for bonbons, 3 stage
8	tambours " " "
12	sweetmeat compotiers, on feet
6	round sugars and covers
8	compotiers on feet
6	large fruit baskets on feet
4	ice cream vases and covers with inside bowls
12	doz plates 8 inch
6	doz plates 7 inch
5	doz Greek form cups and saucers
4	oval sugar dishes
4	cream jugs
	412 pieces, made to order	$1,000.00

Payment for the china was received by L. Veron and Company on January 8, 1834.[101]

The blue and gold china with the eagle which was ordered from France has never been identified. In a private collection, there is a compote with a blue and gold band and decoration of small gold eagles which might be from the dessert service, but the quality of the china and its decoration does not seem elegant enough to come from a French dessert service which cost $1,000 and was handpainted to order.

Portions of another dessert service have survived in the hands of descendants of Daniel Webster with a family legend that he had acquired these pieces from President Monroe. This china has a wide blue marbleized border with a gold rim and the Arms of the United States on each piece. The quality of the china, the elegance of its design, and the use of the Arms of the United States suggest that this is the Jackson dessert service. There were two "decayed furniture" sales; one was in 1851 and one in 1852 when Daniel Webster was secretary of state in the cabinet of President Millard Fillmore. Thus, he could have purchased the china either at private sale or public auction. The repeat of the Monroe eagle in the design of the porcelain would account for the confusion in identifying

French porcelain plate supposed to have been used in the President's House during the administration of President Jackson.

13. Soup plate of white porcelain with a gold line around the edge and a gold circle in the center. There are no marks on this china. Diameter, 9¼ inches.

French porcelain dessert service from the state
china, possibly purchased by President Jackson from
L. Veron and Company of Philadelphia in 1833.

*14. White porcelain plate with a blue marbleized
border edged with gold. The center decoration
is the Arms of the United States in color.
(White House collection.)*

*15. The mark on the reverse of the plate is "M^{ture}
de Madame/ Duchesse d'Angoulême/ P. L. Dagoty
E Honoré/ à Paris."*

14

15

the proper administration at the time Webster acquired the china. Assuming the portion of this dessert service belonging to the family of Daniel Webster is the missing dessert service from the administration of President Jackson, it follows that the firm of L. Veron went back to the same factory in France from which the Monroe service was ordered to acquire the same design. By this time the firm of Pierre Louis Dagoty and Edouard Honoré had been dissolved, but Honoré had continued to work in the same decorating shop on the Boulevard Poissonnière in Paris which had been owned by the partners. The Monroe design was repeated, but in applying it to the Jackson order the eagle was reversed so that in 1833 it faced the viewer's right instead of left. In order not to upset the foreign purchaser, they even used the same manufacturer's stamp that had been used on the earlier service: "M^{ture} de Madame/Duchesse d'Angoulême/ P. L. Dagoty, E. Honoré/à Paris." Pieces of the dessert service, attributed here to the Jackson administration can be seen in collections of the White House, the Smithsonian Institution, the Essex Institute, and the American Museum in Bath, England. There are also pieces in a private collection.

To help pay for the quantity of silver, glass, china, carpets, and elegant furnishings received in 1833, a quantity of old furnishings was sold at public auction by P. Mauro on December 5 and 23 of that year. The list of things sold include the following pieces of china—unfortunately, without descriptions.

2 oval dishes @ 3.12½		6.25
4 oval dishes @ 1.75		7.00
4 " "		4.24
4 round "		6.00
4 round dishes		6.00
4 Pickles & saucers		6.00
3 " "		2.25
15 custards		7.50
15 custards		7.50
2 Centre dishes		17.50
4 oblong dishes		7.50
4 " "		8.00
6 " "		6.75
3 " "		2.25
15 custards		7.50
15 custards		7.50
4 Fruit baskets		6.60
Lot China		10.25

This reference gives an unusually detailed account of the auction sale.

In order to display the Goods to the best advantage I Rented a room on the Avenue, had tables made and hired baize to cover them for which I paid $31 as stated below and have charged you the proportion, the average of which is 1¾ per cent the amount of the sale—My goods sold for $1,059.24— the goods from the President's for $646.18.

He mentions as charges "rent of room, carpenter's work, cataloguers, Baize, wood and candles." [102]

Even with the auction sale in Washington and the sale of some of the old silver, lamps, and hangings by L. Veron in Philadelphia, there was still not enough money on hand to cover all the expenditures. This was pointed out to the chairman of the congressional committee in a memorandum on January 2, 1834. An act of Congress, passed on June 30, 1834, authorized an additional $6,000 for completing the "furniture" of the President's House.

As might be expected, expenditures for the remaining years of the administration were kept to a minimum. There were occasional purchases for miscellaneous household china from local stores by Joseph Boulanger, who had replaced Antonio Guista as the president's steward. Guista had been dismissed in 1833, because Jackson thought the household expenses of $1,000 a month were due to the steward's disinterest. Although Boulanger's household expenses were dramatically lower during the first few months of his service, it was not long before he was spending as much, if not more, than Guista.[103]

In December of 1834, Boulanger purchased one dozen white china cups and saucers and one dozen china chocolate cups and saucers from F. A. Ellery for $5.50.[104]

In the fall of 1836, in preparation for the last social season of the Jackson administration, a purchase for the President's House was made from Charles A. Burnett, a dealer and silversmith in neighboring Georgetown.[105]

1½ doz.	Band and line Deep China			
	plates	@ 6.50	9.75
4 doz.	flat with single band	@ 6.00	24.00
			33.75

In 1965 the Smithsonian Institution acquired two plates of this description which came with the history of having been White House china of the administration of President Andrew Jackson.

The presence of an American porcelain of fine quality on the market at this time leaves speculation about how and why President Jackson disregarded the act of 1826 requiring the purchase of articles of domestic manufacture whenever possible. We know he was aware of the handsome china being produced by William Ellis Tucker in Philadelphia, because on April 3, 1830, he wrote to Tucker acknowledging the receipt of a sample of "the porcelain which it [a letter from Tucker] offered to my acceptance. . . . It seems to be not inferior to the finest specimens of French porcelain. But whether the facilities for its manufacture bring its cost so nearly to an equity with that of the French . . . is a question which I am not able to answer."[106] President Jackson must have been pleased enough with the sample to order some of the china for himself, for on July 13, 1830, Tucker wrote to the president who was then at The Hermitage, his home at Nashville, Tennessee.[107]

About six weeks ago I received an order from you for the manufacture of some Porcelain which I immediately commenced and had it finished excepting the last burning. The kiln in which it was placed for the purpose of completing the process was unfortunately lost, owing to a long continuance of wet weather. . . . Inasmuch as I understood that the porcelain in question was designed for use during your stay at your country seat, I declined recommencing the order . . . until I learn from you your pleasure respecting it.

Perhaps this unfortunate experience and the

subsequent death of Tucker in 1832 made President Jackson wary of ordering from the firm with public funds, though the business continued to operate under Judge Joseph Hemphill until 1838. There is, however, some china identified as ·Tucker in the collections of The Hermitage.

Other china which can be definitely identified today as that used in the President's House during the Jackson administration is some gold and white French china. Andrew Jackson personally purchased it from Mrs. Stephen Decatur in 1833 and took it to The Hermitage with him.

A dessert sett of the finest quality of French China consisting of
4 dozen plates
1½ dozen deep plates
8 dishes
3 baskets
2 Sauce Tureens—The Sett Cost two hundred dollars in Paris
3½ doz of rich white and gold dinner plates—These cost twelve dollars a dozen.

President Jackson paid Mrs. Decatur $350 for the china and eight silver-plated vegetable dishes. She sent him the following note on May 19, 1833.

I will take great pleasure in seeing the articles carefully pack'd up—I have the same cases in which they were imporported [sic] and in which they have been frequently knocked about from one part of the U. States to another without the slightest injury. . . .[108]

In 1817, President Monroe had ordered some French porcelain for Mrs. Decatur, and this was included in the shipment sent to the President's House from the firm of Russell and LaFarge in Le Havre.[109] The order was marked on the shipping invoice sent to President Monroe as being for Mrs. Stephen Decatur and on the bill she was charged 840 francs for the china in addition to shipping charges and postage. In the small community of official Washington in the early nineteenth century, the circle made by the Decatur china—from the time of its order from France in 1817 with furnishings for the President's House to its purchase in 1833 by President

16. *Pieces of the French porcelain dessert service.*
Compote: height, 6-3/16 inches; diameter, 10⅜ inches.
Oval dish: height, 1½ inches; width, 7-9/16 inches;
length, 10-3/16 inches. (White House collection.)

17. *This cup seems to be from the Jackson service*
with the marbleized border, because the eagle's
head is turned toward the viewer's right and because
of the similar technique of painting. (Courtesy
of the James Monroe Law Office and Library,
Fredericksburg, Virginia.)

16

17

Jackson and its possible use there until the end of his administration in 1837—is a perfect example of the way household possessions in the capital city traveled from owner to owner within the same stratum of Washington society.[110]

Despite the fact that an inventory of the furniture in the President's House taken at the end of the Jackson administration has not been located, there is a record of one having been made on March 3, 1837, by order of President Jackson. The inventory is mentioned in a letter from the commissioner of public buildings, William Noland, dated June 12, 1840, and refers to the inventory taken by himself and the second auditor of the Treasury.[111]

Martin
Van Buren

William
Henry
Harrison

John Tyler

*Well the great ball is over and you may congratu-
late us accordingly—It was a magnificent affair—
The company well dressed and as select as* three
thousand *persons could make it—Yes there were
full that number here and of course one quarter
at least were uninvited guests—The east room was
brilliantly illuminated with some hundred additional lights the floor highly polished and orchestra
(with full band in scarlet uniforms) tastefully hung
with blue satin drapery above which floated the
national flag. . . . The supper table arranged under
my own eye was superb, and wine and champagne
flowed like water—eight dozen bottles of champagne were drunk with wine by the barrel . . .
Julia led off the Ball . . . . She looked her best and
was dressed it white satin underdress embroidered
with silver with bodice en sailé and over that a
white [?] looped up all around with white roses
and buds—white headdress hat with three ostrich
feathers and full set of diamonds—We were
arranged as usual along the side of the Circular
room and every one was struck with the beautiful
appearance of the Court.*

Excerpt from the Gardiner Family Papers in the
Yale Library quoted in *The Yale University Library
Gazette,* volume 34, number 1 (July 1959),
"President Tyler and the Gardiners: A New Por-
trait," page 10.

When President Van Buren moved into the
President's House in 1837, it was probably the
most elegantly furnished dwelling ever inherited
by an incoming president. He was definitely
the first president to move into a completely
furnished President's House. In view of the great
expenditures made during the administration of
Andrew Jackson, it seems very generous of the
Congress to have placed a $20,000 furniture
fund at the disposal of President Van Buren
by an act of March 3, 1837.

Despite the fact that the house had been well
furnished in the previous administration, Van
Buren found it needed considerable refurbishing
after Jackson's residence of eight years. He immediately set in motion a great flurry of house-
cleaning, and a thorough renovation of the
interior. Nearly the whole appropriation was
spent for this purpose—most of it on upholstery
and curtain fabrics; repairs of such items as
furniture, chandeliers, and silver; regilding and
repapering—so that the house must have gleamed
with splendor. Very little of the money was
spent on new furniture or furnishings.

All of the china purchases for the administration were made for miscellaneous household
china at the local store of Thomas Pursell. The
orders are much like those of previous administrations, consisting mainly of several dozen plates
at a time, a dozen cups and saucers, single
serving dishes, and similar items. These orders
specifically mention blue printed mugs and plates,
blue-edged dishes, china gold-band coffees, gold-
band china plates, and willow plates.[112] None
of these are identifiable today.

The state china ordered during the administration of President Jackson was still in use for
the elegant formal dinners given by his successor.
This is mentioned in a speech that Charles Ogle,
congressman from Pennsylvania, made on the
floor of the House of Representatives in 1840.
Ogle was outraged by a request in the general
appropriation bill for $3,665 for additional
furniture for the President's House. Small wonder
that Congress was totally out of patience, for
Van Buren had already been granted a supplemental appropriation in 1838,[113] and this was
the beginning of a bitter campaign year. Ogle
was a strong supporter of General William
Henry Harrison, the "Log Cabin" candidate, and
it was an ideal opportunity to point out what
he considered to be the regal pretensions of Van
Buren. Armed with an array of figures, bills,
vouchers, and other documentary evidence to
support his theory, he took up each bill individ-
ually to prove his point that the Nation was
being asked "to support their Chief servant in
a Palace as splendid as that of the Caesars and as
richly adorned as the proudest Asiatic mansion."
Van Buren was personally assailed for every
elegant and costly addition to the house from the
time of its refurnishing in 1817 under President
Monroe to his own administration. With little
regard for historical accuracy or honesty, each
bill and voucher from 1817 on was presented to
Congress as a purchase by Van Buren.

Congressman Ogle could speak with some accuracy when it came to the elegant dinners given by the president, as he had himself been a guest at the President's House. Undeterred by a feeling of obligation to his host, he pointed out with sarcasm:

> How delightful it must be to a real genuine Loco Foco to eat his *pate de fois gras, dinde didosse* and *salade a la volaille* from a silver plate with a golden knife and fork. And how exquisite to sip with a gold spoon his *soupe a la Reine* from a silver tureen.
> I will in the next place call the attention of the committee to the bill for the splendid French China for dinner service and the elegant dessert set of blue and gold with eagle all made to order in France and imported by Louis Veron & Co., celebrated dealers in fancy China, etc. Philadelphia.[114]

Van Buren was not without his supporters. Levi Lincoln, a Whig congressman from Massachusetts, rose to his defense. He pointed out a few of the inconsistencies in Congressman Ogle's speech. At one point, Lincoln said:

> One thing above all seems to have created amazement with the member. He has found in his manly and dignified research an invoice of "cups and saucers" which were in the Closets of Mr. Adams; and he cries out with astonishment at their number. What need, he demands, of so *many* dozens of cups and saucers! Sir, I will tell the member. They are wanted for a purpose which he could never conjecture—the hospitable entertainment of visitors and friends—. They were used for the refreshment of the nation's guests.[115]

The whole dispute was referred to the Committee on Expenditure on the Public Buildings which reported at the first session of the 26th Congress. The report was printed in the United States House Reports, and the greatest value of the accusation against President Van Buren is the printed public record it occasioned concerning the furnishings of the President's house and the manner in which they were acquired.[116]

President Van Buren did not get any more money. One wonders how he could survive without any expenditures for miscellaneous household china which, up to that time, were made almost monthly. That mystery was finally cleared up several administrations later, in 1846. In the account of William W. Corcoran, purchasing agent for President James K. Polk, there is a bill from Thomas Pursell for items sold to President Van Buren in 1839 and 1840 for which Pursell finally was paid in 1846.[117] Again, the account is repetitious. In addition to the blue earthenware purchased in 1836 and 1837 "6 large green-Edged dishes china" were also mentioned.

The inventory for the administration of Van Buren has not yet been located, but one is known to have been taken. In March of 1841, William Noland, the commissioner of public buildings received a letter from R. H. Hammond of Milton, Pennsylvania.

> Statement has been made by respectable men in this neighborhood who were recently in Washington attending the inauguration that the furniture of the chambers of the Presidents were entirely stripped and the articles carried off by the late Prest, Mr. Van B.—prior to the 4th of March—. They even give the number of boxes filled and carried off by the Late Prest. at 75 in number.

Mr. Noland answered him immediately.

> It is true that a number of boxes were sent on to New York from the President's House; but these boxes contained furniture, glass, books, documents, papers, wines etc which belong to Mr. Van Buren and to his son Maj[r] Van Buren—. Mr. Van Buren was a housekeeper in Washington for several years and had collected articles of furniture for his own use, as had his son Maj[r]. Van Buren. It may not be improper here to state that it is customary, at the close of the presidential term to take an inventory of the furniture, plate, etc. belonging to the President's house and that the Commission of Public Buildings did at the request of Mr. Van Buren take such an inventory a few days before the inauguration of the new President, one copy of the inventory was delivered to Mr. Van Buren, one to Col. Chambers, the agent of Gen[l] Harrison and one retained by the Commissioner of Public Buildings.[118]

In spite of the fact that President William Henry Harrison was only in office one month, he spent $1,826.81 out of the usual appropriation voted on March 3, 1841. As a matter of fact, his purchases began before he even assumed office. As early as February 26, 1841, there is a bill for china purchased by him. It was the usual miscellaneous chinaware needed for ordinary household use and was bought from the firm of Hugh C. Smith in Alexandria, Virginia. Perhaps the Harrison ménage could foresee the necessity of more dishes to serve the mobs of people who were descending on the city for the inauguration of the popular "Log Cabin" president and who might be expected to call at the President's House after the inaugural ceremony. It is the consensus that on inauguration day "the crowd at the President's house was immense and the marvel is that serious accidents did not occur." Because of President Harrison's death in April 1841, the payment for the bill presented by Hugh Smith and Company was made in an account set up especially for the purpose without any purchasing agent listed. The bill was personally certified for payment by President John Tyler as "for goods purchased during the lifetime of the late President."[119]

President Harrison's Virginia connections made the purchase of household furnishings in nearby Alexandria, Virginia, a reasonable procedure. Especially in the first half of the nineteenth century, vouchers prove that it was the practice of each president to make his purchases in a locality with which he was personally familiar and in which he felt he could trust the merchants. It is interesting to note that Hugh Smith and Company had already furnished china for the President's House in 1809 during the administration of another Virginian, James Madison.[120] By the time of the Harrison administration, Dolley Madison was living in Washington again, a revered and honored senior citizen of Washington society. She may even have recommended the Alexandria store to President Harrison or members of his official family.

Further purchases for President Harrison are also to be found with the accounts of President John Tyler who assumed office in April 1841 after the sudden death of Harrison. President Tyler's first account, submitted in 1843, included a whole packet of accounts of purchases made by Seth Hyatt for the late President Harrison.[121] More of Harrison's bills are contained in a separate account submitted by Seth Hyatt in July 1843, which covered the last few days of the Harrison administration and the first months of the administration of President Tyler. This account includes a payment of $25 which was made to W. A. Williams[122] "to taking inventory" after Harrison's death. The name of Samuel Redfern appears in two vouchers as furnishing miscellaneous household china for the house during February, March, and April, 1841.[123]

The bill for the final china purchased for President Harrison was paid in 1846 during the Polk administration at the direction of the Comptroller's Office. The bill was for "8 Edged dishes" which were purchased March 22, 1841, from Thomas Pursell for $5.[124]

The state service bought by President Jackson obviously was still being used for formal occasions at the President's House as there is no bill for a complete dining service in either the Harrison or Tyler administrations. President Tyler may have bought some replacements of the more expendable pieces of the Jackson state service in a purchase he too made from Hugh Smith in Alexandria on September 20, 1841. The voucher covers "6 doz. Rich Gilt and Pain^d china plates to pattern @ $12—$72.00" and "6 doz, Rich Gilt and Pain^d coffee cups and saucers at $6 a dozen for $36.00."[125] The cost of these plates, cups, and saucers, the description of "rich" gilt, and the information that they were painted seems to indicate that they were made to match the china already in use. Perhaps the coffee cups and saucers purchased in Alexandria are those with the eagle which are in the collections of the James Monroe Law Office Museum and Memorial Library in Fredericksburg, Virginia. The eagle has his head turned to the viewer's right like the Jackson service rather than to the left as on the Monroe china, or they may be the cups and saucers in the Daughters of the American Revolution Museum in Washington, D.C., which have the same eagle design in gold.

President Tyler purchased cheaper miscellaneous pieces of china from Thomas Pursell, the Washington merchant who was currently enjoying the patronage of the President's House.[126]

Harrison was the first president to die in office and the transfer of the position to the former Vice-President Tyler seems to have complicated the expenditure of the furniture fund. In each act of Congress which appropriates the money for furniture for the President's House, authorization for its expenditure is given only to a specific president who usually designated an agent. After Harrison's death the auditors of the Treasury Department must have been unsure whether or not the authorization to expend the furniture fund was automatically passed to Harrison's successor without further action of Congress. This would explain why Seth Hyatt continued to act as agent until July 1841. His final account for the period to July 1841 was submitted in 1843 at which time John Tyler, Jr., submitted his first account as agent for his father for the two-year period following July 1841.[127]

The last account to be entered during the Tyler administration is dated January 22, 1845, and was simply to settle the balance owed to President Tyler for expenditures on the previous account and does not contain any purchases of china.[128]

II *The Nationalistic Period, 1845–1893*

By 1846 there was a growing nationalistic emphasis in American politics which is reflected in the porcelain ordered for the president's table. Although the china was still manufactured in France, its design was dictated in this country and it was superimposed on blanks manufactured in the rococo style then considered fashionable. On his official dinner service, President James Polk used the red, white, and blue shield of the United States with the motto of the United States across the face of the shield. The scrolled and gilded rims of the plates are typically French as are the beautifully executed flower designs in the center of each of the dessert plates. Succeeding presidents used the American bald eagle and the Arms of the United States to emphasize the suitability of the china selected to be a formal banquet service for the use of the president of the United States.

Nationalistic fervor reached its peak with the extraordinary china designed by Theodore Davis for President Rutherford B. Hayes featuring the flora and fauna of America. A more restrained and more formal expression of this same fervor can be found in the china designed by Mrs. Benjamin Harrison which featured cornstalks and goldenrod as symbols of America's bounty and beauty. All of these porcelains were still being manufactured in France.

The more prosaic wares of this period, purchased as usual in the retail stores of the Washington area, were earthenware and commercial grades of French and English porcelain—rococo in style and floral in design.

James K. Polk

Zachary Taylor

Millard Fillmore

I was very agreeably disappointed in the President [James K. Polk]. I had expected a tall, grim man and to my surprise found on entering the room a short, slender and pleasant looking gentleman with long silvery hair, bowing and congeeing about, shaking hands very cordially with whigs and democrats alike. To be sure he does not care now he's got it, but he might show a little spite to the whigs if he wanted to do so. He resembles Gen. Jackson as a young hickory tree would a stiff old one. Mr. W. arranged the march to the dinner, the order of the polka. There were forty guests and the dinner table was as handsome as any I ever saw in proportion to its size, not even excepting the supper table at the Tuilleries at the Queen's Ball. The servants wore dark blue coats, white vests, cravats and gloves. There were two hundred chandeliers, candelabras and figures around the grand center ornament, all of which were of gilt burnished and very brilliant with vases of flowers. The dining room is the west room of the right wing and corresponding to one half of the east room. Three long windows were hung with purple and gold coloured figured curtains and purple velvet chairs with carved rosewood frames. As the furniture is all new and fresh and all the decorations newly gilded, it was very splendid. Sit! I guess we did sit—for four mortal hours, I judged one hundred and fifty courses, for everything was in the French style and each dish a separate course.

Soup, fish, green peas, spinach, canvas back duck, turkey, birds, oyster pies, cotolettes di mouton, ham deliciously garnished, potatoes like snowballs, croquettes, poulet, in various forms, duck and olives, pate de foie gras, jellies, orange and lemon charlotte russe, ices and "pink mud" oranges, prunes, sweetmeats, mottos and everything one can imagine, all served in silver dishes with silver tureens and wine coolers and the famous gold forks, knives and spoons for dessert. The china was white and gold and blue with a crest, the eagle, of course, and the dessert plates were a mazarine blue and gold with a painting in the center of fruits and flowers.

The President had to be so kind as to drink all our healths, although we looked in pretty good case just then. The glassware was very handsome, blue and white finely cut, and pink champagne, gold sherry, green hock, madeira, the ruby port, and sauterne, formed a rainbow around each plate—with the finger glasses and water decanters. Eating must end when repletion begins and at the finale, with

a number of mottos for each lady who boasted of her children, we danced the Polka in reverse and reached the drawing room in safety. Coffee was served and liquers, and we bade adieu and reached home at ten o'clock.

Excerpt from the diary of Mrs. James Dixon, wife of Congressman Dixon from Connecticut, for December 19, 1845. Permission to quote was granted by Miss Elizabeth D. Welling.

When James K. Polk became president, he asked his good friend, William W. Corcoran to act as his agent in expending the furniture fund which again had been appropriated by an act of Congress on March 3, 1845. Corcoran had begun his business career in Georgetown as a dry-goods merchant and had operated a wholesale auction house and commission firm before going into the banking business. When Daniel Webster left Washington in 1845 at the end of his service as secretary of state in the Tyler administration, Corcoran purchased Webster's house on Lafayette Square. As he was traveling to New York to purchase furnishings for his own recently acquired home, he made purchases at the same time for the President's House as a favor for the newly elected President and Mrs. Polk.

On April 25, 1845, Corcoran purchased from the firm of B. Gardiner at 285 Broadway "1 Elegant Blue Tea Set" which cost $85 and had the bill sent to him at the "Astor House" where he was staying.[129] The elegant blue tea set thus acquired cannot be positively identified, but the Smithsonian Institution has in its collections pieces of a blue and gold tea set which was purchased at an auction of "decayed" White House furnishings in the mid-nineteenth century. The china is English of the type produced at the Rockingham factory. By the time the set reached the Smithsonian Institution in 1933, it had acquired a legendary association with Dolley Madison; unfortunately, Dolley's personal charm was so great that many of the surviving nineteenth-century White House furnishings which were acquired at the public sales attained, at the same time, a history of ownership by Dolley Madison. The set which came to the Smithsonian would certainly be described as elegant and it does seem to date from this period. Perhaps Dolley's name was associated with it because she was an honored guest at the President's House during the Polk administration and must have often enjoyed tea from the elegant blue tea set.

Corcoran also bought household china at the firm of J. J. Joyce in the City of Washington, listing specifically "cream jugs" and "cups and saucers of granite china."[130]

None of the miscellaneous chinaware purchased in these administrations can be identified. It was also time for the purchase of a new state dinner service for the elegant dinner service purchased by President Jackson had now been in use for more than ten years and was undoubtedly much depleted. In March 1846 Alexander Stewart and Company, the famous dry-goods house in New York City, procured a new state service for the President's House for which they received the following bill.[131]

1 porcelain dinner and desert service
445187 francs @ 20 pr. fr. is   890.37
    add 10%   89.03
                       ————
                       979.40

This new state dinner service was white with a rim which was molded in scrolls and gilded. The shield of the United States in red, white, and blue and the motto of the United States "E Pluribus Unum" on a banner swirled across the face of the shield was also placed on the rim of each plate. The dessert service had plates the same size and shape as the plates in the dinner service with the borders painted a light green.

On the dessert service, the shield in color and the banner are in a white reserve on the green rim. The center of each dessert plate was decorated with a different handsome flower in full color. The dessert service also contained fruit baskets and compotes with the green band, gilt scrolls, and floral decorations. The use of the French spelling, the bill, and the notation of the cost in francs indicates that Stewart and Company had procured a French service. The china itself bears the mark in red on a scroll: "E D

Honoré/Boul^d/à Paris/Manufacture/à Champroux Allier." Where the scroll rolls up at the bottom, "N°" and "Prix" are printed.

Once again the state service had been made at the same factory in which the first service was made in 1817. After the partnership between P. L. Dagoty and Edouard Honoré was dissolved in 1820, Honoré continued operation in the decorating shop on the Boulevard Poissonnière. In 1824 he moved the factory from Paris to Champroux (Allier), keeping only the decorating shop in Paris. The mark was in use until Edouard Honoré died in 1855. The shield which decorates each piece of the service contains 27 stars, the number of states in the Union from 1845 to 1846, which was the year the china was ordered. Stylistically, this French porcelain is a revival of an earlier period with its rococo rim and the flowers decorating the center of the dessert plates. This was in keeping with the other products of the industrial nineteenth century which borrowed from an earlier period of creative art. The undecorated "blank" plate used for the service was not exclusive to the service painted for the President's House as the Smithsonian Institution's staff was shown other plates made on the same blank which have portraits of ladies decorating the center of the plates.

This service of official tableware of the Polk administration is represented in the collections of the Smithsonian Institution, the White House, the President James K. Polk Home in Columbia, Tennessee, and in many private collections of White House china. Individual pieces still turn up in public auctions today. Many people consider this service the most beautiful of all the state china—especially the dessert plates with their green borders.

These dessert plates were reproduced sometime later in the nineteenth century with the green border and the seal painted on a blank plate which did not have the scrolls molded into the blank china. On these plates, the scrolls are simply gilded on the flat rims of the plates. There has been no evidence that these plates with the flat borders were ever made to be used in the President's House as no vouchers were found for painted china ordered before the purchase of the

French porcelain dinner and dessert service purchased
by President Polk in 1846 from Alexander Stewart
and Company of New York City.

18

19

20

21

18. *Reverse of the dessert plate showing the mark of the Honoré factory.*

19. *White porcelain dinner plate with the rim molded and gilded in a scroll design decorated with the United States shield in color. Diameter, 9½ inches; depth, 1¼ inches.*

20. *Soup plate, similar to the dinner plate. Diameter, 9½ inches; depth, 1½ inches.*

21. *White porcelain dessert plate with border of light green. The rim of the plate is molded and gilded in a scroll design with the decoration that of the United States shield in color. Diameter, 9 inches.*

next state service by President Franklin Pierce. Most likely, they were made in the late nineteenth century to be sold as souvenirs at the same time the souvenir plates of other presidential administrations were produced for sale to the general public.

The first account submitted by William Corcoran also contained a voucher for payment of a bill for "1 doz Edged dishes" which President Tyler had purchased from Thomas Pursell in 1842.

President Polk had more than President Tyler's unpaid bills charged to his appropriation fund. In the account which Corcoran submitted in 1847, he was directed by the auditor of the Treasury to also pay Thomas Pursell for items sold to Martin Van Buren in 1839 and 1840. The following were included in this bill as having been purchased on January 28, 1840.[132]

2 doz cc. plates	$1.50
1 Blue pr[td] Pitcher	1
1 Ironstone "	1
1 White China cream	.75
6 Large green Edged dishes	6

He was also instructed to pay Pursell for "8 Edged dishes sold to "Gen'll Harrison" on March 22, 1841.[133]

Corcoran's last account covers the period from 1847 to 1849. Only miscellaneous china was purchased in this period from merchants in the Washington area. One was C. S. Fowler who furnished one dozen banded cups and saucers.[134] Another was the firm of Boteler and McGregor who furnished the President's House with "4 doz. plates, 3.50; 2 doz. [plates], 3.50;" and "1 doz. French Gold Band Teas, 4.50."[135]

The name of Boteler which appears frequently with the china of later administrations is first found on this voucher submitted during the Polk administration. The Boteler family, beginning with this bill dated March 13, 1848, furnished china for the President's House until late in the century. It was primarily miscellaneous china for general household use, but by the time of the Grant administration the firm was trusted with orders for the state dinner service.

The imprint left on the President's House of the sophistication and elegance of William Corcoran is unmistakable when the accounts and vouchers are studied. Corcoran, who helped finance the Mexican War for the administration of President Polk and who was the dominant force in Washington's social and cultural life in the middle of the nineteenth century, deserves equal recognition for his influence on the style in which President Polk and succeeding presidents have lived. From the time of the Polk administration to the present day, presidents of the United States and their authorized purchasing agents have recognized the quality of the household furnishings available in New York City and almost all the major purchases of furniture and decorative accessories since 1845 have been made there.

The Polk administration is one of the few for which the inventory of furniture is still on record. The inventory dated January 1, 1849, is found in the letter book of the commissioner of public buildings [136] accompanied by a letter dated December 31, 1849, from Commissioner Ignatius Mudd to Col. William W. Bliss, the secretary, son-in-law, and authorized purchasing agent for President Zachary Taylor. Mudd in his letter identifies this inventory as one taken in November 1848 by his immediate predecessor who was Charles Douglas. The following listing of china is part of the inventory.

15-3/12 doz.	dinner plates
3 doz.	soup plates
9-5/12 doz.	dessert plates
2 stands for confectionary	
4 fruit stands	
10 fruit stands, common	
8 stands for confectionary	
4 Vegetable dishes with covers	
2 Sallad Bowls	
8 Meat dishes different patterns	
3 large wine coolers, china	

In the words of Mudd, he felt the inventory would "afford but a limited estimate of the stock on hand"—a reasonable conclusion when we reflect on the amount of china purchased for the house in the interim since the last known inventory which was taken during the administration of President John Quincy Adams.

The accounts kept by Colonel Bliss are a model of specificity in comparison with the confusion which came before and which was to follow. His familiarity with keeping accounts for the United States government acquired during his education at West Point and his years of active duty in the United States Army is obvious. First of all, he submitted his accounts quarterly and the first account covering the second quarter of 1849 is prefaced by an authorization duly filed with the account stating that "Lt. Col. W.W.S. Bliss, U.S.A. is hereby appointed to make the disbursements out of the appropriation for furnishing the President's House made by the Civil and Diplomatic Appropriation Law of 3d March 1849 as well as balance of former appropriation for that object." The authorization is signed "Z. Taylor" and was dated April 3, 1849.[137]

Thomas Pursell had not been discouraged by the slow payment for china supplied for the President's House for, on March 9, 1849, he furnished "1 doz p^d cups and saucers, $1.25" and "2 doz willow plates, 2.50."[138]

There was no china purchased in the third quarter of 1849; in the fourth quarter, C. S. Fowler, another faithful Washington dealer, submitted bills for "1 doz Gold Band Coffee, 6.00"[139] purchased on July 20, and "3 doz banded cups and saucers, 13.50" which were purchased on December 11, 1849, probably to take care of the additional entertaining anticipated during the Christmas season.[140] In the first three months of 1850, Colonel Bliss purchased from the same dealer "2 doz Gold Band china plates" for $9 which may have been used with the cups and saucers.[141] The next account covers the period from April 1 to July 24, 1850.[142]

President Taylor died in office on July 8, 1850, and Colonel Bliss submitted his account to cover the end of the Taylor administration. On the following July 24, President Millard Fillmore personally certified that he had received from the colonel the unexpended amount of $717.36.

Commissioner Mudd during 1849 and 1850 was certainly conscious of his obligation to take

the inventory of the contents of the President's House as his comments to Colonel Bliss on December 31, 1849, indicate.

It appears to be one of the proscribed duties of the Commissioner of Public Buildings to exercise a supervisory care over the furniture, plate, etc. of the President's House. ... to comply with the obligation I am under I have thought it would be proper to take another and fuller inventory at such time and in such way as may be most convenient and agreeable to the President's family.[143]

Either it was never convenient to make the "fuller inventory" or that is just one more inventory which has disappeared from the letter book.

President Fillmore submitted his own accounts for purchases from the furniture fund. Purchases of banded china from C. S. Fowler continued, and in November the Fowler bill showed delivery of the following pieces.[144]

1 doz banded plates	$4.00
6 banded dishes	6.25
1 doz deep banded plates	4.50
1 " flat " "	4.50
also ½ doz banded cups and saucers	8.00

In October of 1851 from the same source, the following were purchased.[145]

1 banded butter	$3.00
½ doz coffees	3.25
1 doz banded plates	2.50
½ doz banded cup plates	.63

The popularity of the gold-band china can be explained by its availability on the local market and the fact that the simplicity of the design made it suitable for use with the large services still in use from previous administrations.

The continual reorder of what is called on the bills "banded" or "gold band" is one of the most interesting facts to emerge from a study of the invoices for miscellaneous china purchased during the first half of the nineteenth century. This china, which is assumed to be French tableware of good quality, was white porcelain deco-

22. Fruit basket and two compotes from the dessert service described for figure 21. Basket: height, 9¾ inches; diameter, 10¾ inches. Compote on left: height, 4½ inches; diameter, 9½ inches; depth of bowl, 1½ inches. Compote on right: height, 4⅝ inches; diameter, 9½ inches; depth of bowl, 1¼ inches.

Tea set purchased at a White House auction in Washington, D.C., in the mid-nineteenth century and tentatively identified as the "Elegant Blue Tea Set" purchased by President Polk from the firm of B. Gardiner in New York City in 1845.

23. Teacup: height, 2¼ inches; diameter, 3½ inches. Teapot: height, 6 inches; width, 10 inches. Coffee cup: height, 2¾ inches; diameter, 3 inches. Rear, plate diameters, 6 and 7½ inches. There are no marks on this china.

rated with a narrow gold band and variations thereof. It was being produced in the Paris factories and was advertised by American dealers as early as 1820.

According to account 107778, there were two sales of "decayed" furnishings during Fillmore's administration—one on November 22, 1851, conducted by Dyer and McGuire and one on April 22, 1852, conducted by James C. Mc-Guire.[148]

Franklin Pierce

James Buchanan

May 20, 1858

My Dear Harriet!

Learning that you were about to purchase furniture in New York [for the White House] *I requested Dr. Blake* [commissioner of public buildings] *to furnish me a statement of the balance of the appropriation unexpended. This balance is $8,369.02. In making your purchases, therefore, I wish you to consider that this sum must answer our purpose until the end of my term. I wish you therefore not to expend the whole of it; but to leave enough to meet all contingencies up till 4 March, 1861. Any sum which may be expended above the appropriation I shall most certainly pay out of my own pocket. I shall never ask Congress for the Deficiency.*

Letter from President James Buchanan to his niece, Harriet Lane, who served as First Lady at the White House during the administration of her bachelor uncle. Quoted from *The Works of James Buchanan* by James Buchanan, collected and edited by John Bassett Moore (1908–1911), volume 10, page 214.

Before President Pierce took office, Congress had already voted him an appropriation of $25,000 for the furniture fund on the advice of John Blake, commissioner of public buildings. Blake had advised the committee of the House that extra money was needed for repairs to the house to put it in the best of condition for the new president.[149]

President Pierce moved into the presidential mansion on March 4, 1853, mourning the death of his only remaining son, Benjamin, a boy of eleven, who was killed in a railroad wreck just two months before his father's inauguration. His wife joined him later.

The emphasis on the physical condition and decoration of the mansion seems strange in light of the Pierces' mourning. The purchases made by President Pierce may indicate that he felt an obligation to the office to live in fine style even if public entertaining was to be kept to a minimum for the four years of his administration. The president's former law clerk, Sidney Webster, came to Washington to act as his secretary, and it was to him that President Pierce entrusted the expenditure of the furnishings fund.[150]

Soon after Pierce took office, he was invited to take part in the opening ceremonies of the country's first World's Fair in the Crystal Palace in New York City on July 14, 1853. This fair was American response to England's famous Great Exhibition in the Crystal Palace which had been held in London in 1851. Like its English counterpart, the New York exhibition was intended to present "The World of Science, Art and Industry," with special emphasis on progress being made in these fields by the United States. At least one of the firms represented at the exhibition seemed to have been anxious to do business with the fair's most distinguished guest. In one of the publications publicizing the fair, the following entry is found.

The remaining illustrations have been selected from the goods exhibited by Messrs. Haughwout and Dailey of New York. These gentlemen are engaged in decorating porcelain which is imported or manufactured for them. The designs are chiefly copies from works executed abroad, and present, therefore no point worthy of particular remark.— Two plates with the cypher of the President and the arms of the United States form part of a service for the use of that functionary.[151]

The illustrations accompanying the text show one plate with a scalloped edge, dark rim, stippled border, and a dark line enclosing the border. There is a rococo shield in the center of the plate containing the initial "P' which is printed as a mirror image.[152] The other plate has a cable around the rim, a wide colored border, and an interpretation of the Arms of the United States in the center. Horace Greeley in his account of the New York exhibition says that "Haughwout and Dailey have in the gallery of the American Department a very fine collection of decorated Porcelain—the whole collection reflects credit on the exhibitors who have established the art of decorating in this city." [153]

The report of the British Commission to Queen Victoria on the New York exhibition states that Haughwout and Dailey had about one hundred people working for them in 1853, most of them English, and that women did the gilding.[154]

President Pierce must have been pleased with the compliment paid to him and evidently liked the china prepared for his approval. While still in New York, he ordered from Haughwout and Dailey a dining service consisting of the following pieces.

2 Salads, 2 Pickles, 2 Cust^d Stands, 2 Doz. Custard Cups, 2 high & low Comports, 2 Strawberry Bowls, 2 Dessert Sugars, 2 Round high Baskets, 2 Oval high Baskets, 2 Butters, 2 Bakers, 5 Doz. Dining Plates, 2 Doz^n Soups, 3 Doz^n Dessert Plates, 2 Doz^n Oyster plates, 2 Doz^n Tea plates, 2 Doz^n Breakfast Coffees, 2 Doz^n Teas, 1½ Doz^n After Dinner Coffees, 2 Bowls, 4 Square Cake plates, 2 Water pitchers and 1 centre piece.

The cost of the service was $536.24 plus insurance paid by "H & D" of $8.00.

The president also ordered a large service of glass from the same company. He was allowed $180.11 for old glass and china from the President's House which had been turned in to the firm. The bill is dated July 1853; the china was received by Sidney Webster on October 22, 1853, and the bill was paid on that date.[155]

The discovery of illustrations in a publication about the New York fair of the china offered to President Pierce by Haughwout and Dailey seems to settle the question of the proper attribution of the blue, gold, and white porcelain previously thought to have been ordered by Dolley Madison or by Andrew Jackson. The attribution is further substantiated by the listing of "1 centre piece" on the voucher. The "centre piece" is the large bowl supported by three Parian figures which is probably the best known piece in the White House China Collection since the time of its rediscovery by Mrs. Benjamin Harrison in the attic of the Executive Mansion and its attribution at that time to Dolley Madison. The centerpiece is similar to one shown by the Minton factory at the Crystal Palace exhibition in London in 1851. Included in the Minton display and illustrated in the catalog of the London exhibition is a tea service selected by Queen Victoria in 1851 as a royal wedding present. The large centerpiece of the service was a basket on a pedestal with three Parian figures supporting it

"in every way beautiful and appropriate. They are allegorical and represent Love, Peace and Abundance."[156]

The Pierce porcelain decorated with blue and gold scrolls and a stipple of gold on the rim, but without the "P," is in collections in the White House and the Smithsonian Institution, and in various private collections. Occasionally, individual pieces come up at public auction where they are invariably misidentified as part of a service which belonged to Dolley Madison. This china does not have a mark so it cannot be identified by country of manufacture, but there does not seem to be any doubt about its date.

The miscellaneous china of the Pierce administration was still being purchased from C. S. Fowler and Company of Washington. A bill dated December 26, 1853 included "1 Wedgwood Tea Set" which cost $6.00 with other miscellaneous pieces amounting to $19.49. On this bill, there is still the "c.c."—cream color—designation for "2 nappies" costing $.38.[157]

On January 2, 1857, Sidney Webster wrote to the Honorable Elisha W. Whittlesey, comptroller of the treasury, transmitting the last of his disbursements from the fund for refurnishing the President's House and enclosing a check for $3.62 for the balance of the money due to the United States on the account. He says: "You will observe that I have not at any time made charge for the care and annoyance during four years which the disbursement of this appropriation have occasioned me. I hope that by your act I will now have full and speedy release."[158]

The somber Executive Mansion during the administration of President Pierce gave way in 1857 to the sophisticated type of life to which the newly elected James Buchanan was accustomed. He was the country's first bachelor president—his fiancée having died shortly before their wedding date. As a result, his official First Lady was his niece, the youngest daughter of a sister. When Harriet Lane was orphaned at the age of ten, she became his ward and, from that time, he supervised her education and

French porcelain dinner and dessert service decorated by and purchased from the New York City firm of Haughwout and Dailey by President Pierce in 1853.

24. White porcelain dessert plate with blue and gold decoration. The rim of the plate is stippled with gold dots, and there is a blue and gold cartouche in the center of the plate. Diameter, 8¼ inches.

25. A group of china from this service. Oval fruit basket: height, 10 inches; width, 16¼ inches; length, 10-5/16 inches. Dinner plate diameter, 9¼ inches. (White House collection.)

24

25

26. *Centerpiece. This is the last item listed on the voucher. It is the most spectacular piece in the White House China Collection and has been variously and erroneously identified as belonging to Dolley Madison or to Andrew Jackson since it was rescued from oblivion in the White House attic by Mrs. Benjamin Harrison in the 1890s. Dimensions: height, 24¾ inches; diameter of bowl, 14⅝ inches. (White House collection.)*

27. *Design of plates with the cypher of the president and the Arms of the United States which was exhibited by the New York City firm of Haughwout and Dailey at the 1853 World's Fair. Left, the design of the china with the cypher which was purchased by Franklin Pierce in 1853. Right, the design of the china with the Arms of the United States which was chosen by Mrs. Abraham Lincoln in 1861 from the same firm. (Illustration from* The World of Science, Art and Industry Illustrated from Examples in the New York Exhibition 1853-1854, *edited by Professor Benjamin R. Silliman, Jr., and C. R. Goodrich, Esq.   New York: G. P. Putnam and Company, 1854.)*

training. She was his official hostess in Washington, D.C., and later when he was minister to Great Britain. Thus, at the age of twenty-six, she was well qualified for the duties of First Lady at the President's House in Washington.

Having been in public life during most of his career, Buchanan came to the presidential office experienced in the correct procedures for the expenditures of public funds. During his administration, he spent large sums of money for flat silver and silver serving pieces, for draperies, rugs, chandeliers, upholstery, and furniture; however, his only expenditures for china are for chamber china purchased from Tyndale and Mitchell of Philadelphia[159] and china flower vases from the same firm.[160] There is no bill for a dining service, so it is presumed that the one purchased by President Pierce was still in use in the President's House. The traditions of the Buchanan family identify several personally owned services as having been used in the mansion during that administration. Both President Buchanan and his niece, Harriet, owned large services of china which they had acquired during the years when Buchanan, as a public servant, had entertained extensively. They may well have preferred to use these services when additional china was needed. The president's personal china was a handsome pink-banded Sèvres set, each piece elaborately decorated with flowers which Buchanan had purchased at a sale of the household belongings of the French minister to Washington during the period of 1845–1849 when he was secretary of state under President Polk.[161] Harriet Lane's china was a red-edged set which she had purchased in France, probably when she was the official hostess at the embassy in London during her uncle's term as minister to Great Britain from 1853 until his return in 1856. The members of the family to whom Harriet Lane Johnston left the red-edged china thought it had been used by her in the President's House.[162]

This family tradition seems to be substantiated by the account of Theodore R. Davis, artist-correspondent for *Harper's Weekly,* who twenty years later recalled having seen the table at the White House set for an elaborate dinner given for the Prince of Wales, later Edward VII, in 1860 with pieces of the blue, gold, and white china—now identified as that purchased by President Pierce—and with a red-edged set which Davis thought was the set purchased by Pierce.[163] Instead, the red-edged china must have been Harriet Lane's own and not china purchased with government funds.[164]

Davis was the first person to write about presidential china and his incorrect identification of the Pierce china as "red-edged" began a confusion which has been handed down to the present. As a matter of fact, a small illustration which accompanied an article of his in *The Ladies Home Journal* of May 1889 is identified as "Pierce China" and shows pieces of the rose dinner service purchased by President Grant in 1869.

Abraham Lincoln

Andrew Johnson

A magnificent supper had been provided in the state dining-room by Maillard, of New York, but when the hour of eleven came, and the door should have been opened, the flustered steward had lost the key, so that there was a hungry crowd waiting anxiously outside the unyielding portal. . . . Then the irrepressible humor of the American people broke forth—that grim humor which carried them through the subsequent misery. "I am in favor of a forward movement!" one would exclaim. "An advance to the front is only retarded by the imbecility of commanders," said another, quoting a speech just made in Congress. To all this General McClellan, himself modestly struggling with the crowd, laughed as heartily as anybody. . . . Finally the key was found, the door opened, and the crowd fed.

The table was decorated with large pieces of ornamental confectionery, the centre object representing the steamer "Union," armed and bearing the "Stars and Stripes." On a side table was a model of Fort Sumter, also in sugar, and provisioned with game. After supper promenading was resumed, and it was three o'clock ere the guests departed. The entertainment was pronounced a decided success, but it was compared to the ball given by the Duchess of Richmond, at Brussels, the night before Waterloo. People parted there never to meet again. Many a poor fellow took his leave that night of festivity forever, the band playing, as he left, "The Girl I Left Behind Me."

Excerpt from *Perley's Reminiscences of Sixty Years in the National Metropolis* by Ben Perley Poore (Philadelphia: Hubbard Brothers, 1886), volume 2, pages 119–120.

President and Mrs. Lincoln entered the President's House in 1861 under the cloud of the impending Civil War. Nevertheless, Mrs. Lincoln soon saw that there was not enough left of the Pierce china service to set a formal dinner, and that chinaware was not the only thing needed in the Executive Mansion in her opinion. Fortunately for Mrs. Lincoln, Congress appropriated the usual funds to supply furnishings for the house so in May 1861 she set forth on a shopping excursion to New York and Philadelphia. Mrs. Lincoln was accompanied on the trip by a favorite cousin, Mrs. Elizabeth Todd Grimsley, who had come to Washington for the inauguration in March and stayed on at the White House for a six months' visit. Their arrival in New York on May 12 was duly noted in the newspapers. *The New York Daily Tribune* of May 16, 1861, recorded the visit under the heading of "Personal."

Mrs. Lincoln employed the greater portion of Wednesday forenoon in making purchases. Among other places she visited the establishments of Lord & Taylor and Messrs. E.V. Haughwout & Co. At the latter establishment she ordered a splendid dinner service for the White House in 'Solferino' and gold with the arms of the United States emblazoned on each piece. The purchases also included some handsome vases and mantel ornaments for the blue and green rooms.

This was not the first presidential patronage of the firm E. V. Haughwout and Company for under the name of Haughwout and Dailey, they had sold a dinner service to President Pierce. In the Haughwout and Dailey exhibit at the Crystal Palace fair of 1853 in New York City, they had displayed two plates hopefully designed for a service for the use of the president. These two plates are illustrated in a catalog on the exhibition. One of the plates is the china design of the set purchased by President Pierce in 1853. The other design was the china chosen by Mrs. Lincoln in 1861. This latter plate was described in the catalog as a "specimen plate with blue band, Alhambra style, of a dinner service manufactured for the President of the United States."[165] The only change that Mrs. Lincoln made in her order for this china design was to have the blue border changed to "Solferino," a bright, purplish red color which had become fashionable since its invention by the French in 1859. Shades of purple were favored by Mrs. Lincoln, and she often chose purple for her personal attire as well as for interior decoration at the mansion.

The Alhambra border refers to the gold tracery around the edge of the plate. This Moorish motif—of which the decoration of the Alhambra in Spain is the great example—was used to decorate the Crystal Palace in London in 1851.

It achieved great popularity because of the success of the British exhibition. A catalog on the 1853 New York fair explains that "the Moorish system of which the Alhambra furnishes a familiar example [shows that] the colors almost invariably employed are pure blue, red and yellow or gold. The essential feature of this style then consists in the exquisitely varied and harmonious tracery which breaks up the surfaces."[167]

The new china was not unnoticed by the press. In Columbus, Ohio, the editor of *Crisis,* in an article in the paper on May 30, 1861, commented that "the silver plate from Haughwout and the china services from the same, all with the United States coat-of-arms emblazoned upon them, will admirably suit the mulberry-colored livery of her footmen, etc. in Washington and possibly may help very nicely to get rid of the apparently exhaustless $25,000 a year salary of Mr. Lincoln. ... Should Jeff Davis get into the White House *par hasard,* in a manner as unexpected the brilliant silver service and the China sets, with their Solferino borders, would delight his troops, I fancy, as well as the viands thereupon; but I trust there is no such humiliation in store for my country nor for Mrs. Lincoln."[168]

Mrs. Lincoln had an opportunity to see and approve the new china when she returned to New York for more shopping in August 1861. The china was delivered on the following September 2 with an itemized bill.[169]

One fine Porcelain Dining Service of One Hundred, and ninety pieces ... 190 ... decorated Royal purple, and double gilt, with the Arms of the United States, on each piece, for the Presidential Mansion ... namely. ...

Two Bowls for Salad
Four Shells do Pickles
Four Meat Platters 9 inch
Four   do   do 10 do
Four   do   do 13 do
Two   do   do 15 do
Two   do   do 18 do
Two   do   do 20 do
Four Fish   do various sizes, and forms
Two Butter Dishes, with drainers, and covers
Six uncovered vegetable dishes or bakers

Ninety-six Dinner Plates 9 inch
Forty-eight Soup   do 9 do
Four Large Water Pitchers.
Two Bowls for Ice.

Eleven Hundred, and ninety-five dollars

One fine Porcelain Dessert Service, consisting of Two hundred and eight pieces ... 208 ... richly decorated to match Dining Set. . . namely.

Two Stands for Custard Cups
Thirty-six . . .   do   do
Eight High Comportiers for fruit.
Two   do   do large do   do
Four shell   do
Two Bowls for Strawberries
Two Dessert Sugars
Six Round High Baskets for fruit
Two oval   do   do   do do
Sixty Dessert Plates 8 inch
Thirty-six after Dinner Coffees.

Eight Hundred, and thirty-seven dollars

One fine Breakfast, and Tea Service, containing Two Hundred, and sixty pieces, richly decorated to match Dinner Service . . . namely.

Forty-eight Tea Plates 6½ inch
Thirty-six Preserve do 4½ do
Thirty-six Coffees for Breakfast
Twenty-four Egg Cups
Thirty-six Teas
Eight Plates for Cake

Seven Hundred, and fifty-nine dollars

Four Small Sevres Centre Pieces for Bon Bons, decorated to match Dinner Service @ Twenty-five = One Hundred

Two large Centre Pieces, Sevres, supported by "White Pelicans" and decorated to match dinner service @ One Hundred = Two Hundred

Two Punch Bowls, decorated to match dinner service @ Fifty = one Hundred

Packages   Four Dollars

Total Amount
Three Thousand, one Hundred and Ninety-five dollars.

By the end of the nineteenth century, it was thought that this china had been specially designed to symbolize the country engaged in the civil war between the states. Writing in 1895, Edwin

The French porcelain dining, dessert, breakfast, and tea service—known as the "royal purple" set—was purchased by President Lincoln in 1861, and the design was reordered by President Andrew Johnson in 1865. Additional orders were made by Presidents Grant in 1873 and Arthur in 1884. The first two orders during the Lincoln and Johnson administrations were for French porcelain decorated by the New York City firm of E. V. Haughwout and Company; the later orders were made and decorated in France by Haviland and Company and purchased from the firm of J. W. Boteler and Brother of Washington, D.C.

28. Dinner plate of white porcelain with a royal purple border, gold cable design around the edge, and gold dots inside the purple border. The Arms of the United States are in color in the center of the plate. Diameter, 9 inches.

29. Mark on the plates which were reordered during the Grant and Arthur administrations.

30. *Pieces of the royal purple china of the Lincoln administration. Oval basket: height, 8-1/16 inches; width, 9-13/16 inches; length, 10-1/16 inches. Covered custard cup: height (with lid), 4 inches; diameter, 2⅞ inches. Footed after-dinner coffee cup: height, 2½ inches; diameter, 2⅛ inches. (White House collection.)*

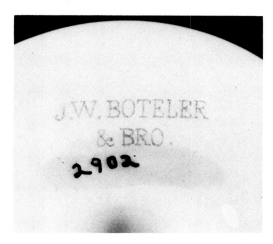

31. *The mark on the footed cup identifies the "violet and gold" china ordered by President Grant in 1873 as another order of the Lincoln china, because it specified "on foot" cups and saucers. (White House collection.)*

Atlee Barber commented that the design was selected after much consultation among officials at Washington. He said that the border of the plate was a gold guilloche or cable of two strands entwined and that they mutually strengthened each other, and his interpretation was that it intended to signify the union of the North and South. He theorized that the eagle in the center was intended to symbolize the United States with sunlight breaking through the surrounding clouds. This 1895 interpretation was inspired by the political events of the Lincoln administration, but would scarcely be appropriate for a design created in 1853, eight years preceding the Civil War.[170]

There is no maker's mark on the Lincoln china acquired in 1861. The Haviland factory in Limoges, France, has a tradition of having made it, but this china was purchased ten years before they started to mark their ware.[171] The undecorated "blank" porcelain does seem to have come from the Haviland factory for it is of the same quality and from the same mold as other table services of a later date which have the Haviland mark; however, the letterhead of E. V. Haughwout and Company, successors of Haughwout and Dailey identifies that firm as continuing in the decorating business which had been so well established in 1853. As the design was one produced and exhibited by the New York company in 1853, there is no reason to doubt that both this order and the reorder in 1866 were decorated in New York City. There is also no doubt that Haviland and Company both made and decorated, in France, the additional pieces of the Lincoln china design ordered in 1877 during the administration of President Grant and by President Arthur in 1884. The pieces of these later orders were marked "fabriqué par Haviland & Co./ pour/J. W. Boteler & Bro./Washington."[172] In 1881 Theodore R. Davis attached the following note to a plate of the Lincoln china stating that "this plate One of the Lincoln Set made by Haviland & Co. was used by President Garfield when upon his deathbed. The plate was broken in bringing it from the President's room and was given by Wm. Crump to Theo. R. Davis Sept. 1881."[173] The plate is now in the collections

of the State Historical Society of Wisconsin, but it is not marked with the name of the Haviland and Company so it must have been from either the 1861 or 1865 orders.

The use of the word "Sevres" for the serving pieces listed in the 1861 order was confusing, because Haviland produced at this early period a pattern they called "Sevres." It is illustrated in an early pattern book in the archives of Haviland and Company, but it does not match the surviving pieces of the Lincoln service; however, a close examination of the stand for custard cups in the White House collection revealed the printed mark "S60" on the base, a mark used by the Sèvres factory in 1860 to identify the manufacturer who made the blanks for the ornamental pieces which were the most beautiful part of the service.

Pieces of the Lincoln state china are in the White House and in many museums including the Smithsonian Institution; the Henry Ford Museum in Dearborn, Michigan; the Lincoln National Life Foundation in Fort Wayne, Indiana; and in many private collections. Though the service was never sold at public auction, broken and odd pieces were sold both at public and private sale and, occasionally, still are found on the antique market. Some confusion in identification has resulted from the fact that the Lincoln state china was reproduced for sale to the public as souvenirs later in the nineteenth century. These pieces of china, of which this writer has only seen plates, are marked on the back: "Administration/Abraham Lincoln" in either black or red.

It is obvious that the official dinner service delighted Mrs. Lincoln, for she ordered a similar set for herself. On the personal service, the initials "M.L." were substituted for the Arms of the United States as decoration. Her cousin, Mrs. Grimsley, wrote that "this latter, I know, was not paid for by the district commissioner, as was most unkindly charged when it was stored away."[174] It has been suggested that the personal china was paid for by a withdrawal of $1,106.73 from the president's account with the bank of Riggs and Company in Washington, D.C.

The personal china was an indiscreet purchase,

at best, and Mrs. Lincoln was soon accused of buying the china out of public funds. In the midst of the campaign in which Lincoln ran for reelection in 1864, an opposition newspaper, *The New York World,* published a bitter attack on the president and his wife charging that the bill submitted by E. V. Haughwout for the state service had been padded to include the cost of personal china.[175] According to the newspaper's editorial, the deceit was discovered when the amount of the bill was questioned by a clerk in the Treasury Department and "Honest Abe," when cornered, made payment out of his own pocket. This story seems to be refuted by the evidence on the Haughwout bill, which was for only the pieces in the state service. The bill was signed by the comptroller for payment on September 16, 1861, within two weeks after the china arrived in Washington, and only three days after President Lincoln had approved the bill.

The extent to which this controversy spoiled Mrs. Lincoln's pleasure in the handsome purple service perhaps can be measured by the fact that after President Lincoln was reelected, she purchased another large porcelain service for the White House. Also, the Solferino china must have been somewhat depleted, for in November 1864 it had become necessary to send out to the local firm of Webb and Beveridge for "1 dozen Band China cups and saucers" which cost $11.[176]

A bill at the National Archives documents the new set as being ordered by Mrs. Lincoln from J. K. Kerr of 529 Chestnut Street, Philadelphia, whose establishment, known as "China Hall," specialized in French and English china and glassware.

On January 9, 1865, Mrs. Lincoln telegraphed James K. Kerr of China Hall: "We must have the China tomorrow—Send what you have. Our dinner comes off Monday, & on Saturday, the articles must be ready for use here—" It is signed "Mrs. Lincoln." She telegraphed again on January 10: "What is the meaning, that we do not have the China." It, too, is signed "Mrs. Lincoln" followed by *"Answer* immediately."[177]

Despite her urgency, the bill accompanying the china was dated January 30, 1865. It was for

"One extra large French China Dining, Dessert and Coffee Service decorated on a White ground delicate Buff border with burnished Gold Lines consisting of the following pieces.[178]

12 dozen dining plates
 6 dozen soup plates
 6 dozen dessert plates
 6 dozen ice cream or peaches and cream plates deep
 1 large dish for head of table
 1 foot dish
 2 second course head and foot dishes
 2 more dishes
 2 more dishes
 2 more dishes
 4 vegetable dishes with covers
 4 more vegetable dishes with covers
 4 sauce tureens
 4 sauce boats
 4 stands for sauce boats
 4 pickle shells
 2 salad bowls
 2 custard stands
48 custard cups with covers
 2 large rich oval fruit baskets
 4 smaller round fruit baskets
 4 fruit comports shell form for fruit
 4 fruit comports high round
 2 dessert sugar bowls with covers
48 after dinner cups and saucers
 1 large dish for fish

The price is given as $1700. The records show that the china was brought to Washington by Harnden Express. There is a voucher "for freight on 5 casks from Philadelphia, Pennsylvania to Washington, D.C., mkd Mrs. A. Lincoln $28.50. China from J. Kerr Phila. Pa. for dinner." It is signed "J. K. Kerr," and "Mrs. Lincoln" and is dated Feb. 13, 1865.[179]

Again, Mrs. Lincoln seems to have been pleased with the new porcelain for just one week later, on February 20, J. Kerr of Philadelphia sent a bill for some additions to the service. The original order had included after-dinner cups and saucers, but no larger size cups; this oversight was corrected in a new order for additions to the service.[180]

32. A group of royal purple china of the Lincoln administration. Round basket: height, 7¾ inches; diameter, 8-9/16 inches. Cup: height, 3⅛ inches; width, 3⅞ inches. Saucer diameter, 6½ inches.

33. Another group of the royal purple china of the Lincoln administration. Oval basket: height, 11 inches; width, 15-15/16 inches, length, 15-5/16 inches. Footed bowl: height, 4¼ inches; diameter, 8¾ inches. At rear, fish platter: width, 7-15/16 inches; length, 23⅜ inches.

32

33

A French porcelain dining, dessert, and coffee service—the so-called "buff and gold" set—was ordered in 1865 and delivered shortly before President Lincoln was assassinated. This service was purchased from the firm of J. K. Kerr of Philadelphia.

34. Soup plate of white porcelain decorated with a delicate buff border with burnished gold lines and a gold circle in the center. Diameter, 9 inches.

2 dozen coffee cups and saucers				
Delicate buff border and gilt			20.00	40.00
4 water pitchers	do	do	10.00	40.00
4 do smaller	"	"	8.00	32.00
4 " "	"	"	6.00	24.00
4 " "	"	"	5.00	20.00
6 bowls			2.50	15.00
		Package		2.50
		For a total of		173.50

Two months later President Abraham Lincoln was assassinated. The china so recently ordered could have been little used by Mrs. Lincoln, and evidently payment had not been made. At one of the first conferences which B. B. French, the commissioner of public buildings and grounds, had with President Johnson in April 1865, he spoke of a bill for purchase of china so recently ordered from "China Hall" by Mrs. Lincoln and asked President Johnson to approve its payment.[181]

In spite of Commissioner French's concern, the bill for the new buff china was not receipted as having been paid until August 29, 1865, at which time the bill was endorsed: "Received from B. B. French Commissioner of Public Buildings and Grounds the above amount of 2332.50 dollars in full of this account." The second order for additional china of the same service was not paid for until October 1866, a year and a half after the pieces were delivered. On the bill is the notation: "Rec'd payment in full 10/66 J. K. Kerr."

Pieces of the buff and gold china which Mrs. Lincoln ordered in 1865 are at the White House and in the Smithsonian Institution. Miscellaneous pieces are in private collections, where they are often incorrectly identified as either Monroe or Grant china.

The inventory of the White House made on May 26, 1865, when Mrs. Lincoln turned over the house to President Andrew Johnson lists under china and glassware "One full set China" which was most certainly this buff and gold service and "3 small remnants of china sets nearly all broken up" which must have included the remaining pieces of the royal purple service.[182]

Evidently the buff china did not appeal to the Johnsons, for within less than a year they ordered replacement pieces of the purple set. On January 17, 1866, E. V. Haughwout received an order for "rich China Ware with the Arms and Crests of the U.S. to replace the pieces broken and lost of the Solferine sett."[183]

1 salad dish
4 pickles
31 custard cups
24 egg cups
18 dishes—4/10 inch, 6/11 inch, 6/13 inch, 1/15 inch, 1/18 inch
6 comports—3/high, 2/low and 1/shell
2 dessert sugars
2 round baskets
2 butter dishes
31 dinner plates
57 dessert plates
48 tea plates
25 soup plates
26 preserve plates
36 breakfast coffees
36 black coffees
36 teas
1 cake plate
4 pitchers
1 ice bowl

The name of the most famous professional china painter in America, Edward Lycett,[184] has been associated with this second official order for the Lincoln china. Lycett worked for John Vogt and Company of New York City, a firm which was rapidly surpassing E. V. Haughwout and Company in the quality and quantity of china which was being decorated in this country. Though there are no contemporary records which have survived to prove this point, E. V. Haughwout and Company could have commissioned Lycett even though he was working for the Vogt firm to decorate the large order for the Lincoln china design that was placed in 1866 by President Andrew Johnson. The story of the artist's work on the service first appeared in an article by Edwin Atlee Barber in 1895 and again in 1897[185] when Lycett was still alive and which he did not contradict. In fact, Lycett and succeeding generations of the family have always boasted of his work on the service.[186] Certainly, the variations in the surviving china suggest that the two orders were produced differently. Barber states in his article that the decoration of the second set was more carefully done than that of the first, being wholly painted by hand, while the Haughwout designs were first printed in outline and afterward filled in with the brush. The difference in workmanship can be detected on close examination.

An act of the 39th Congress on July 23, 1866, provided for the appointment of an official steward for the Executive Mansion "who shall have the custody of the plate, furniture and other public property in the President's House." The law required the steward to give bond to the United States for a sum to be determined by the secretary of the interior for faithful discharge of his trust.[187]

In order to comply with the law, Secretary of the Interior Orville H. Browning directed Benjamin B. French—still acting as commissioner of public buildings—to take the inventory, file it, and obtain from William Slade, the steward, a receipt for the legal custody of the items on the list. French carried out the orders and on February 28, 1867, he advised the secretary that he had taken the inventory himself assisted by Mrs. Martha Patterson, the daughter of President Johnson who served as his First Lady; a Colonel Stevenson; the upholsterer; and Job Angus, general superintendent of public buildings and grounds.[188] Slade's receipt indicates that in addition to the copy retained by him, lists went to Mrs. Patterson and to the secretary of the interior.

In an effort to arrive at a realistic value of the china and glass, Benjamin French sent a letter to E. V. Haughwout to ask for an appraisal of the items furnished by his firm in the preceding years. The firm set a value of $22,000 for the handsome Solferino service and the plate and cut glass purchased from Haughwout during the Lincoln and Johnson administrations. The inventory, dated February 28, 1867, lists as the "Rich China Solferino Set" all of the china of that design which was then in the President's House. Everything else is included under a heading "Old China" and the small number of pieces

listed are hard to reconcile with even the quantity of buff china so recently acquired.[189]

The inventory taken on December 14, 1869, nine months after President Grant took office, continued to list the Solferino set and also listed a buff set which must be the one ordered by Mrs. Lincoln, for the set with the yellow border ordered by President and Mrs. Grant had not then arrived at the presidential residence.[190]

The later orders of china matching the Lincoln "Royal Purple" state service design are discussed in the chapters on the administrations of Presidents Grant and Arthur.

Ulysses S. Grant

. . . Dinner was served at the White House promptly at five o'clock, and every member of the family was expected to be punctual. General Grant's favorite dishes were rare roast beef, boiled hominy, and wheaten bread, but he was always a light eater. Pleasant chat enlivened the meal, with Master Jesse as the humorist, while Grandpa Dent would occasionally indulge in some conservative growls against the progress being made by the colored race. After coffee, the General would light another cigar and smoke while he glanced over the New York papers. About nine o'clock, a few chosen friends would often call, sometimes by appointment, but business matters were generally forbidden, and offices were not to be mentioned. The children retired at nine o'clock, Mrs. Grant followed them about ten, and between ten and eleven General Grant sought his pillow.

Excerpt from *Perley's Reminiscences of Sixty Years in the National Metropolis* by Ben Perley Poore (Philadelphia: Hubbard Brothers, 1886), volume 2, pages 259–260.

When President and Mrs. Grant moved into the Executive Mansion in March 1869, Mrs. Grant began at once to renovate and refurnish it to her own taste. Her first purchases for the house commenced on March 6, and she continued to buy for the next six months. The summer of 1869 was spent in having painting, cleaning, and alterations taken care of while the Grants enjoyed a family holiday at Long Beach, New Jersey. By the time they returned to Washington at the end of September, the workmen were putting the finishing touches on all of the downstairs rooms.

The first evidence that new china was being considered as part of the refurnishing project is found in a letter addressed to the commissioner of public buildings and grounds, Gen. Nathaniel Michler, from a firm in New York City named Covell and Company. The letter dated June 28, 1869, asked if a decision had been made about the dining service "for the White House." Concerning the sample plates shown to Mrs. Grant by Mr. Spaulding of the firm of Brown and Spaulding in New York City, Covell and Company wrote that "we would be happy to receive the order for the service of China and assure you *our facilities* for getting up the set, *are second to no house* in the country." [191]

It was evidently easier to order the china from a Washington, D.C., dealer for the Grant state china was purchased through the firm of J. W. Boteler and Brother, importers and dealers in "china, glass, crockery ware and house furnishings" at 320 Pennsylvania Avenue, N.W., who had been supplying miscellaneous china to the Executive Mansion since 1865. The Washington firm ordered the china from Haviland and Company whose products had been achieving recognition and winning prizes at each world's exhibition since the Great Exhibition at the Crystal Palace in London in 1851.

On October 5, 1869, Charles Haviland, in Limoges, France, wrote to his brother Theodore in New York City about the new presidential service. The following is a translation of a portion of the original letter, written in French.

For the service of the President and the others, I am having made 24 samples for the 8½-inch plate by Lissac and these samples will be used for the engravings after they have been used for the services now being made. . . . I find the flowers at 1.25 francs received from Walton infinitely less pretty than those you have had made on the 7½-inch plate and I am more than ever convinced that we will never make pretty flowers . . . without printing and sampling them for the colors. We have already 15 samples of the 24 flowers for the 8½-inch plates and I assure you they are truly beautiful. But it will be very expensive. Lissac only averages about three sketches every two days because I first let him study his flower from nature then I pester him about each leaf until I am satisfied with the effect and arrangement. We will at last have good flowers that will endure because they are, at the same time, accurate, simple in arrangement, and beautiful. [192]

The painter Lissac referred to in this letter was one of the finest painters and engravers employed by Haviland and Company, and from 1868 to 1885 he was in charge of their decorating department. He is perhaps best known for his work on the elaborate state service ordered dur-

A state dinner service of "587 pieces with flowers and Coats of Arms" was purchased by President Grant in 1870 from J. W. Boteler and Brother of Washington, D.C. It was made by Haviland and Company in Limoges, France. Additional pieces were ordered by President Grant in 1873. The service is of white porcelain with a narrow buff band edged with gold and black lines. There is a modified version of the United States seal in red, gold, and black in a white reserve on the buff band. Each piece has a different flower in color in the center.

35. Dinner plate, diameter, 8½ inches. The flower in the center is the trumpet vine.

ing the Hayes administration.

The man named Walton mentioned in this letter is more difficult to identify. Charles Haviland writes of Walton's sketches as having been "received," and it is possible that he was an American artist who was sending sketches of native flowers for use on the president's china.[193]

On February 10, 1870, the new porcelain arrived at the Executive Mansion, and the bill for $3,000 was submitted by J. W. Boteler and Brother who describe it as "one State Dinner Service 587 pieces with flowers and Coats of Arms."[194] This bill was paid on the following May 12 by General Michler.

The success of Charles Haviland's method of encouraging his artists can be seen in the many charming flowers which adorn the Grant state service—the wild rose, lilac, peony, Virginia creeper, orange field lily, mimosa, to mention only a few. The flowers are encircled with a buff band on the border of the plate, and in that border was placed a very small, accurate rendering of the coat of arms of the United States in red, gold, and black.

Col. William H. Crook, chief usher at the White House from the Lincoln administration to that of Theodore Roosevelt, in his book *Memories of the White House* reported that the Grant state service became known as the "Flower Set" and that in "each of the scores and scores of dinner plates in this Flower Set of the White House china may be found almost every flower native to the United States at the time the set was made, and there are no duplicates in the whole service."[195]

President and Mrs. Grant obviously liked the new porcelain so well that when preparations began for the wedding of their beloved, only daughter, Nellie, in May 1874, they ordered additional pieces of the state service for use on that occasion. Like the original order, it came from the local firm of J. W. Boteler and Brother and was delivered to the mansion on December 10, 1873. The voucher lists the following pieces.[196]

6	compotes	"coat of arms"					$51.30
6	compotes		"coat of arms"				58.80
6	fruit bowls	"coat of arms"					51.80
6	round baskets	"	"	"			103.15
37	cups and saucers	"	"	"		coffee	170.75
39	"	"	"	"	"	" tea	140.50
39	"	"	"	"	"	" after dinner	140.50
37	butter plates	"	"	"			60.00
74	dinner plates	"	"	"		8½ in.	370.00
49	deep plates	"	"	"		8½ in.	245.00

None of the plates in the Grant state service have a maker's mark on the reverse, but the compotes ordered in 1874 are marked in orange-red: "Fabriqué par Haviland & Co./pour/J. W. Boteler & Bro./Washington."

One other piece of Grant china among those at the Smithsonian Institution which is marked is a dessert saucer which is 7¾ inches in diameter. The mark, in an oval of orange-red, is "Haviland & Cie/——/Limoge."

This must have been a trial mark used for the first order in 1870, for in the later order, there were no dessert saucers. The use of the French abbreviation "Cie" for company does seem to indicate that it is an early mark used before Haviland and Company recognized the importance of making the name of the company recognizable to the American market.

The theory that the mark "Haviland & Cie/ Limoges" dates from 1870 is reinforced by the fact that another service, privately owned, has the identical flowers used on the Grant service. The letter from Charles Haviland of October 5, 1869, discussing the presidential china states that "these samples [of the flowers] will be used for the engravings after they have been used for the service now being made. . . ." The pieces of the privately owned service are marked "Haviland & Cie/Limoges."

The additional pieces which Abby Gunn Baker mistook for pieces of Grant china "without the Coat of Arms and flower decorations," and which she thought had been ordered for the wedding of Nellie Grant are actually pieces of the buff service ordered by Mrs. Lincoln in 1865.[197] The Lincoln buff china was displayed with the Grant china in the White House China Collection from its establishment in 1903 until the collection was sorted and reorganized in 1958 at the direction of Mrs. Eisenhower and with the assistance of a staff member of the Smithsonian Institution.

For Mrs. Grant, probably the most disappointing part of the handsome new china was the fact that it was delivered on February 10, too late to be used at the state dinner which the president gave in honor of Prince Arthur, third son of Queen Victoria, on January 26, 1870.

The Grant state china is represented in the collections of the Smithsonian Institution, the White House, and other private collections. On occasion, individual pieces of this china can still be found at auction sales. It should be remembered, however, that this china did *not* have any mark on the plates. Plates that occasionally come on the market today which are marked in red or black "Administration/President Grant" are reproductions which were made later in the nineteenth century for public sale as commemorative souvenirs.

Because the handsome new state service was intended to be a banquet service, Mrs. Grant ordered another porcelain dinner service for less formal use from J. W. Boteler and Brother. This service, delivered on January 3, 1870, was a "Rose Band Dinner Set" which cost $550.[198] The White House chief usher, Colonel Crook, wrote that this rose-band set was used primarily for a breakfast service, and he writes that "the porcelain breakfast plates were of a delicate pearly white excepting the broad border which was a soft old-rose tone with a very fine line of gold around the outer edge." [199] The rose-band set was also French porcelain, and one of the big platters has the impressed mark "H & Co," which identifies it as another set of Haviland china.

The confusion of the Grant china with the rose band with that of the administration of President Pierce began with an article by Theodore R. Davis which appeared in *The Ladies Home Journal* in 1889, where it is illustrated and labeled as Pierce.[200] This confusion was discussed at some length in the earlier chapter on the china of Presidents Pierce and Buchanan. The mistaken attribution by Davis continued until the recent discovery of an illustration in a con-

temporary catalog of the china President Pierce had chosen during his visit to the opening of the New York fair of 1853.

It should be noted that a number of pieces of the rose-band china were sold at the public auction held during the later Chester A. Arthur administration. A few pieces with this attribution to Pierce—a covered vegetable dish, an open-work fruit compote, and two plates purchased by William Crump at the sale—eventually were returned to the White House by his daughter when Mrs. Theodore Roosevelt began to assemble the White House China Collection. Others with the same incorrect attribution have been added since.

Preceding the wedding of the Grant's only daughter, Nellie, many things were ordered for the President's House so that it would be in elegant condition. In preparation, the state apartments were freshly decorated, and the portraits of the presidents were removed from the East Room, where the ceremony was to be held, to the corridors. As previously stated, new pieces had been ordered for the state service. One of the most surprising purchases was a group of additional pieces to supplement the Lincoln state china. This time, it was ordered from J. W. Boteler and Brother, and on December 10, 1873, the following assortment was delivered to the Executive Mansion.[201]

48	Plates	Violet and Gold, Coat of Arms						$210.00
72	”	”	”	”	”	”	”	306.00
73	Plates	”	”	”	”	”	”	310.25
10	Compotes on foot	”	”	”	”	”	”	120.00
72	Cups and Saucers on foot	”	”	”	”	”	”	360.00

This order can be definitely identified as more of the Lincoln state china design, because the White House has among the surviving pieces of the Lincoln service a number of small, footed, after-dinner coffee cups and saucers marked "J. W. Boteler & Bro." and there are Lincoln plates and compotes in the White House China Collection marked "Fabriqué par Haviland &

36. *Dessert plate, diameter, 7½ inches. The flower is a pink rose.*

37. *The mark on the dessert plate is the earliest printed mark of Haviland and Company.*

38. *Mark on the three standing pieces from the Grant dessert service.*

36

37

38

39

40

39. *Deep plate, diameter, 8½ inches. The flower in the center is the red field lily.*

40. *Three standing pieces from the Grant dessert service. Round basket: height, 9 inches; diameter, 8½ inches. Compote: height, 3½ inches; diameter, 9 inches. Fruit bowl: height, 5½ inches; diameter, 9½ inches.*

The rose-band dinner service ordered by President Grant in 1870 was purchased from J. W. Boteler and Brother and was made by Haviland and Company in Limoges, France.

41

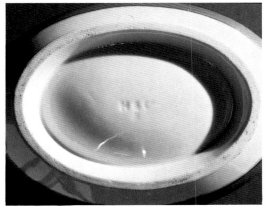

42

41. *A group of china from the Grant rose-band set. Basket: height, 7¼ inches; diameter, 9-3/16 inches. Vegetable tureen: height (with lid), 5¾ inches; width, 7½ inches; length, 11¼ inches. Cup: height, 2½ inches; diameter, 3½ inches. Saucer diameter, 5 inches. Plate diameter, 8¼ inches. (White House collection.)*

42. *Impressed mark, "H & C°," on the vegetable tureen of the Grant rose-band service. (White House collection.)*

Co. pour J. W. Boteler and Bro. Washington."
This confirms the tradition of Haviland and
Company that china of the design of the state
china of the Lincoln administration was both
made and decorated at their factory in France for
the Executive Mansion. Pieces of the Lincoln
china with the J. W. Boteler and Brother mark
are in the collections of the Smithsonian Institution, the White House, the Henry Ford
Museum in Dearborn, Michigan, and in many
private collections.

Rutherford B. Hayes

James A. Garfield

Now for the grandest and most beautiful entertainment of all—Cousin Lucy's Lunch given to her guests. . . . There was nothing on the table, which was in the shape of an H, but beautiful flowers, fruit and fancy candies. . . . I can't begin to tell you what a beautiful sight it was. At each plate was a tiny Boutonniere of carnations and smilax and a vase of half-blown buds. While in the center of the table was a long narrow glass-looking glass-on this was a stand of Camilias [sic] white as snow and scarlet Poinsettia and Smilax. There were other flowers on the table but this one stand absorbed all my admiration. The new china, which is superb, was used at the lunch. The ices were loveliest of all. One was a hen surrounded by 8 or 10 little chickens of various colors and the nest looked like spun glass. Another was a beautiful swan in the same sort of nest. We were at the table about one hour and a half or two hours.

Letter written on Executive Mansion stationery, dated January 7, 1881, by Dora Scott of New Orleans to her mother while visiting the mansion during the administration of Rutherford B. Hayes (Smithsonian Institution accession 284904).

Negotiations for a new state dinner service for the Executive Mansion began very early in 1879 with a request from Mrs. Rutherford B. Hayes to Col. Thomas L. Casey, the current commissioner of public buildings and grounds. A letter was sent to Collamore, Davis and Company and to Haviland and Company, both "Importers of Fine China" in New York City, asking them to submit samples of decorated china which would be suitable for a state dinner service. Collamore, Davis and Company were asked for samples of Wedgwood and Minton china, and Haviland was asked to send samples of its own ware. The Haviland firm replied immediately with samples and expressed a great interest in the project.

On January 19, 1879, Haviland sent an estimate for a dinner set to Colonel Casey which was described as being of the best quality and decorated by their best artists.[202]

10 dozen Dinner Plates flat plain 8¾ fronce Decoration, pearl grey on border with line of dead gold, Rich Persian Border by Renaud in rim of Plate in gold and colors, with Crest of U. S. & figures 1879 in gold.	$498.50
5 dozen Soup Plates deep plain, 8¾ fronce Same Decoration	249.25
5 dozen Fish Plates Shell Shape 7½ fronce, Color under glaze Grand fire, and Marine plants and shells by Pallandre	198.50
5 dozen Game Plates Engraved border 8 fronce Decoration similar to Dinner Plate, and Game Birds in centre by Bellet	299.50
5 dozen Dessert Plates Coupe (thin), 8 fronce Color under glaze Grand fire, and subjects by Bracquemond, with Crest, etc.	376.75
5 dozen Dessert Plates Coupe (thin), 7½ fronce Color under glaze Grand fire with Flower and Fern centres by Lyssac & crest	258.50
4 Fruit Baskets Saxon round. Color under glaze Grand fire, flowers in panels by Chaubunnier with Crest, etc.	45.00
2 Fruit Baskets Saxon oval Same decoration, assorted colors	48.70
4 Jardinieres Meissen 2nd Same decoration, assorted colors	61.60
2 Jardinieres Meissen 1st Same decoration, assorted colors	59.20
6 Bonbon Stands Laced edge Fern decoration in centre by Lyssac	60.90
4 Bonbon Stands Same shape, high foot Same decorations	40.60
30 Pairs After Dinner Coffees Anchor Shape (thin) Deep saucers. Persian border by Renaud, with crest, etc.	148.50
30 Pairs Teas Parisian (thin) Same decoration	175.50
30 Pairs After dinner Coffees Crystal (thin) Rich decoration by Jochuin [?], with crest, etc. Cups tinted inside, twelve colors	225.00
30 Pairs Teas Parisian 1st. Same decoration	250.50
	$2996.50

Colonel Casey compared the figures submitted by Haviland with those submitted by Davis, Collamore, and Company; as the cost of the Haviland china was less and as Haviland had stated that the order could be filled in not less than three nor more than five months, a contract was negotiated for the state service based on the estimate.

This contract, signed on February 20, 1879, stated that the firm would make, in the best

State dinner service ordered during the administration of President Hayes in 1879 from Haviland and Company of New York City and Limoges, France. Additional orders were made by President Arthur in 1884 and by President Cleveland in 1886.

43. Oyster plate diameter, 8½ inches.

44. *Seafood salad plate*
diameter, 7½ inches.

manner possible, a porcelain service of 562 pieces for the state dinner table of the Executive Mansion for the estimated price of $2,996.50. The price was to include the coat of arms of the United States and the date on each piece. The service was to be completed and delivered within six months of the start of work or sooner. Payment would be made upon delivery and acceptance. A bond was attached to the contract binding Haviland and Company to the United States for $1,000, payable if the contract was not properly completed.[203]

The work of the artists in the Haviland firm named in this original contract had been known in this country from the time of the Haviland exhibit at the Centennial Exposition in Philadelphia in 1876. *Harper's Weekly* in reporting on that exhibit commented that "Haviland's porcelain is too well known to require extended notice." The article states that one table set shown at the exposition had been decorated by Pallandre and another by Bracquemond. The latter artist was especially complimented for a set of twelve plates which were painted with great delicacy and originality.[204]

The dinner service proposed by Haviland was undoubtedly much in the style of those shown at the Centennial Exposition, but fate was to decree the production of a radically different set of china. Theodore Haviland had asked Colonel Casey to send him clippings of ferns which Mrs. Hayes wished to be used in decorating the dessert plates and the bonbon stand. Mrs. Hayes was in the White House conservatory pondering over her selection when two gentlemen entered. One of them was Theodore R. Davis, well-known artist-reporter for *Harper's Weekly* who had come to the mansion to supervise the taking of a picture of a meeting of President Hayes's cabinet for an illustration in the magazine. He had with him a photographer named G. W. Pach who was to make a photograph of the cabinet from which Davis would work. They had come into the conservatory so that Pach could test his chemicals by taking some trial pictures and, thus, had found Mrs. Hayes. They were quick to seize the opportunity to take some pictures of the First Lady. Mrs. Hayes then asked the

photographer to photograph the ferns and told the men about the new dinner set and the use of ferns as decoration on the dessert plates. Davis expressed regret that the new china could not be made in the United States and suggested that she had a marvelous opportunity to create something especially American by using the flora and fauna of this country as decoration on the new china. The idea so appealed to Mrs. Hayes, and Davis's enthusiasm was so contagious that Mrs. Hayes immediately called Colonel Casey to the conservatory to have him write to Haviland and Company to propose the change, and she asked Davis to assume personal direction of the new state china.[205]

When Theodore Davis returned to New York, the project was given the enthusiastic support of his employer, Fletcher Harper, the publisher of *Harper's Weekly.* Harper greatly respected Davis's talent, and he was reported to have told his "faithful" artist that "I don't ask you to try to surpass everything of the kind that Haviland has done. I expect you to beat them, and I'll have one of the duplicate sets for myself."[206]

Davis himself was a little more restrained in his version as shown in a letter, dated February, 26, 1879, which he wrote to Webb Hayes, son and personal secretary of President Hayes.

I am pleased to be able to report to Mrs. Hayes that Messrs. Harper & Brothers, commend the proposed designs for the State service and sanction the the [sic] use of my time and name in connection therewith, feeling an interest in the advancement of art, and culture, and a desire that, in work in any way pertaining to a national character should be in a measure the production of our Country.

Mr. Theo. Haviland, though at first under the impression that a service so novel, in form and decoration could not be produced in a limited time is now convinced, that, with with [sic] the facilities at his command, the Ser [sic] will be in readiness for use during next winter.

He is greatly pleased with the change and enters cordially into the new thought, saying that the set will be at once the most interesting and appropriate which has been seen in this country. . . .

Will you also say to Mrs. Hayes, that as soon

as Mr. Haviland & myself decide upon the form, size & special selections both as regards design and character, a memorandum will be forwarded, together with a few sketches which may serve to make our ideas somewhat comprehensive.

Mr. Haviland expresses a willingness to discard old shapes, which pleases me. I wish to add a few unthought of things, do you think that it will be advisable? I hope so.[207]

Theodore Davis had gotten to know Theodore Haviland when Davis was covering the Centennial Exposition for his magazine, and this friendship was to be put to test in the project on which they were about to begin.

Theodore Haviland wrote to Colonel Casey to confirm that it was agreeable to Mrs. Hayes and to the colonel to follow Mr. Davis's proposals. Colonel Casey assured him that it was, but queried "generally upon what pieces and to what extent modications are proposed and are to be designed."

In an attempt to answer this question, Haviland wrote Davis a letter on March 20, 1879, in which he outlined his ideas of how they should proceed with the work.

1st. Give us some definitive designs for each size plate, as you have already *done so well* for the Game service and fish service. Soup plate with design/Dinner plate with design/Salad plate with design/ Dessert plate with design/Cheese plate with design/Tea cup with design/ Coffee cup with design.

Then make 2 series of the plates & cups, alike so that I can give one series, viz. a design of each size plate and cup to Mr. Love [New York representative of Haviland and Company], for him to submit the same to Mrs. Hayes—and have the order regularly settled in a business-like way; and the other series for me to take to Europe and with it prepare the work we will have to do.—

I will sail on the 3rd of April, I would be much more at ease if you could give me the necessary papers a week from next Monday.

2nd. When that portion of the work is settled, I would then suggest to you to finish the/Game series/Then the Fish series/and so on, and so on, until you reach the end, when you can make the fancy pieces such as the chocolate cups and pot, etc.

If we do not adopt at once some plan and *stick* to it, we shall never be able to get through with this tremendous task before us.

You have undertaken to do in a few weeks the work of five and six months and we shall be obliged to do in a few months a work the difficulty of which you cannot even conceive.

In ordinary times I would not undertake to do all the engraving, trials of color etc. this set will necessitate in less than two years.

I hope we shall both find our reward by and by but for the present there is nothing but work, and work before us.

If you do your part as promptly as you have commenced it with, all will be well.[208]

In April 1879, Haviland was able to submit to Colonel Casey for approval a list of the subjects which Davis was considering for the new china. In this letter, he advised Colonel Casey that the designs were so much more elaborate than the originals that it would increase the cost of the service and require an extension of time for completion to May 1, 1880. This list was attached ot the letter.

Soup Course:	Tomato, Sweet potato, Buckwheat, Snap Bean, Corn, Amolu (Soapweed), Cactus.
Fish Course:	Shad, Florida Red Snapper, Raritan [River] . . . Smelt, California Salmon, Freshwater Lobster, Buckpike, Striped Bass, Pompano, Spanish Mackerel, Washington white perch, Brook trout, Black bass.
Dinner Course:	Buffalo & Coyotes, Antelope, Racoon, Black tail deer, Big horn sheep (Rocky Mountain), Bear, Opossum, Buckeye & grey squirrel, Virginia deer, Ohio goldenrod, May flower, Virginia creeper.
Game Course:	Quail, Canvass-back duck, Prairie hen, Partridge, California Quail, Yellow leg Snipe, Teal Duck, Woodcock, Wild pigeon, Reed birds, Ptarmigan, Rail, Wild Turkey.
Fruit Course:	PaPaw, Chincapin, Wild apple, Persimmon, Blueberry, Pecan, Currants in 3 Colors, Delaware grape, Wintergreen, wild cherry, Thimble berry.[209]

45. *Obverse and reverse of the soup bowl. Diameter, 9 inches.*

45

46. Fish platter, "The Shad," and fish plates, "Pompano" and "Mackeral."
Platter: length, 24 inches;
width, 9¼ inches.
Plates: diameter, 8½ inches.

47. Fish plate, "The Smelt":
diameter, 8½ inches.

46

47

No reply has been found from Colonel Casey to Mr. Haviland.

Davis had gone into seclusion at Asbury Park, New Jersey, which he selected as a place to work because of its convenience to New York, the variety of flora and fish available to him there, and its relative isolation. For his studio, James A. Bradley, the developer of Asbury Park, gave him three of the dressing rooms in the bathhouse facing the sea. The partitions were removed, and a large space was cut out for a window, affording a view of the ocean. The studio was in the shape of the letter L and was about four feet wide and six feet long. Here, Davis worked with "his watercolor board on his knee, his colors at hand, the everchanging sea before his eye" surrounded by the specimens from which he drew his inspirations.

He worked through the late spring and summer of 1879, drawing on the knowledge of flowers, animals, birds, and fish which he had acquired during his many years as a special artist for *Harper's Weekly*. "Professional duty, and love of adventure, had led him to study the native flora and fauna in every part of the country" to which his assignments took him. "He had fished in the rivers of the East and West and in the sea; hunted fowl and game in the forests, swamps, and the mountains; shot the buffalo on the plains; and visited historic haunts of the Indians in the East; met the Indians in their wigwams, and studied their habits on the prairies· of the far West." It was this knowledge which inspired the more than 130 different individual designs produced for the new state service.[210]

The designs were made in watercolor, and though they were bold and striking, they were difficult to reproduce perfectly upon porcelain with hard mineral color. It was necessary for Haviland and Company to invent new methods to produce the designs on the china.

According to Davis, the watercolor drawings were rolled and sent to Europe each Saturday. When they arrived at the Haviland factory in Limoges, France, an etching was made. The outline thus obtained could be quickly transferred to the number of plates required for each subject. Then, the basic colors of the design were applied to each plate by a chromolithographic or decalcomania process.[211] Finally, the plate was taken by the decorator who shaded and colored the design to match the original watercolor drawing. The last step in decoration was the gilding.[212]

The work was even more complicated, because Davis had designed new shapes for the dishes of each course which had to be successfully modeled at the factory and approved before the art work could begin. He credits the interest, enthusiasm, and ceaseless care of Theodore Haviland himself with the success of their production.

This care is reflected in a letter Haviland sent to Davis in January 1880. The designs had been finished in October and sent to France, but, there, the work was just beginning. Haviland informed Davis of the following.

We have sent to New York, as samples of the President's set/4 dinner plates/ 4 game plates/4 fish plates/half of these plates are decorated as were the first plates sent you and they are submitted to you on account of the *subjects*—the other plates are decorated according to a new method.

We hope you will like them for outside of any other merits, they look well on the china, they have not that harsh look which was so conspicuous in the first plates sent to you—

The crab, the fishes, are delightful plates, the dessert plate with the cranberry design is also excellent. You must not take any notice of seeing a soup subject on a game plate and a game subject on a fruit plate, we simply make trials on whatever plates nearest at hand. It is particularly requested that you should not show any of the plates to any one but Mrs. Davis.

In justice to yourself and to ourselves we do not care to have anyone see our trials and have them pass a judgment on a plate incomplete as to the China, shape, decoration, etc. It would be as if a director should admit the public to witness the first rehearsals of a new piece.—Not a plate must be shown either in France or in America until it is perfect according to your and our idea—

If the plates suit you—then the almost impossible feat of decorating plaisantly on china the president's plates will be an accomplished fact and we need not trouble ourselves except for the details which can always be corrected to suit you—

You must not fear asking us to commence and commence over again we do not mind the trouble— If these last plates suit you as to the style of decoration we shall then finish all the subjects and send them to you for correction of details.

Now for the Models of the Set 1st dinner plate:—

The corn plate sent you cannot be made to look nice, we have tried and tried different way but we cannot make it look right— It is a clumsy affair in china— We cannot make the plate as you designed it, we do not like the coupe plate first selected by you, because it is not a dinner plate, it is a plaque, and we think the first thing for a dinner plate to be is to be like a plate. We have tried several, and we think a very simple coupe plate with the addition of a very small and thin rim will answer the purpose [here Haviland sketched a profile of the plate], the rim will be thin only to give to the plate a look of dinner plate. The shape is after a chinese plate, it is unlike any plate ever made in china, it is very simple and we think just the thing. We have made five and as soon as decorated we shall send them to you.

The letter took up each part of the service in turn and discussed the problems of making the shape and the compromise arrived at, but always deferred to Davis's opinion and asked for his approval. Haviland wrote that "the whole set has been a long series of trials and no one will ever appreciate the set for the work it has cost you and is costing us. However we hope when it is finished, we shall both be pleased." [213]

The difficulty of manufacturing the china was only one of Theodore Haviland's worries. Five months before, on August 14, 1879, he had written to Colonel Casey that to that date sufficient progress had been made on the service to permit making a more accurate estimate of its cost. He requested an additional $2,000 to partially reimburse the company for the sculpture, decoration, and time which making the

service had entailed. He said that Davis had also designed some extra pieces not mentioned in the original contract such as oyster and salad plates, a fish and game platter, an individual butter plate, and a cup and saucer for chocolate. He asked what quantities would be needed of each, and said he would submit an estimate of the cost. Colonel Casey did not answer this letter immediately, so Haviland wrote again on September 4 repeating the same questions.

The colonel answered Haviland's earlier letter on September 5. He wrote that he did not feel authorized to recommend an additional sum of $2,000 for the dinner set nor did he feel authorized to ask for an estimate for the additional pieces. His duty was to keep the cost to the original contract, and he asked how many and which pieces of the dinner set could be furnished by June 30, 1880, for the original price.

This obviously came as quite a blow to Haviland. His indignation and displeasure were evident in the letter he wrote to Colonel Casey on September 18, 1879. In it, he said he would regret having to deliver a set imperfect in quality or quantity to the Executive Mansion.

Haviland was so distraught that he personally came to Washington to try to persuade Colonel Casey to reconsider, but in vain; so, on October 2, he proposed a list of the pieces Haviland could furnish under the original contract.

60 Dinner Plates	— 10 copies of 6 of Mr. Davis's designs.
60 Game Plates	— 10 " " 6 game subjects
60 Fish Plates	— 10 " " 6 fish "
60 Soup Plates	— 10 each of 6 subjects.
60 Dessert Plates	— 10 " " 6 fruit designs
60 Pairs of teas	
60 Pairs of After Dinner Coffees.	

He asked for a reply, stating that this proposal was acceptable; if not, Haviland would deliver the set exactly as described in the original contract, without any more ado.

Colonel Casey replied that a reduction from 562 pieces to 420 was too great, and he proposed that the company revise the order and make 80 dinner plates and 80 dessert plates. With this

48. *Game platter, "On Chesapeake Bay," and game plates. Platter: length, 18 inches; width, 11½ inches. Plates: diameter, 9 inches.*

49. *Turkey platter: length, 19½ inches; width, 13 inches.*

48

49

amount the set would be usable, and the offer could be accepted.

Theodore Haviland again reminded Casey that the set of 420 pieces that the company was offering would cost the company 3,200 francs more than the 562 pieces in the original contract, including the cost of designing and modeling the new forms. He offered to change the amount on the proposed list in order to give the White House more dinner and dessert plates; this could be accomplished by cutting all the other quantities of the service to be supplied from 60 of each to 50.

Colonel Casey finally capitulated and asked permission of the commanding general, chief of engineers, to modify the contract on those terms and to allow the time extension to June 30, 1880, for delivery. When Casey wrote Haviland about the change in the contract, he reminded him that the coat of arms and date required in the original contract were to be put on the china as designed by Davis.

Haviland replied that the company would proceed at once with the decoration of the china. He also told Colonel Casey that as the coat of arms would be out of place as part of the decoration on the face of the plate, they had given instructions to have it in color on the back of each plate. Colonel Casey agreed to this arrangement of the crest, and production began on November 1, 1879.[214]

In March 1880, Haviland wrote to the colonel stating that the dinner service—with six designs per course—would be ready by June, but they would like to use all twelve designs. Should this be the case, he said that delivery could be made by October 31. Colonel Casey replied that no further extension of time could be made and they would expect the delivery of six designs on June 30, 1880.[215]

The month of June brought a flurry of correspondence between Haviland and Company and Colonel Casey relating to the shipping, the arrival of the china, and its duty-free entry into the United States. On June 29, 1880, Haviland advised Colonel Casey that the china was on its way from New York to Washington. The letter said that it "seemed such a pity" not to use all

of the designs made by Theodore Davis so that in place of only six designs, they had sent nine of the soup course and nine of the dinner course and all twelve designs of the game, fish, and dessert courses. The other three designs of the soup and dinner course needed to complete the service would be ready in October, and if Mrs. Hayes wished to set aside some of the plates in those courses, they would be willing to exchange them as soon as possible. The letter said that Theodore Davis would be glad to come to Washington to explain the designs to Mrs. Hayes when the china was opened.[216]

The china arrived on schedule, June 30, with only four saucers broken.[217] Davis did come to Washington when the china was delivered, but Mrs. Hayes was not at home. The service was described and explained for Mrs. Hayes and others in great detail in a booklet which was printed by Haviland and Company to accompany the china. It is entitled *The White House Porcelain Service, 1879, Designs by an American Artist illustrating exclusively American Fauna and Flora* which is reprinted in its entirety in Appendix I. Theodore Haviland mentioned the booklet in his letter of January 1880 to Davis:

At the same time as we shall have the President's set ready, we shall publish a pamphlet giving an history and a description of each plate. The pamphlet will be illustrated by a sketch in pen and ink of all your designs—

The illustrations will be very well made, and under each design there will [be] a little description of the subject presented.

I have made the catalogue by copying the descriptions out of Mrs. Davis's charming and interesting letters and this circular I will send to you next week for correction and additions.[218]

A copy of the booklet on extra-fine paper was sent to the White House. It cautions that the set was designed to be seen as arranged on a table, and that those plates which seemed less attractive when examined singly would not seem inferior when so viewed. Davis also advised Mrs. Hayes that "many of the designs were made with a view to their effect under strong gaslight and for this reason some of the decorations are quite imperfectly seen by day light." It was the flamboyant realism and strong color of the designs which made the new service so unusual and caused so much comment.

The oyster plate was one of the most admired pieces in the new service. The deep blue of the sea contrasts strikingly with the irridescent white interior of five blue-point oysters molded into the plate. They are arranged against ribbons of vivid green seaweed and clusters of oysters. Touches of gold sparkle on the design and ornament the scalloped edge of the plate. The soup bowl was molded in the shape of the laurel blossom and twelve different scenes decorated the individual bowls. They included such flights of fancy as "American Soup of the XV Century" which shows an Indian seated beside a steaming pothole in the rocks with a slain deer beside him to indicate the kind of soup which is to be made. "1776" shows the giant fireplace of a New England home with a Dutch oven on the swinging crane. Willow plates, a flint-lock rifle, and a grandfather's clock can also be seen in the decor of the room. The explanatory booklet entitles one soup plate as the "Green Turtle" and shows the turtle on a Florida reef crawling between the ribs of an old shipwreck by the light of the rising moon. It seemed a prophecy of twentieth-century "pop art."

The plates in the fish series are in the form of a scallop shell, two of which combined form the plate. The larger white shell below was designed to hold the food. The smaller shell above was decorated with fish found in the rivers, mountain streams, and the Eastern seaboard. The series included among the twelve different designs, the red snapper, the trout, and the striped bass. The handsome platter with rolled and gilded corners shows a large shad enmeshed in a net of gold.

The platter for the main course also has rolled and gilded edges, and upon its surface is painted a magnificent wild turkey silhouetted against a rosy sunset sky. The form of the dinner plate is coupe with a narrow rim and each of the twelve plates is painted with a different scene. Many of them depict the larger game animals of

this country, such as the bear, the buffalo, and the Rocky Mountain big horn sheep. One of the most picturesque scenes is entitled in the Haviland booklet "On the Plains at Night" and is from a sketch made by the artist while on the Indian campaign with Gen. George B. Custer in 1867.

The game platter is entitled "On Chesapeake Bay" and the coupe-shaped game plates are slightly smaller than the dinner plates. The designs are twelve different game birds pictured in their native habitats.

The fruit plate design is modeled from the leaf of the. wild apple and the twelve different designs mainly portray fruit and nuts indigenous to America. In this series is found a plate which was designed as a compliment to the First Lady, Mrs. Hayes, showing a swallow darting over tufts of Ohio goldenrod. Another plate is decorated with a portrayal of the artist's bathhouse at Asbury Park and is entitled: "The Studio."

The tiny after-dinner coffee cups are creamy white, simply ornamented with bamboo leaves— a sprout being twisted for a handle. The cup rests in a circle of bamboo on a nearly flat saucer. The teacups in the shape of an inverted mandarin's hat have a delicate green interior. The outside of the cup is decorated with dead gold and a design of the pinkish blossoms and green leaves of the tea plant.

The Haviland booklet described the platters which were designed for each course, but which were not in the china delivered in June 1880. The handsome oyster plates were also pictured and described, but were not among the pieces delivered in the first order.

The Executive Mansion received a listing of the designs made by Theodore Davis for the dinner service which was not in the original order. This listing came in a memorandum from Albert A. Love of Haviland's office in New York City, dated July 3, 1880. A few weeks later Haviland and Company advised Colonel Casey that they could complete the state dinner set, all of which were designed by Davis and in the process of manufacture, with delivery promised by January first. The following offer was furnished.

50

51

50. "Bison" and "Big Horn" dinner
plates: diameter, 10 inches.

51. "Goldenrod and Swallow" and "Artist's Studio"
dessert plates: length, 8 inches; width 9 inches at widest.

52. Ice cream platter and plates. Platter: length,
18¼ inches; width, 11½ inches. Plates: length,
7¼ inches; width, 6½ inches.

4	Fish platters	Shad
4	Sauce boats	Water lily
4	Game platters	"On the Chesapeake"
4	Dinner platters	Wild turkey
4	Ice Cream trays	Snow shoe
80	Ice Cream plates	Individual
50	Salad plates	"Washed ashore."
50	Oyster plates	Blue points and racoon oysters
50	Indian plates	"Crackers, Cheese, & Cigars"
80	Independent butters	Lily leaf

330

The 330 pieces for the sum of $3205.40.

Colonel Casey replied on August 9 that, taking into account the silver platter used at state dinners, the following selection of pieces would be more useful.

2	Game Platters	2	Dinner Platters
2	Fish Platters	2	Sauce Boats
2	Ice Cream Trays	50	Ice Cream Plates
50	Salad Plates	50	Oyster Plates
50	Indian Plates	50	Independent Butter Plates

This totals 260 pieces, plus 40 dinner plates including the 3 designs lacking in the original order: Bear in a Bee Tree, Buffalo, and Antelope, Prong Horn.

The final price agreed on for the order was $3,120, with Haviland and Company pointing out that the reduction in price was slight because a greater number of the more expensive pieces were being ordered.[219]

The new order included a seafood salad plate entitled "Washed Ashore." It was a round plate painted a pale blue watery color, applied in translucent layers over a lobster and other shell-fish molded in relief into the body of the plate. The "Indian" plate referred to a plate designed to look like an Indian basket with a willow switch bent in a circle and thin strips of reed woven across it. Davis said this was an "after-coffee" plate designed to serve the "crackers and cheese and cigars," if, as was frequently the case, the dinner ended "in smoke." His choice of the Indian design was to give a "breezy Western whiff from the plains to an Eastern dinner."

The so-called "Independent" butter plates were shaped like pale green water-lily leaves with crystal drops of water, here and there, on the surface of the leaf. The ice-cream trays and plates were models of a Canadian snowshoe against the winter snow, rosy in the reflected light of the setting sun. The latter addition seemed especially appropriate when the rest of the service arrived at the Executive Mansion on December 29, 1880, in the midst of a driving snowstorm.

Each piece delivered to the White House in June and December 1880 was marked on the reverse with the United States coat of arms in color and with the words "Fabriqué par/ Haviland & Co./d'après les dessins/de/Theo R. Davis" in red except for the artist's signature which is in black. They were also marked "H & Co." in green and "Limoges." The most important mark is an acrostic made of the artist's initials "T.D." formed from a red, white, and blue pennant suspended from a crossbar with the date "1879." This latter mark is important, because it is the distinguishing mark for the first edition of the Hayes china and was used on all the china furnished the White House in 1880. Haviland intended to make 25 artist proof sets to help recompense the company for the cost of the set supplied to the White House. Theodore Haviland's letter of January 1880 mentions these 25 sets and states that "as soon as we are ready here we shall try to sell a set to the Prince of Wales, after that the rest will be very easy."[220] Perhaps it was not as easy as he had hoped, for no record can be found that the Prince of Wales bought a set.

According to the newspapers, eight duplicate sets were sent to this country to be exhibited in stores in the metropolitan areas. One set or portion thereof was exhibited at J. W. Boteler and Son in Washington, D.C., as early as July 31, 1880. This was not a complete set as Boteler borrowed a few pieces, some of which were from the Executive Mansion, to give the public a more complete look at the new state service. Another could be seen at Van Heusen Charles and Company at their New York store on Broadway, and a third was shown at Jones, McDuffee and Stratton's in Boston. A newspaper article about the set exhibited in New York gives the price of a complete set as $1,200.[221]

It seems doubtful that any full set of the china was sold in this country other than the one purchased by the Executive Mansion, because none has ever been brought to the attention of the Smithsonian Institution or the White House.

In 1950 an antique dealer in Montreal, Canada, wrote to the White House that he had acquired a complete set of china of the same design as the Hayes state service which belonged to the Honorable J. A. Chapleau, the lieutenant governor of the Province of Quebec in 1892. Each piece was marked with the signature of Theodore R. Davis, but instead of the coat of arms of the United States this set was marked with the Canadian crest or coat of arms made up of the emblems of the five provinces which were in confederation in 1871—Quebec, Ontario, New Brunswick, Nova Scotia, and Manitoba. The White House did not pursue the matter, and the present location of the Canadian service is unknown.

Theodore Haviland wrote to Davis on September 28, 1880, and mentioned a set being exhibited in Paris

. . . where its novelty attracted great deals [sic] of attention. The subjects were found very interesting. The only criticisms I have heard have been to the effect that the designs were too complicated for the taste of the French whose academic educations taught them to like simple lines, but all were loud in their praises of the quiet and elegant tones of each plate. The fruit plate and a. d. [after-dinner] coffee were said to be the handsomest pieces ever made in china.[222]

The new state service created a tremendous sensation after it was received at the White House and first viewed by the press in 1880. Everyone had something to say about it, pro-and-con. The metropolitan newspapers carried stories about the elaborate service and art critics were vocal in their opinions. The new china inspired either strong support or violent dislike and condemnation. Mrs. Hayes was strangely silent in her own personal opinion about the end result of her impulsive action that day in the conservatory. On July 24, 1880, Theodore Davis finally wrote her personally.[223]

With the exception of Colonel Casey's very cordial reception I have had no direct word from anyone connected with the Executive Mansion, though I should have been particularly pleased to have learned something of the reception that the services met with.

I am convinced that a short autograph note from your hand would be very valuable to reproduce (facsimile) and introduce in a few copies of the descriptive volume. Such a letter would serve to connect your name pleasantly with this first American set, now as well as in the future and if it is not trespassing too much upon your time, and good nature, I shall be very glad to learn from you personally your impression of the new service and whether any particular design is regarded as the favorite.

Mrs. Hayes's letter in reply, dated August 2, 1880—a facsimile of which is reproduced in Appendix I—is curiously impersonal.

My absence from home when the beautiful porcelain set arrived is my apology for the delay in sending you my thanks. The exquisite State dinner service executed by Haviland & Co. from original designs by you is universally admired by all competent judges of works of art who have seen it. It is a delight to study the beautiful forms and paintings. One almost feels as if such Ceramic Art should be used for no other purpose except to gratify the eye. I congratulate you in the accomplishment of the task which you so kindly imposed upon yourself in the production of the beautiful designs which have added fresh laurels to American Art. With best wishes for yourself and my little friend. [signed] Sincerely   Lucy W. Hayes.[224]

The immediate furor raised by the china and the interest in the china shown in the stores prompted Theodore Davis to take out design patents for each of the series of plates in the state service. In the patent papers, Davis assigned the right to Haviland and Company to produce the designs for private and public use, for the following seven years. In the words of the application, which was filed on July 20, 1880, the "highly

53. *Teacup and saucer and after-dinner cup and saucer. Teacup: height, 2 inches; diameter, 3 inches; saucer diameter, 6 inches. Coffee cup: height, 2 inches, diameter, 2½ inches; saucer diameter, 4½ inches.*

54 *The Indian plate, according to Theodore Davis, was designed to be an "after-coffee plate" for serving "crackers, cheese and cigars." Diameter, 8⅞ inches.*

55. *Sauceboat: height, 4 inches; width, 5 inches.*

56. *Marks on the Hayes china: left, mark used on china received at the White House in 1880; right, mark used on china on the open market and found on White House china purchased in 1884 and 1886 during the administrations of Presidents Arthur and Cleveland.*

53

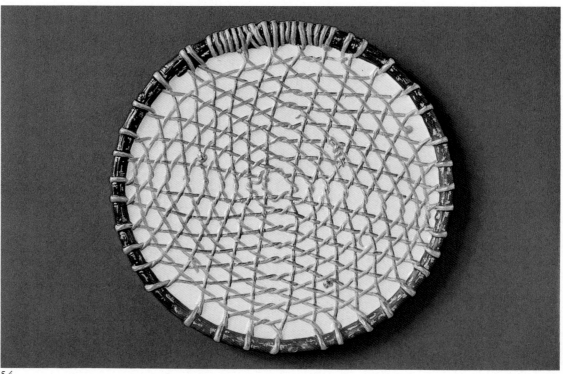

54

114

55

56

artistic dishes or plates by reason of their elegant and unique design are well suited for use in holding various articles or as attractive means of ornamentation." The patents were given the numbers 11932 for the game course, 11933 for the soup course, 11934 for the dessert set, 11935 for the fish course, and 11936 for the dinner plates. Pieces of the Hayes china design marked with the inscription "Design Patented/August 10th, 1880/N̲o̲ 11932—" and subsequent numbers through 11936, are pieces which were produced for sale to the general public.

These pieces also have the United States coat of arms and the words "Fabriqué par/Haviland & C̲o̲/ d'après les dessins/de/Theodore R. Davis" as was on the White House set; however, instead of the artist's initials and the date 1879, the china made for sale to the public has the number and date of the patent.

Judging from the number of pieces still in existence which bear the patent number, the Hayes china enjoyed quite a vogue when it went on the open market. Perhaps the public dispute about the artistic merits of the service only enhanced its desirability to the general public.

Theodore Davis's ambition was to design a set that was distinctively American and he had "aimed at striking originality and strong, bold effects of color and form combinations." [225] It was the view of more than one art critic that the designs were neither decorative nor original. One *New York Tribune* critic made some scathing comments.

It is the treatment that ought to make the Americanism of the designs and the treatment of these subjects is distinctly Oriental and founded on the superficial study of Japanese ornamentation. . . . It is amusing to see the efforts made to convey the impression of originality in the forms of the dishes, for fish, meat and game all of which are essentially the same and directly borrowed from the Japanese as may be seen even in the commonest of our shops for the sale of Japanese wares. [226]

The critic goes on to say that "the professional French china-painters have subdued Mr. Davis drawings to the style they themselves work in. . . . Every touch portrays the professional hand working in the skilled routine of the professional workshop."

This judgment of the china does seem to be unduly harsh. Davis may have been influenced, perhaps even unconsciously, by the china exhibited at the Centennial Exposition of 1876 which he had covered so thoroughly. The Japanese wares at the centennial were described as "with strikingly faithful reproduction of leaves, vines and other forms of nature. [227]

An article on ceramic art at the exposition states that "the best for all purposes is the French Haviland. . . . In one dinner set the knobs are modeled after different vegetables; in another called the "water lily" the dishes and covers are shaped after the plant and the ornamentation shows the flower itself." [228]

Another review of the Haviland display comments that "the ground color is generally rather dark and always very uneven and full of gradations and clouds." [229] The effort to present a great variety of subjects in one service and the intensity of the presentation is typically American, however, and the Hayes china has a strength and a vigor that is lacking in the more stereotyped state china of the twentieth century.

The new state service was first used for an intimate dinner given by out-going President and Mrs. Hayes for the newly elected President and Mrs. Garfield in November 1880. Its first use for state entertaining was at the formal dinner given in honor of President and Mrs. Grant on their return from a triumphal tour around the world. [230] This dinner for forty was given on December 20, 1880, with members of the cabinet, Supreme Court, Congress, military officers, and civilians present.

The Hayes china continues to evoke strong reactions from those who view it today, and its merits as a dinner service are still controversial. The feeling was probably best summed up by Mrs. James G. Blaine, wife of the senator from Maine, who once wrote of seeing the Hayes service and commented: "It is worth a trip from New York to Washington to see the table at a State Dinner at the White House." [231]

Information about reorders of the Hayes state

57. Carte-de-visite *of Theodore Davis bearing his signature.*

58. *View of Theodore Davis's studio in Asbury Park, New Jersey, taken in 1879. Davis is shown sketching by the open door.*

59. *Seafood salad plate designed by Theodore Davis for sale to the general under public Patent 1193– to replace the plate shown in figure 44 which was part of the White House service.*

118

60. *Picture taken in the White House conservatory in 1879 by the photographer Pach of New York City. The little girl wearing the white apron is Carrie Paulding Davis, daughter of Theodore Davis. Mrs. Rutherford B. Hayes is seated in the chair with her son, Scott Russell, at left, and her daughter Fanny, at right. (Courtesy of The Rutherford B. Hayes Library and Museum.)*

61. *Snowshoe from which Theodore Davis modeled the ice-cream platter and plates for the Hayes service.*

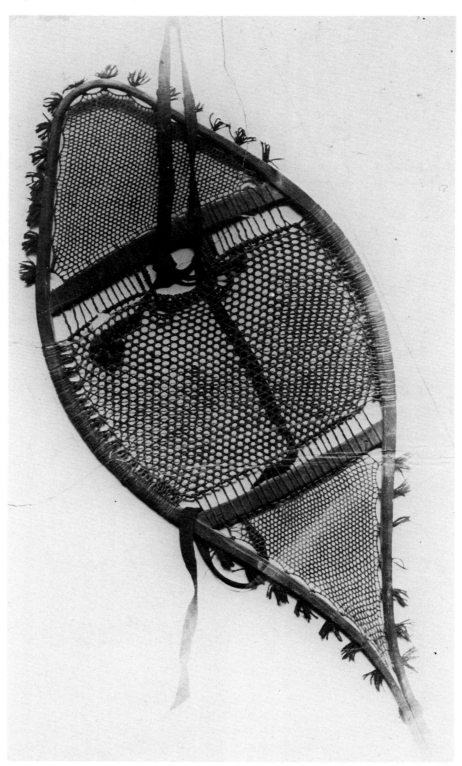

china are discussed in the chapters on the administrations of Presidents Arthur and Cleveland.

Pieces of the Hayes service with the mark of the official service are in the collections at the White House and in the Smithsonian Institution. The White House still has in its possession all of the serving platters received in 1880 and multiple examples of all the pieces in the service with the exception of the independent butter plates. Two independent butter plates with the original marks are in the collections of the Falmouth Historical Society. It is possible that the sample china which came into this country to the stores in Washington, New York, and Boston during the summer of 1880 had the same mark as the set delivered to the White House, for the patent on the designs was not secured until August.

The Hayes china was in pristine condition and hardly had been used when President and Mrs. Garfield moved into the Executive Mansion in March 1881. It was the major service used by them until the social season of the spring of 1881 was curtailed by the illness of Mrs. Garfield. She was convalescing when President Garfield was shot on July 2, and the long summer that followed was devoted to the care of the president until his death on September 19.

Chester A. Arthur

Grover Cleveland

. . . President Arthur's first state dinner was given in honor of General and Mrs. Grant. The parlors and the East Room were profusely decorated with flowers, and in the dining-room were palm trees and other exotics massed in the corners, while the mantels were banked with cut flowers. There were thirty-four plates on the long table, in the centre of which was a plateau mirror, on which were roses and lilies of the valley. On either side of it were tall gilt candelabra bearing eleven wax lights each, and beyond these large gilt epergnes overflowing with Marechal Niel roses. At the end of the mirror were pairs of silver candelabra bearing shaded wax lights and oval cushions of white camelias [sic] set with roses and orchids. At the extreme ends were round pieces of bon silene roses and lilies of the valley. Around this elaborate centre decoration were ranged crystal compotes and cut-glass decanters. Large, flat corsage bouquets of roses, tied with satin ribbons, were laid at each lady's plate, and small boutonnieres of rosebuds were provided for the gentlemen. The cards were of heavy gilt-edged board, embossed with the national coat-of-arms in gold, below which the name of each guest was written. The Marine Band performed selections from popular operatic music. . . . Dinner was served in fourteen courses, with which there were served eight varieties of wines, each variety having its appropriate wine-glass. The guests were two hours at the table, and the menu was eulogized, especially the terrapin, which was highly commended by the epicures who enjoyed it.

Excerpt from *Perley's Reminiscences of Sixty Years in the National Metropolis* by Ben Perley Poore (Philadelphia: Hubbard Brothers, 1886), volume 2, pages 459 and 462.

Amid the tragic circumstances that placed Chester A. Arthur in the presidency, he managed during the first autumn of his administration to make a long and serious study of the furnishings of the Executive Mansion, which was being extensively redecorated before he actually moved into the house on December 7, 1881. During the period of the renovation, President Arthur, personally, with the assistance of the doorkeeper, Carl Loeffler, carefully evaluated all the old furnishings they found in the attic and basement storerooms. They divided the items into two groups—pieces which were to be sold and those which could be repaired and used. The president went through the china closets of the mansion with the same thoroughness. Unfortunately, he seems to have been totally unaware of the historical association of the china. At that time, there was a considerable amount of old china in the house consisting of broken sets and odd pieces that dated back to the Monroe period. He had William Crump, the steward, clear the large original kitchen and into that room the pieces that were to be discarded were packed into thirty barrels.[232] The pieces to be kept were crammed into an unfinished closet which had been made from part of the little hallway by the elevator. A newspaper article of the 1890s noted that "there were two rows of shelves about three feet deep and there the three sets which belong to the service are kept; one third of them being on the floor."[233] The three services referred to would have been the state china from the administrations of Presidents Lincoln, Grant, and Hayes.

The Hayes service, which had arrived in 1880 was still new when President Arthur assumed the presidency, so there was no reason for him to order another state dinner service. Indeed, the china ordered by Mrs. Hayes was very much to his liking, so it is doubtful that he even considered ordering more. At his direction, the two ornate sideboards in the family dining room were crowded with a display of the more spectacular pieces of the Hayes china.

Theodore Davis wrote in 1889 that President Arthur not only used the china on state occasions, but frequently on the family's table.[234] Davis also wrote that many pieces admired by President Arthur were removed from the Executive Mansion during the summer months and taken to decorate the dining room of "the Soldiers Home, when for health's sake the President removed to that place."

The type of china he did need was prompted by the large receptions and afternoon teas which were his preferred style of public entertaining. In preparation for these parties, the Executive Mansion bought the following from J. W. Boteler and Son in November 1881.[235]

62. Plates in the White House collection identified as from the administration of President Arthur. These could be from the twenty-three plates purchased from Tiffany and Company in 1882. (White House collection: no mark; "SM," Limoge. At rear, Brownfield and Son; Worcester for Tiffany and Company; and impressed mark "C.")

Nov. 26, 1881

1 Doz. Dresden Tea Cups and Saucers	40.00
1 Doz. Haviland " " " "	40.00
1 R. W. A. D. Coffee cups and saucers	50.00

Nov. 29, 1881

1 Doz Dresden " " " "	35.00

Nov. 30, 1881

2 Doz cups (Coffee and Saucers)	72.00

This bill is interesting, because it is the first indication of the many varieties of china which were appearing in the retail stores of the city after the Civil War. None of these pieces can be identified today.

When Abby Gunn Baker began her work on White House china less than twenty years later, she noted that President Arthur ordered only miscellaneous pieces during his administration and the inventory of 1901, based primarily on the work done by Mrs. Baker and Colonel Bingham, lists for the Arthur administration "25 dessert plates odd, 5 Dresden cups and saucers, small and 1 dessert plate [the latter must have been either more spectacular than the other 25 or of a different size.]" [236] A selection from the dessert plates represents the Arthur administration in the China Room in the White House. One lovely plate is decorated with a big red rose and gold butterflies, and another has alternating wedge-shaped segments of blue and gold and red which is on a tracery design of the so-called Alhambra style popular in mid-nineteenth-century America. Neither plate has a maker's mark.

Vouchers in the National Archives show that on May 16, 1882, President Arthur through Col. Almon F. Rockwell, officer in charge of public buildings and grounds, purchased from Tiffany and Company, 23 china plates ranging in price from $2.75 each to $10.50. Nine of these plates are single entries. There are two listings of three plates each and two listings of four plates each. . . .[237]

The plates which Mrs. Theodore Roosevelt asked Mrs. Baker to select to represent the Arthur administration in the White House China Collection must have been chosen from those bought at Tiffany's. Their handsome decoration suggests that they were intended for ornamental rather than table use.

Among the curious entries for the year 1884 are the weekly charges made by J. W. Boteler and Son for "hire of Decorated china and cut glass." In the month of February, the weekly charge was $16.90, and in March $23.44 was paid.[238]

The same voucher which covered the rental of the decorated china from Boteler also listed a purchase in April 1884 of "1 Square Decorated Ice Cream Plate @ 2.00, 1 Decorated Fish Plate @ 4.50," and "1 Decorated Fruit Plate @ 2.25." [240] These are specific individual replacements for the Hayes dinner service. It is known that the firm of J. W. Boteler and Son was the Washington, D.C., outlet for the china designed by Theodore Davis for the Hayes administration, a design which was later sold to the general public; therefore, it is possible that the china rented to the White House in February and March may have matched the Hayes state china.

By the end of March, the social season was coming to an end, which may explain why the next order from Boteler is dated July 1884. At this time, the Executive Mansion ordered "2½ doz. dishes, Purple and Gold with U.S. Coat of Arms, Decorated to Order @ $60.00 costing $150.00." This was for another order of the Lincoln china,[239] accounting for still more of the Lincoln china with the Boteler mark being used in the White House. After the Lincoln-design plates were purchased in July, there is no record of charges for rental china.

President Grover Cleveland came into office as a bachelor and the accounts for the Executive Mansion for the rest of 1885 and 1886 reflect the lack of interest being taken in the house and its furnishings by the president. The news of his forthcoming wedding in June 1886 revived the interest of the commissioner of public buildings and grounds, and Col. John M. Wilson requested and received a memorandum from William T. Sinclair, steward of the Executive

Mansion, listing the number of pieces of the Hayes china dinner service which were still in good condition.

50 Oyster plates
38 Soup plates
46 Fish plates
91 Dinner plates
45 Game plates
49 Snowshoe plates
47 Cheese plates
78 Dessert plates
47 Salad plates [241]

Colonel Wilson then wrote to Mr. A. A. Love, who still represented Haviland and Company in New York City. Wilson wrote that he had talked with artist Theodore Davis a few days before about replacing some of the celebrated Hayes china which had been broken and that Davis had referred him to Haviland. In order to have at least 60 of each kind, he hoped to be able to order the following and inquired about the price of "10 oyster plates, 22 soup plates, 14 fish plates, 15 game plates, 11 snowshoe plates, 13 cheese plates, 13 salad plates."

Love immediately replied that they could furnish soup, fish, snowshoe, and cheese plates in the quantities desired. He felt that they also might be able to provide a few oyster, game, and salad plates. He wrote that if Colonel Wilson was not too particular about the design of the various plates that they could complete the courses requested. The price would be the same for each piece, $12.50 a plate.

Colonel Wilson was horrified by the price quoted and wrote back that it was so excessive compared to the original service that he thought that he would have to forego the idea and make arrangements for another style of plate.

Love wrote back immediately to say the original dinner set was ordered duty free and the price they quoted for replacements included the 60 percent duty.

After much correspondence, a satisfactory price of $7 was agreed on for each piece except the cheese plates which would cost $8; the order was placed in anticipation that Congress would make the usual appropriation for the Executive Mansion before July 1. If the appropriation was not made, which Colonel Wilson assured them hadn't happened in years, the plates could not be accepted. Arrangements were made for the china to come in duty free, and it finally arrived on September 25, 1886. The shipment contained the following plates at $7 each: 12 soup, 4 fish, 5 game, 1 ice cream, and 3 salad. The delivery also included 3 Indian plates at $8 each. The bill was marked: "To replace plates broken at various times in China set purchased in 1880 for use in the Executive Mansion on State Occasions." [242] There is no information on the marks of these later additions, but the surviving pieces in the White House with the patented mark seem to indicate they were marked like those which were made for sale to the general public.

On September 27, Colonel Wilson wrote to Haviland and told them that the three salad plates received were different from those in the rest of the set. The original salad plate entitled "Washed Ashore" was without feet and the lobsters and shell fish were white on a light-blue ground with white clouds above; the new ones painted in dark colors with shell feet. He asked if they could be exchanged. He felt that the newer ones were more handsome, but could not be used with the original order.[243] Haviland apologized for the mistake, and said that three plates would be made in France to match the original order, for matching plates were not available in the United States. These plates were sent to the Executive Mansion on December 16, and the three that did not match were returned to New York on December 17, 1886.[244]

The only other china order for the first Cleveland administration was an order in January 1888 for "2 doz. cups and saucers." As these cost only $2.00 a dozen, they may have been intended for kitchen use.[245]

Benjamin Harrison

[*The First Lady's*] *most cherished project just now is a class in china painting, for which she has invited to come to Washington an expert Polish teacher from Indianapolis. With Mrs. Harrison presenting so much of her own handiwork to church bazaars and her friends, the craze for painting china has revived, and twenty-five enthusiastic ladies are already wielding their brushes upon delicate white porcelain under the direction of this gentleman. The class includes the daughters of the Vice-President, ladies of several Cabinet families, and leaders of Washington society. Their finished work is baked in Mrs. Harrison's own kiln, which she brought here from Indianapolis and which is set up in the home of Mrs. John Wight, at Kendall Green.*

A certain closet at the White House is now filled with unpainted porcelain dishes, awaiting Mrs. Harrison's expert brush. Vases and platters, and many other odd pieces have been sent her by Washington ladies with the request that she decorate them, after which they will become prized heirlooms in their families. Many a baby whose parents have named him for the President has received a milk set painted by Mrs. Harrison with cunning Kate Greenaway children. . . . Invariably there will be found somewhere in her designs a tiny four-leafed clover, which serves not only to wish good luck to her friends, but as her signature.

Of all his grandmother's work, Baby McKee likes best his porcelain bathtub, which is painted with pink magnolia blossoms. Young Benny is so fond of the beautiful flowers on its sides that he can hardly sit still in the water. When he leans out to kiss them and the tub upsets, flooding the carpet, he thinks it a fine sport.

Excerpt from *Carp's Washington* by Frank G. Carpenter, pages 300-301. (Copyright 1960 by Frances Carpenter Huntington. Used with permission of McGraw-Hill Book Company.)

Mrs. Benjamin Harrison's arrival at the White House in 1889 brought to the position of First Lady a woman of many cultural interests. She had an appreciation of historical relics connected with American history, and it was her ambition to make the White House a comfortable and stylish residence for a president while at the same time preserving such things as the furniture, silver, glass, and china associated with its past history. She was particularly interested in the china of the past administrations as she was an accomplished artist who especially delighted in china painting.

Mrs. Harrison found a large assortment of broken sets and broken pieces in the pantries and closets of the Executive Mansion. What was possible to mend, she had glued and riveted in order to retain in service some of the old sets. Though the large service of the Hayes china was still adequate to set a state dinner, she decided to spend some of the furnishings' appropriation for the purchase of new china. It would seem that this purchase was not prompted so much by necessity as it was by a change in taste. Mrs. Harrison decorated china in a rather conventional and dignified style, and she may have found the Hayes service too overpowering in its decoration.

Once Mrs. Harrison had decided to order new china she enlisted the aid of Paul Putzki, a professional teacher of china painting, in arranging the design.[246] Putzki had come to Washington at the invitation of the First Lady, who had studied under him in Indiana, and was teaching a china-painting class.[247]

President Harrison was elected on a platform favoring high tariffs to protect American industry and Mrs. Harrison was a firm supporter of his "American first" philosophy. It must have distressed her that there was no china manufactory in the United States which could produce the china she wished to buy for the president's mansion, but she determined to make its design symbolic and meaningful to Americans. For shape, she chose the undecorated "blank" porcelain that had been used for the Lincoln state china. The representation of the Arms of the United States on the center of the plates is adapted from the eagle used on the center of the Lincoln plates. The rim of the plates were to be a rich dark blue shot with tiny gold stars with a lacy gilt tracery of corn and goldenrod. The design was Mrs. Harrison's own inspiration, but she owed the professional execution of her design to Paul Putzki.

Mrs. Harrison had selected corn in the design to typify the produce of the United States and as a delicate compliment to the Hoosier state.[248]

The goldenrod was selected because President Harrison considered it the most beautiful of our native flowers; for that reason, it had also been chosen by his daughter as the design in the fabric used for her inaugural ball gown.[249]

The designs were turned over to the Washington firm of M. W. Beveridge at 1215 F Street, N.W., importers of French china, who requested sample plates from several china firms. Artists in many factories in Limoges competed and from the samples Mrs. Harrison chose the design made by the factory of Tressemannes and Vogt in Limoges.[250] This factory was represented in New York by the firm of Vogt and Dose "whose productions of fine goods are known throughout the country."[251]

On October 21, 1891, Col. Oswald H. Ernst wrote from the Office of the Commissioner of Public Buildings and Grounds to the Beveridge firm.

The order for decorated dinner plates given you recently by Mrs. Harrison for use in the Executive Mansion is confirmed as follows, viz.

Six dozen soup plates according to Sample A @ $31.00	186.00
Six dozen dinner plates according to Sample A @ $31.50	189.00
Six dozen breakfast plates according to Sample B @ $31.00	186.00
Six dozen tea plates according to Sample B @ $28.50	171.00
	732.00

Colonel Ernst closed his letter by stating that "it is understood that the plates will be delivered before the first of January next."[252] It had been decided to give the breakfast and the tea plates a narrow rim of the deep blue with a garland of corn and goldenrod and on the edge another band of white of the same size containing 44 stars in gold representing the states of the Union. Abby Gunn Baker writes that the different and lighter design for the smaller plates was suggested by William H. Martin, part owner of the firm of M. W. Beveridge who was evidently handling the order.[253]

The voucher for payment of the china indi-cates that it was received on December 30, 1892.[254] The bill from Beveridge shows that the delivery was short one soup plate as payment was asked for "5 11/12 dozen" soup plates and the charge was only $183.42.

The voucher is marked "Paid on January 21, 1892," and is stamped "procured in open market at lowest market rate, the public exigencies requiring immediate delivery of the articles and performances of the work." The missing soup plate was delivered on April 15 and a separate bill for $2.58 was submitted.[255]

The china received was marked on the reverse "T & V, France" in green; also "T & V" in a bell and "France décoré pour M. W. Beveridge Washington, D.C." in gold. The mark "Harrison 1892" was also stamped in gold on the reverse as a matter of record and to prevent theft.

The soup plate and dinner plate, with the wide blue border designated as "Sample A" on the voucher are 9 and 9½ inches in diameter, respectively. The diameter of the breakfast plate with the two narrow borders of white and blue is 8½ inches and that of the tea plate, also with the narrow borders, is 7¼ inches.

Examples of all of the pieces ordered are in the White House collection. The Smithsonian Institution has examples of the dinner plate and the breakfast plate, so both varieties of borders are represented in the collection. There are also pieces in the President Benjamin Harrison Memorial Home in Indianapolis, Indiana, and in private collections.

The china was very well received by the public, and Mrs. Harrison was pleased with the results. In August 1892, Colonel Ernst again wrote a letter to M. W. Beveridge confirming the firm's proposal of July 27 to furnish the Executive Mansion with five dozen after-dinner coffee cups and saucers with "wide blue border decorated like the plates furnished last Autumn at the rate of $30.00 a dozen."[256] These were delivered on January 3, 1893, and paid for in February.[257] Again only "4 11/12 dozen" were delivered; the other cup and saucer probably had been submitted as a sample.

Collectors of White House china should be aware of the fact that only after-dinner cups and

The state china purchased by President Benjamin
Harrison in 1892 was made by Tressemannes and
Vogt in Limoges, France, and ordered through the
Washington, D.C., firm of M. W. Beveridge.
Orders for the Harrison china were made again
in 1898, 1899, and 1900 during the McKinley
administration. Harrison plates were reordered in
1908 during the administration of President
Theodore Roosevelt.

63. *Mark on the Harrison china
purchased in 1892 and possibly
on the same china design
purchased during the period of
1897–1901.*

64. *White porcelain dinner plate with
wide, dark-blue border etched in gold
with a design of goldenrod
and corn and the Arms of the
United States in color in the
center of each plate.
Diameter, 9½ inches.*

65. *Mark on the Harrison china
which was reordered during the
administration of Theodore
Roosevelt.*
(White House collection.)

64

65

66. *White porcelain breakfast plate with divided border, half is white and half is dark blue. The white section is etched in gold with goldenrod and corn and the blue section has a circle of 44 gold stars. Diameter, 8½ inches.*

67. *After-dinner cup and saucer. Cup: height, 2¼ inches; width, 2¼ inches. Saucer diameter, 4½ inches.*

66

67

saucers of the Harrison state china were ordered by the White House in 1892. Teacups and saucers with this design occasionally turn up marked like the original service. These must be considered as being reproductions of the design which were made for sale as souvenirs to the general public; none were ordered for the White House. It is also well to note that the breakfast plate and the dessert service in the original order had the double border.

Unfortunately, Mrs. Harrison did not live to see the handsome after-dinner cups and saucers as she died in the White House on October 24, 1892. She had contributed to the White House what many people think is the most handsome of all the formal dinner services designed specifically for that house. At the same time, her interest in china painting had contributed to the great popularity of that hobby which swept the country at the turn of the century. While china painting had been Mrs. Harrison's hobby, her contribution to the Harrison service was just the design. The trade publication *China, Glass and Lamps* reported on March 9, 1892:

> Vogt & Dose received by the S.S. Aurania a consignment of new samples etc. which they hope to have on exhibition by the middle of next week. Some new shapes of white ware for decoration, in which line this house does a large business, will be found among the samples. There has been quite a boom in this trade, always very lively at this season and the notoriety given to the White House china painted [designed only] by Mrs. Harrison and purchased of Vogt & Dose, may in part account for the present activity.
>
> In this connection it may be well to note that the meeting of the Ceramic Club, held at the studio of Madame Le Prince of New York City last week goes to prove that the number of persons who like china painting is increasing.

China of the same design as that of the Harrison administration was reordered during the administrations of Presidents McKinley and Theodore Roosevelt. A discussion of these later orders and their distinguishing marks are in the chapters on those administrations.

III The Contemporary Period, 1893 to the Present

Shortly before the end of the nineteenth century, the designs of the state dinner services purchased for the White House began to have a restrained elegance and sophistication. These designs were influenced by porcelain manufactured in the finest European factories for official use in European palaces. There is again the revival of the classical motif, but this time miniaturized and underplayed with elegance drawn more from the quality of the porcelain than the quality or quantity of the decoration. The state china of the twentieth century has become stereotyped, characterized by formal variations on a single theme; however, the state china selected by Mrs. Lyndon Johnson seems to indicate that this period is coming to an end and more variation will probably be seen in the future.

Grover Cleveland

William McKinley

January 12, 1897

. . . the President's [William McKinley] first reception came off successfully this week, and society hopes now to keep its gait.

During Cleveland's administration the evening receptions became just free-for-all jams. McKinley has wisely adopted a rigid censorship of the invitation list and, what is more important, a closer inspection of people who come to the door. But even with these changes you take your life in your hands to go to the White House on a cold evening. It is strange that in all these years no way has been devised to prevent a blast of north wind coming in with every guest.

As the crowd increased Tuesday night it became impossible to close the door at all, so the gale, with a spray of fine snow, was continuous. The front hall with rows of coat racks and a flock of women with bare arms and shoulders looked like a municipal bathhouse. The time spent getting wraps checked and ourselves into the double line moving almost imperceptibly to the right seemed interminable, but it was a good-tempered crowd, full of apologies for the crush which no one could have prevented except by staying at home. It began to get warmer too as we got into the family dining room. Through the long corridor there was a nice warm view of the conservatory where the red-coated Marine band sat playing the Wedding March. In the Red Parlor, enlivened by the portraits of Andrew Jackson and Mrs. Hayes, a quiet but compelling voice said, "Single file, please," and before I knew it I had shaken hands with the President, bent down a moment to hear Mrs. McKinley, who was seated and spoke very softly, the Cabinet ladies had smiled at us across their barricade of blue velvet sofas, and it was all over. In the East Room, for the first time in a trifle more than an hour, we thawed out and began to enjoy ourselves. The ceiling and the crystal chandeliers were veiled with gleaming smilax; the national shield done in flowers occurred at intervals around the room, and every mirror, mantel and window was banked with fern and poinsettias. Also, ambushed in every corner, was a detective in plain uniform. I don't see the use of them. . . ."

Excerpt from *Washington Wife: Journal of Ellen Maury Slayden from 1897–1919* by Ellen (Maury) Slayden (New York: Harper and Row, 1962), pages 23–24.

The second Cleveland administration began in 1893, four years after President Cleveland first left the office of the presidency. In the intervening years, Mrs. Benjamin Harrison had added the service she designed for the Executive Mansion, and the Hayes service was still in use on state occasions.

As state china was not a problem, Mrs. Cleveland evidently felt free to indulge her own preferences in purchasing for less formal occasions. In October 1893, at the beginning of the social season, she purchased ten dozen plates from J. W. Boteler and Son.[258] Five dozen were "Minton Decorated plates" for $150 and five dozen were "Wedgewood [sic] Decorated plates," also for $150. Just before the end of the year on December 30, she placed another order with Boteler.[259]

12	Coalport Plates	@ $7.50	$90.00
1	” ”		10.00
1	Dresden Plate	@	7.50
1	F. C. ”	@	5.25
1	Minton ”	@	6.25
3	R. W. Plates	@ $7.50	22.50
6	Minton ”	@ $8.50	51.00

In April 1894, Col. J. M. Wilson, the commissioner of public buildings and grounds, wrote to J. W. Boteler and Son and ordered an additional five dozen Wedgwood plates to be delivered to the Executive Mansion between July 1 and December 1 of that year. The letter has a note on the bottom: "Bill for 60 plates—$200.00. Paid October 10, 1894."[260] The variety of these plates, both in manufacture and pattern, is reflected in the number of miscellaneous plates in the White House today which have been tentatively identified as being from the Cleveland administration.

An inventory made in 1901 by Abby Gunn Baker and Col. Theodore Bingham, then the commissioner of public buildings and grounds, lists the following pieces for the Cleveland administration.[261]

Plates, dessert, turquoise	95
Plates, dessert, ivory and gold	18

68. Selection of Wedgwood and Minton plates
in the White House China Collection which
are identified as being from the second administration of President Cleveland. The china was
purchased from the Washington, D.C., firm of J. W.
Boteler and Son. The bills are for plates only,
presumably selected from stock available for public
sale at the store. (White House collection:
Wedgwood and Minton. At rear: Wedgwood,
Wedgwood, and Minton.)

Plates, dessert, odd	13
Plates, dessert, scalloped-edge, blue	11
Plates, dinner, blue border	84
Plates, dinner, red & gold border	84
Plates, dinner, pink and gold border	95
Plates, breakfast, green & gold	96
Platter, Ice cream, pink & gold	1
Plates, Ice cream, pink & gold	3
Dishes, bonbon, flags of nations	18
Plates, breakfast, rolled edge	396
Cups, tea	191
Saucers	190
Cups, after-dinner	190
Saucers, after-dinner	193
Plates, Haviland, odd	3
Plate, deep red, dinner	1
Plates, rolled-edge	3

In 1906, some years after the Clevelands left the Executive Mansion, Mrs. Baker visited Mrs. Cleveland personally to learn from her what tableware she had selected for the mansion.[262] Photographs were taken to her with the hope of identification. The former First Lady told Mrs. Baker that she had purchased very little china and glass, because the congressional appropriation for the furnishings of the house was quite small during her husband's second administration. She said her selections had been largely confined to plates and cups and saucers. Her own favorite among those plates, identified by Mrs. Baker in her inventory, was a piece of Minton decorated with a narrow border of dainty pink flowers, edged at each side with a narrow decorated border in gold leaf. The plates which she had selected also include Minton china with a border design in medallions and floral loops in gold. There are also two Wedgwood patterns, one with a wide red border outlined in gold and another of almost the same pattern except that the wide border is green instead of red. Out of all the pieces listed on the inventory, the above pieces are the only ones identified by Mrs. Cleveland personally as her own purchases and the purchase orders seem to verify her memory. After visiting Mrs. Cleveland, Mrs. Baker deleted from the 1907 inventory a number of pieces which had previously been credited to the Cleveland administration.[263]

During their conversation, Mrs. Cleveland told Mrs. Baker that the "flags of the nations" bonbon dishes, so often credited to her husband's administration, were not chosen by her. They were used at a diplomatic dinner during the Cleveland administration, because—though she considered them cheap and crude—they seemed appropriate for the occasion.

The pattern of buying continued to be much the same for the McKinley administration which followed—small quantities of miscellaneous china usually purchased directly from stock on hand in the better local retail stores. Additions to the Harrison china during Mrs. McKinley's years in the Executive Mansion attest to her fondness for this china.

Research on the china purchased for the White House from the year 1897 on is difficult, because the miscellaneous treasury accounts with the vouchers attached are no longer in the National Archives. Fortunately, before this set of records was deactivated, the vouchers for the state dinner services purchased after this date were removed from the records by the National Archives, but all the vouchers for miscellaneous expenditures are missing.

The commissioner of public buildings and grounds started to keep a list of expenditures in 1897. The first entry for china on the list is on May 26, 1898, when one dozen decorated plates costing $42.50 were recorded under "Miscellaneous Furnishings." For the following October 29, there is a list of purchases for the private dining room which includes "one dozen large plates (Harrison set) $31.50" and two dozen breakfast plates (Harrison set) $60.00." [264] The dinner and breakfast plates added to the Harrison china which are listed in the itemized expenditures for 1898 were furnished by the estate of M. W. Beveridge and could have been marked just like the original order received during the Harrison administration.

The inventories taken during the McKinley administration and the surviving china in the White House suggest that the breakfast plates ordered during the administration of President McKinley were 8½-inch plates made with the wide blue border. From the evidence at hand, it is conjectured that the only order for the design which was called "Sample B" was made during the administration of Benjamin Harrison.

In addition to the reorders of the Harrison china delivered on October 29, 1898, the itemized expenditures for the private dining room lists two dozen each of decorated plates of green Wedgwood, $74; pink Minton, $92; and turquoise, $44.[267]

In an illustration accompanying her early articles on the White House collection, Mrs. Baker identified some of the miscellaneous porcelain plates purchased by Mrs. McKinley. One is a Minton plate from the M. W. Beveridge firm with a narrow border of bright blue and festoons of pink roses; another is a Haviland plate with the Dulin and Martin stamp which has a border of large pink roses, a narrow dark blue and gold rim, and a gold medallion in the center of the plate. The White House also has in its collections a Minton plate with a bright yellow border and colorful bouquets of flowers which are identified on the 1901 inventory as being from the McKinley administration. The inventory also lists a Minton plate with a narrow turquoise-blue border which could possibly be the turquoise plates purchased in 1898.[268]

Again, manufacturers' marks and the variety of styles reveal what was available on the local market and what was popular during the period. The exuberance of the designs of the two floral plates suggests Mrs. McKinley's personal preference in contrast with the classic simplicity of the plates chosen by Mrs. Cleveland.

All of this miscellaneous china purchased during the Cleveland and McKinley administrations was what would now be called "open stock" patterns. It could be purchased by anyone who shopped at retail stores in large cities that carried the same stock. It is impossible to say that any china of this same pattern is White House china unless it can be documented as coming from the White House. The Minton plate with the bright blue border and festoons of pink roses hanging from the border seems to have been especially popular in 1900, and when one turns up at auctions today it is almost always identified as McKinley china. Instead, it should

be considered as china of the same design as that purchased by Mrs. McKinley. The wise collector must remember that Mrs. McKinley purchased only two dozen plates of the Minton china, and there is no record of any of them having been sold by the White House.

Perhaps the most significant part of the story of china purchased during the McKinley administration concerns the ever-increasing pressures to purchase china for the Executive Mansion which was manufactured in the United States.

The weekly trade journal, *China, Glass and Lamps,* in an 1897 article entitled "Then and Now" again pushed the idea of an American-made state service.[269]

. . . this country has relied in the past mainly on France for table services to be used in state functions, though they have usually been decorated by American artists. In the earlier days of the republic, before our ceramic industry had reached its present development, this condition of affairs was perhaps unavoidable but there is no longer any excuse for patronizing foreign establishments.

In East Liverpool, Trenton and other centers of the pottery industry wares are now being produced which are fully equal in composition and artistic treatment to anything made abroad. What the present administration will do in this respect we cannot predict, but we would respectfully suggest the propriety of giving our own pottery the opportunity of furnishing to the White House its official china for the next four years.

It is not surprising that with this type of pressure, President McKinley turned to the company of Knowles, Taylor and Knowles in his native state of Ohio. Edwin Atlee Barber in his book, *Pottery and Porcelain of the United States,* published in 1893, commented that this firm made vitreous-translucent hotel china of a superior quality in large quantities for the trade, and it was just beginning to produce a number of excellent designs in extra-thin china which was sold both plain and decorated.[270] In addition to its good reputation, the president of the company, Col. John N. Taylor, was a warm personal

These plates in the White House China Collection
are attributed to the administration of President
McKinley.

69   70

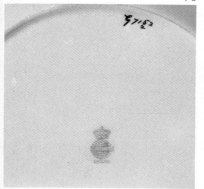

71

69. *Mark of the Washington,
D.C., firm of M. W. Beveridge,
the Minton trademark, and the
word "England." 71, reverse*

70. *Minton trademark and the
word "England." 72, reverse*

71. *English porcelain plate which
has a white ground with a narrow
scroll border in bright blue
and gold around the rim of the
plate and festoons of
pink roses and blue forget-me-
nots on the inside of the rim.
There is a bouquet of roses in
the center. Diameter, 9 inches.*

72. *English porcelain plate which
has a white ground with a wide
yellow border decorated with
gold. There are small blue and
pink floral bouquets in the
center of the plate.
Diameter, 9 inches.*

72

73. *The "Dulin & Martin" mark on this plate links it to the McKinley administration rather than that of Cleveland, because the Dulin and Martin Company succeeded the firm of M. W. Beveridge in 1899.*

74. *French porcelain plate which has a cream ground with a narrow, dark-blue and gold design around the edge. Full-blown roses encircle the inside border with one rose dropped into the center of the plate. The reverse of this plate is marked "Haviland/France" in green and "Haviland & Cº./ Limoges/ for/ Dulin & Martin Cº./ Washington, D.C." in red. Diameter, 8½ inches. (White House collection.)*

friend of William McKinley dating back to the days before he was in Congress. Knowles, Taylor and Knowles had produced a campaign plate for the 1896 election which had a blue border with a stenciled gold design and a portrait of William McKinley in the center.

In June 1899, Commissioner Bingham wrote to Colonel Taylor asking for a bill for three-dozen plates furnished by Knowles, Taylor and Knowles for the Executive Mansion in November 1898. Evidently two previous requests had been made for the bill, and it had never been submitted, for at the bottom he added in longhand, "or if there be no bill please inform me."[271] Colonel Taylor replied that "the plates were criticized so severely and seemed to give such poor satisfaction that I have felt it would be wrong to ask pay for them, presuming that others more suitable had to be purchased to replace them."

The source of the criticism has not been discovered, but a laudatory comment on the firm's work appeared in *The Crockery and Glass Journal* for December 1, 1898.

One of the most perfect pieces of pottery ever made in this section [East Liverpool, Ohio]. was shown at Knowles, Taylor & Knowles Company's office last week. It was a sample from an order they are making for the White House at Washington. The plate has a blue rim of exquisite shade, delicately illumined with sprays of gold. In the white center is the seal of the United States, very artistically executed.[272]

These plates have not survived; however, if the decoration and the ware was comparable to the campaign plate, they were not of the quality of the English and French china usually purchased for the Executive Mansion.

Under the miscellaneous expenses itemized for the year 1899 is "one tete-a-tete set (4 pieces) with coat-of-arms $54." The tête-à-tête set was a tea set for two designed as a single unit which was popular at the turn of the century. The devotion of the president to his invalid wife suggests afternoon teas together using this set.

On January 26, 1900, the "Itemized Expendi-

tures for the State Dining Room" lists two dozen each of dessert plates at $16 per dozen and oyster plates at $25 per dozen. This list also includes two dozen of the Harrison soup plates at $30.00 per dozen.[264]

The 1900 listing is supplemented by a letter in the correspondence of the Office of Public Buildings and Grounds from Dulin and Martin whose letterhead identified the firm as "Successors to M. W. Beveridge." In a letter to William Sinclair, steward of the Executive Mansion, they advised him that they could furnish "two doz. soup plates 8" full blue border Harrison 1892 at $30.00 a dozen." Commissioner Bingham replied that the proposal was acceptable and that the plates should be delivered in October 1899. This letter has a notation: "Pd bill $144 [for the Harrison china and other china] on January 26, 1900." [265]

In April 1900, Commissioner Bingham wrote to Dulin and Martin to confirm another order for a dozen Harrison dinner plates for $31.50 and a dozen Harrison breakfast plates for $30.00. At the bottom of the letter, Bingham noted in pencil that the Harrison plates could not be delivered until autumn and then later wrote: "Pd bill $187.75 [for plates plus some cut glass] November 26, 1900." [266]

Both the 1899 and 1900 orders of the Harrison china design from Dulin and Martin may have been filled from porcelain already in stock for sale to the general public and possibly bore the name and marks of their predecessor, Beveridge, which were discussed in the chapter on the Harrison china.

In 1901—despite the exchange of notes in 1899—George Cortelyou, President McKinley's secretary, approached Knowles, Taylor and Knowles again with an inquiry about making a dinner service for the Executive Mansion. Colonel Taylor replied:

. . . it would not speak well for our progress if, after all these years of his [the President's] fostering care over the Pottery Industry, we could not make a dinner service suitable for the Executive Mansion.

As this is strictly an American administration, it would seem very unAmerican, considering all the circumstances, to go abroad for such goods, provided a suitable service can be made here.

We can make the service and we believe to the full satisfaction of all interested. . . .[273]

The letter went on to inquire about such matters as the size of the service, when it would be wanted, and the designs and cautioned that as each piece would require special modeling and special decoration, it would require a longer than average amount of time to complete it.

Colonel Bingham advised Cortelyou that it should be a complete service for one hundred people, and that there should also be a breakfast service for fifty people. He requested that plain white samples and colored designs be submitted for approval, and that each article be marked "Executive Mansion" and dated. The magnitude of the ideas expressed by Colonel Bingham must have been discouraging to the potters for Colonel Taylor replied on March 29, 1901 that "I fear now that on account of labor troubles that are looming up and contemplated changes we will possibly make, that we would not be justified in taking up the making of Dinner Service for the Executive Mansion just at this time."

A glimpse of the complications facing the Executive Mansion and any china manufactory which would undertake such a commission is found in a letter addressed to the officer of public buildings and grounds in October 1899. A letter from Miss Mary Lester Nash of Chicago asked for information about the new state china that was rumored to be under consideration for the White House. She queried whether the designs submitted would be restricted to members of the National League of Mineral Painters or whether other ceramic workers might have the opportunity. She wrote that she was delighted to find such encouragement being given to those whose life work it was and asked for information for publication.[274] The reply to the letter was a curt: "No china contemplated at present."

Despite the discussions of a new state service during the McKinley administration, no service was ordered after Colonel Taylor declined. Less than six months later, President McKinley was assassinated and Theodore Roosevelt entered the White House. Nevertheless, the agitation for a state service made in the United States had begun, though it would not meet with success for another twenty years.

Theodore Roosevelt

William Howard Taft

The East Room is here seen in gala attire. There are no broad stretches of carpet, with their painful associations with dreary receptions, when an over-worked President had to receive smilingly the thousands who trooped in to shake his hand. There are no great chairs, stiffly placed as though no human being ever was to sit in them. Moreover the decorations seemed to grow more tawdry with each succeeding administration, are here relieved, or masked, by greens and flowers. And then state apartments are always seen to best advantage when the light of day has deserted them. The most beautiful ball room has a garish look in the day-time. All has now been softened by the artificial light from the great crystal chandeliers, from electric lights in the ceiling and hundreds of smaller bulbs, grouping themselves into stars, or twined among the greens that hang in long festoons overhead, or droop with the hangings, or climb the fluted shafts of columns,—not to mention the shaded candles upon the many candelabra. One may doubt whether the old East Room was ever more beauti-fully illuminated, from the time of John Adams to the present than on the evening of February 24th, 1902. *It must have seemed to the German prince very much like a dinner in a Christmas tree,—a tree, which unlike most German specimens of that variety, blossomed with the greatest profusion of rare roses and smilax. The broad expanse of linen sweeps around in a great curve to the left, with its succession of roses and candelabra and centre-pieces, its array of cut glass and silver, of decorated plates hiding themselves modestly under snowy napkins. There is every sign of a royal welcome to the gallant prince, every indication of a nationl hos-pitality warm in its greeting to royalty, without departing from the republican traditions of the past, and the old-time memories of the East Room.*

Description of the East Room of the White House decorated for the state dinner given in honor of Prince Henry of Prussia on February 24, 1902, taken from the back of stereograph number 8174 made by H. C. White Company, Bennington, Vermont, and now in the collection of the Smithsonian Institution.

When Mrs. Theodore Roosevelt commenced her duties as First Lady of the White House, she found that the china most often used for large receptions was the service that had been selected by Mrs. Hayes in 1879. For smaller dinner parties there were also the plates designed by Mrs. Benjamin Harrison, but the first social events given by the new administration proved that neither of these was adequate. A new state service for the house was clearly a necessity late in 1901, and the First Lady requested assistance from The Van Huesen Charles Company of Albany, New York, who were importers of china, glass, and house furnishings. Mrs. Roosevelt must have been a customer of this store during her husband's administration as governor of New York. Mr. Van Heusen himself came to Washington to discuss the new service. He was commissioned to submit to the White House a collection of samples from the leading factories of this country and Europe. The president had hoped that the new china might be made at a pottery in the United States, but he met with no more success than had his predecessors. Van Heusen worked on the commission for several months and assembled samples of seventy-eight designs. The President and Mrs. Roosevelt ex-amined these with great care and consulted with several of the leading artists and connoisseurs before making a selection. Mrs. Roosevelt was particularly anxious to select a design that was different and which would be in keeping with the dignity of the mansion.

The president, Mrs. Roosevelt, and Van Heusen agreed on one thing—that the design should be such that the china would be unmistakably known as "White House China." It was finally decided that the distinctive decoration of the new china should be the Great Seal of the United States.

A contemporary article speaks of the seventy-eight samples submitted by the Van Heusen firm.

They ranged in price from $18,000 to $50,000. For months the matter had been the thought of many of the noted decorators of china. It seemed as if any taste could be gratified. Deep, rich reds, beautiful blues and yellows, rose du barries and the different shades of greens to the simplest treatments that can be imagined were submitted.[275]

Mrs. Roosevelt was determined that the design

should be simple rather than ornate. Her tastes were quite simple and restrained. With the assistance of President Roosevelt, she chose for the new state china a plain pattern decorated in gold with the obverse of the Great Seal of the United States enameled in color on each piece. It was the first time the seal in color had been used for this purpose.

Another attempt seems to have been made at this time to purchase American china according to an article in *The Clay Record* of October 30, 1902, which was titled "Didn't Want Roosevelt Order."

An order from President Roosevelt for a $50,000 china set for the White House has been received by the Knowles, Taylor & Knowles Pottery Company, East Liverpool [Ohio]. After due deliberation the order was declined.

It involved special shapes, a distinct line of decorations, and was a large order, involving so much interruption of regular business, or the erection of an entirely separate small plant for its production that its acceptance here was impracticable.

The contract will probably be let to the celebrated Wedgewoods [sic] of England.

That the company turned down the offer is regarded as remarkable.[276]

The porcelain chosen was made by the Wedgwood factory in England. The ware was a translucent cream-white color decorated around the edge with a border of gold lines arranged as a colonnade in what was called by the press a "simple colonial pattern."

The Wedgwood manufactory was already making porcelain with the gold-printed lines such as the china chosen for the White House service. It was their design number x5333 which was called "Ulunda." There are two other variations of the "Ulunda" pattern on the register at Wedgwood as number x5334 with the design in dark blue and x5336 with drab bands. It seems that the "Ulunda" pattern was a current design in 1902, and it does not appear to have been specially designed for the White House service.[277] This design with the addition of the crest in color was registered as a design in the British patent office by Josiah Wedgwood and Sons, Ltd., on October 15, 1902, and given the registry number 399026.[278] It seems reasonable to assume this was done as soon as the design was chosen by Mrs. Roosevelt and The Van Heusen Charles firm had notified Wedgwood of the choice.

The crest for the White House service was entered in the crest book at the factory as number 325 and four sizes of crest are illustrated, the smallest being for the 5-inch plates; no identification given for the next size (possibly cups and saucers); the third, to be used for the 9- and 10-inch plates and the 9-inch soup plates and oyster plates; and the last one unidentified, but it is the largest so it was probably for the 16- and 18-inch platters. The crest book also provides the following information: "Van Heusen Charles Co., Albany, New York," with a date of August 30, 1902, "Patent applied for Rd. No. 399026. First dispatch Dec. 15, 1902. Completed April 8th, 1903."

The Wedgwood Museum has in its collections a small china slab with the seal used on the White House service. Written on the back is the legend "J.E. Goodwin. The first impression of the U.S.A. coat of arms." J.E. Goodwin was the art director at the Wedgwood factory at Etruria in 1902. Contemporary accounts identify Herbert Cholerton, a crest painter employed by the Wedgwood Company, as the artist who painted all the crests on the service.[279]

In October 1902, *The China, Glass and Pottery Review* announced that the new china had been selected by Mrs. Roosevelt and had been ordered from Wedgwood. The article states that there would be 1,296 pieces in the new service and described the design in detail.[280] A newspaper release said that delivery of the service was expected in January 1903.

At the president's request, Colonel Bingham wrote on December 14, 1902, to The Van Heusen Charles Company asking when the new service would be delivered. He also asked for a list of the number of plates of various kinds which constituted the service ordered. The company replied on December 8 that the manufacturers had just been heard from and that in a few days they would make a "good" [sizable] shipment of tea cups and saucers with the rest following shortly.[281] The notation in the crest book at Wedgwood "First despatch December 15, 1902," probably refers to these cups and saucers.

On February 18, Colonel Bingham asked The Van Heusen Charles Company for an itemized bill for the china recently furnished the Executive Mansion. The bill, dated February 20, 1903, was submitted and listed the following, for which receipt was acknowledged by Henry Pinckney, steward of the mansion.[282]

3 doz. dinner plates		78.00	234.00
1 doz. breakfast plates			78.00
1 doz. fish plates			75.00
1 doz. tea plates			69.75
2 doz. B & B plates		61.50	123.00
4 doz. soup plates		78.00	312.00
1 doz. A. D. coffee cups & s.			117.00
3 doz. tea cups and saucers		119.25	357.75
1 doz. oyster plates			99.75
			1,466.25

Receipt of the first shipment of the china was followed by an application to the United States Patent Office for a copyright on the design filed on April 13 by Armand Leger of Fenton, England, and granted to him the following June 16 as patent design 36363. In the application, Leger identifies himself as having invented a new, original, and ornamental "Design for Decoration" for a plate or similar object.[283] He was probably the designer at Wedgwood who had originally created the design called "Ulunda."

The remainder of the order was received on May 4, 1903.[284]

12 doz. dinner	plates @	78.00	936.00
9 " breakfast	plates @	78.00	702.00
9 doz. fish	plates @	75.00	675.00
6 doz. tea	plates @	69.75	627.75
6 doz. soup	plates @	78.00	468.00
3 doz. bread & butter	plates @	61.50	184.50
7 doz. AD cups & saucers	@	117.00	819.00
7 doz. tea cups & saucers	@	119.25	834.75
9 doz. oyster	plates @	99.75	897.75
12 - 16"	plates @	17.00	204.00
12 - 18"	plates @	23.25	279.00
			6,627.75

These two deliveries indicate that the full service was basically for 120 people with extra dinner plates included, and that there were somewhat less than 120 of the bread and butter plates and after-dinner coffee cups and saucers.

As was frequently the case, payment to The Van Heusen Charles Company was slow. After several letters from the firm, Col. Thomas W. Symons, who, by this time, had replaced Colonel Bingham as commissioner of public buildings and grounds, confessed that funds for payment of the china could not be made available until after July 1, the beginning of the new fiscal year.[285] This payment—in four checks—was finally made for the two shipments on July 30, 1903, and totaled $8,094.[286]

The sample plates of the seventy-eight designs originally submitted occasionally turn up in private hands today, so it can be assumed that the rejected patterns were sold by The Van Heusen Charles Company. These are usually identified by the Great Seal of the United States, which was the single motif common to each of the sample plates; by the mark on the back of the plate of a china manufactory in business in 1901; and by the fact that only one piece can be found of each specific design.

The state china of the administration of Theodore Roosevelt is in the collections of the Smithsonian Institution and of the White House. This porcelain is marked with the Wedgwood vase and the words "Wedgwood/England/From/ The Van Heusen Charles Co./Albany, N.Y./Rd No 399026/Patent Applied for."

Some sample pieces of the china have been made by Wedgwood for public relations use by that firm. These are marked with the vase and the words "Wedgwood/made for/England."

Even the new china was subject to the vicissitudes of use. Correspondence in the letter book of the commissioner of public buildings and grounds concerns the breaking of one of the dinner plates of the Roosevelt set on January 19, 1905, by a dishwasher employed by Charles Rauscher, the caterer at a diplomatic dinner. A new plate was ordered at the price of $78 a dozen from The Van Heusen Charles Company and paid for by Charles Rauscher. The final payment was for $7.10—$6.50 for the cost of the plate and the remainder for the express charge.[287]

Mrs. Roosevelt apparently admired the china designed and ordered by Mrs. Harrison, for two dozen Harrison plates were reordered on March 25, 1908, for $80.[288] M. W. Beveridge, the firm from whom the china originally had been ordered in 1892 had been succeeded by a firm named Dulin, Martin Company. There are at present in the White House plates of the design of the Harrison service with both the marks of M. W. Beveridge (who supplied the original order) and of his successors, Dulin and Martin, for the re-order by the Theodore Roosevelt and, possibly, the McKinley administrations.

"The Inventory of public property, Executive Mansion, June 30, 1908," lists in addition to the two dozen plates ordered in March, another 36 which are specified as breakfast plates which were received on January 6, 1908, from Dulin and Martin at a cost of $120.[289] The two dozen plates had the wide, dark-blue border with the design of goldenrod and corn and have 8-inch diameters as compared with the earlier 9-inch dinner plates. The mark on the back is "Décoré/par/Limoges/T.V. [in a bell]/pour/Dulin, Martin Co/Washington/Limoges/France/Harrison 1892."

The interest in the collection of White House china which began at the White House during Mrs. Roosevelt's administration prompted the making of a number of good reproductions of the earlier services for sale to the public. The firm of Dulin and Martin had copies of the Lincoln, Grant, and Harrison china on sale as well as the copies of the Hayes service.

When Mrs. William Howard Taft became First Lady on March 4, 1909, most of the Wedgwood china was still intact. She had been advised however that, if she wished, she could purchase her own set of china from the governmental appropriation. Thanks to Archie Butt, military aide to both Presidents Roosevelt and Taft, Mrs. Taft's choice is known. In a letter dated March 11, 1909, he wrote:

I suggested to her, as she was going to New York next week, that she might look into the question of china for the White House. She [Mrs. Taft] said very directly:

'I have given that question a good deal of thought, and I have made up my mind to continue with the Roosevelt china, as it is called. I shall try to make it the White House China. It is perfectly absurd to change the china with each new administration. The consequence of this custom is that the closets are loaded up with a mass of china most of which is hideous and ordinary and which I would not use on my private table. Mrs. Roosevelt, evidently, gave this question of china a great deal of consideration and her choice in design and quality is in excellent taste and the best I have seen here. She told me once that it was Minton, but it is not. It is Wedgwood and moreover her contract with the manufactory makes it impossible for them to put it on the market, and none can be used anywhere else. I shall do all in my power to make it the china of the White House. The Hayes and the McKinley China is too awful for words.' [290]

True to her words, Mrs. Taft reordered the Wedgwood china through The Van Heusen Charles Company, and on September 23, 1910, the White House received her order which had the same mark as the pieces received during the Roosevelt administration.[291]

5 doz. Bread & Butter	plates @	61.50	307.50
10 doz. 7 inch	plates @	69.75	697.50
10 doz. 8 inch	plates @	75.00	750.00
5 doz. After dinner cup & saucers	@	117.00	585.00
5 doz. Breakfast coffee cups & saucers	@	180.00	900.00
			3,240.00

The state china purchased by President Roosevelt in 1903 was made by Wedgwood in England and purchased from The Van Huesen Charles Company of Albany, New York. This design was reordered by President Taft in 1910.

75. English porcelain dinner plate is white with a gold border. The Great Seal of the United States in color in cavetto is on the rim of the plate. Diameter, 10⅜ inches.

76. Mark on the reverse of the service. Below the Wedgwood trademark are the words "Wedgwood/England/from/ The Van Huesen Charles Cº./ Albany, N.Y./Rᵈ Nº 399026/ Patent Applied for."

75

76

77. *A group of state china from the administration of Theodore Roosevelt. Bouillon cup: height, 2 inches; diameter (without handles), 3½ inches; the saucer diameter, 5½ inches. Bowl diameter, 9 inches. At rear, plate diameter, 10⅜ inches; salad plate diameter, 7⅞ inches.*

Woodrow Wilson

Warren G. Harding

Calvin Coolidge

Herbert Hoover

. . . Almost every afternoon I [Mrs. Wilson] would receive different Ambassadors and Ministers with their wives who had written for appointments to call. It seemed a little more of a courtesy to them and the countries they represented to receive them severally rather than in groups; so my secretary and I worked out a plan to ask them thirty minutes apart, for a perfectly informal cup of tea before an open fire in the Red Room. We would begin at four for the first; four-thirty for the second, and so on at half-hour intervals until six, leaving time between to have the tea table rearranged. Often the butler would be waiting with fresh cups and plates to rush right in if we overlapped our time. We always tried to find out beforehand a little of the background of the guests. When they were recently arrived and did not speak English with ease, I would try to make the interview as brief as seemed courteous to relieve them of any embarrassment. By these little informal tea parties a bond was established which became personal, as well as official, and instead of their being only a matter of routine we really enjoyed these varying and interesting contacts.

Excerpt from *My Memoir* by Edith Bolling Wilson (New York: Bobbs-Merrill Company, Inc., 1938), pages 92–93.

Fifteen years had gone by since the order was placed for the state service purchased by President Theodore Roosevelt, and the White House was again in need of a complete dinner service. By this time, the commissioner of public buildings and grounds was Col. William Harts, and he was the first to have official professional advice in selecting appropriate china for the White House. The Commission of Fine Arts had been established in 1910, and Colonel Harts, by virtue of his position, was automatically secretary to the commission. He enlisted the help of William Mitchell Kendall of New York City who was also a member of the commission. On June 5, 1917, Kendall wrote to Colonel Harts in Washington informing him that he had carefully looked over all the china in Tiffany's and had seen nothing that seemed to meet the ideas expressed by the First Lady, Mrs. Edith Bolling Wilson, and the commission. He had, however, picked out a plate

that might serve as a basis for a design, and he hoped the commission could meet in New York City to discuss its possibilities. Instead, the plate was sent to Washington, and the inference in the correspondence is that Tiffany was encouraged to proceed with a design.

Later in June, Kendall told Colonel Harts that Dr. George F. Kunz, of the firm of Tiffany, was of the opinion that there was a special coat of arms for the president of the United States and requested an impression so that it could be put on the sample plate.

Colonel Harts secured a colored engraving of the seal and forwarded it to Dr. Kunz at Tiffany's. The receipt of the engraving was acknowledged, and it was hoped that samples could be submitted within the week. It was an optimistic prediction, for in August Kendall wrote to Colonel Harts that Dr. Kunz's sample plates were "far from being satisfactory," although the general idea was good. Kendall discussed the changes proposed in more detail in a letter dated August 20, 1919. He stated that the wreath was satisfactory; however, the eagle was not quite right, but was improving. Kendall wrote that he would like to have as much care expended on the eagle as was taken with the recently designed gold coin. He felt that with the help of the coins for matching the details of such parts as the wings, that the Tiffany modelers should be able to obtain good results.

Harts wrote a letter to Kendall on September 20, 1917, which must have been prompted by the submission of the sample plate.

I had the opportunity today of discussing with both the President and Mrs. Wilson the selection of the glass ware and china for the White House. The discussion was very frank and the expression of preferences clear enough to establish a basis on which some new designs should be submitted.

With regard to the plates,—it was preferred that the china with a white base and slightly creamy color on the border would be preferred, and with a gilt border around the outside edge containing perhaps small stars or similar figures; then, with a border on the shoulder of the plate gilt, but broader than the plate recently submitted, with the President's seal in rather heavy gilt placed upon the border of the plate instead of in the center. Both the President and Mrs. Wilson didn't like the central ornamentation. Could not a plate of pure white china, with two gilt bands as above mentioned and another plate slightly cream in color with somewhat deeper colored band around the border be sent in, with the coat of arms, conventional but with the President's seal?

On the back of the plates and on each article of china should be the device U.S. in one line, *White House* below it, and the date below that, in small compass.

Can you take this up anew with Dr. Kunz and see whether it would be agreeable for Tiffany and Company to prepare these samples? Personally I would much prefer to have Tiffany . . . than to try anywhere else.
. . . He [Dr. Kunz] should not overlook the distinction of having the Tiffany mark on the back of the White House china if the order is given him.

Colonel Harts attached an impress of the president's seal to the letter to indicate that he was speaking for the president.

In the following month, October, Col. C. S. Ridley succeeded Colonel Harts as the commissioner of public buildings and grounds, and he inherited Harts's correspondence with Kendall of the Commission of Fine Arts and with Dr. Kunz of Tiffany's concerning the White House china. In November, Kendall wrote to Ridley stating that he thought that Tiffany's was now on the way toward something worthwhile which would prove satisfactory to the President and Mrs. Wilson. Adolph Weinman, the well-known sculptor who designed the new gold coins, would draw the eagle so that it would be satisfactory. The new sample plate was submitted to the White House through Colonel Ridley on December 8, 1917. In reply, Colonel Ridley wrote to Tiffany and Company on January 8, 1918.

The plate . . . was duly received and submitted to President and Mrs. Wilson. I regret to advise, however, that they do not find it satisfactory and I shall therefore be unable to place an order with you as had been hoped. Moreover a design submitted directly to the President by another firm has received his approval and in view of the long delay

up to this time, I see no other course than to order the china from that firm.

Ridley went on to say that the plates were being returned and that if Tiffany felt they should be reimbursed for their expense in making the sample, they should send a bill. This short letter seems to be an abrupt ending for a negotiation which had been going on for over six months, but the colonel went into more detail in a personal letter to Kendall who had written on behalf of Tiffany and Company to protest the decision. On January 14, he wrote Kendall:

I have your letter . . . in regard to the China for the White House.

In order that my position in this matter may be perfectly clear, I would like to put it before you.

The appropriation for the China was made last June, about six months ago. As I understand it, Colonel Harts at that time, took the matter up with you with a view to having Tiffany submit a design. The design was submitted about September 1st, was disapproved by the President as explained in Colonel Harts letter to you on September 20th. In that letter Colonel Harts stated that the President preferred a plate with a slightly creamy colored border and with the President's seal in heavy gilt on the border instead of in the center.

When I took charge of this office in September, it was my understanding that Tiffany was preparing a sample in accordance with Colonel Harts letter as to the President's wishes. Once or twice, Mrs. Wilson and the President spoke to me about the long delay in securing the China, but I thought Tiffany would soon produce what was wanted, so I did nothing further than write to you about it.

When the second plate came, about December 10th, it did not meet the approval of either the President or Mrs. Wilson, and it did not comply with their desires as stated to Colonel Harts when the first plate was presented. They thought it a very beautiful plate but they wanted the seal and the creamy tone on the border.

Now, to go back, it seems that another firm in this City had, last summer, without request from this office, submitted directly to the White House a design with a cream colored border and the President's seal on the border. At the time I submitted the

The first porcelain state service made in the United States was purchased by President Wilson in 1918. It was made by Lenox, Inc., and purchased through the firm of Dulin and Martin in Washington, D.C. This china design was reordered during the administration of Presidents Harding, Coolidge, and Hoover.

78. *The ivory porcelain service plate has a deep blue and gold border with a large presidential seal in raised gold in the center of the plate. Diameter, 10½ inches.*

79. *The ivory porcelain dinner plate has a deep ivory border edged with gold. There is a small presidential seal in raised gold on the border of the plate. Diameter, 10½ inches.*

78

79

Tiffany plate to Mrs. Wilson, she showed me this sample and said that the President liked it very much.

The conditions, therefore, at that date about December 15th were as follows: Tiffany had failed to produce anything that was satisfactory; another firm had, without the knowledge of this office, submitted a design which was very satisfactory; the matter had been delayed at least six (6) months; certain portions of the china were urgently needed; there was no assurance that Tiffany would produce anything better than the other firm had done; I could not, under the circumstances describe the design of the other firm and ask Tiffany to submit it.

In view of all this, I submitted the matter to you at your last visit here and accepted your advice to write Tiffany and ask them to submit a bill for their services to date, and then take up the matter of purchase with the other firm.

I am extremely sorry that it has all turned out this way, but I hope I have made my position clear in this matter, and I don't see that anything else can be done now. It seems to me that the design as submitted by the other firm, while quite conventional, is at the same time very good and dignified. Moreover, it pleases the President and Mrs. Wilson, and this of course is of prime importance.

Kendall replied to this somewhat curtly stating that it seemed Colonel Ridley had done all he could in a difficult situation.[292] The explanation to Kendall, however, does not reveal completely the circumstances under which the new china was selected. Fortunately, Abby Gunn Baker was still interested in White House china. She requested and received permission to write about the newly chosen design for the state service, and it is in her articles that the story of the china actually accepted by President and Mrs. Wilson is told.

Mrs. Baker's publicity for the new china stressed the strong satisfaction felt by the President and Mrs. Wilson that, at last, the White House could have a state dining service made in the United States—the first to have ever been used there. She thought it also should be a source of pride to every patriotic citizen that the porcelain made at the Lenox pottery in Trenton, New

Jersey, was now equal in body and utilitarian features to the best products of European manufacture and that, in its decorative capabilities, it was even superior to that made in the Old World.

Walter Scott Lenox had been striving to meet this challenge since the turn of the century. When he realized he had achieved his goal, he began to send displays of Lenox china to the leading ceramic stores in the country. One of the firms selected for the display was the Dulin, Martin Company—among the best and oldest of such establishments in the City of Washington. It is certain that Mrs. Wilson knew both Mr. Dulin and Mr. Martin personally, for not too many years before, as Edith Bolling Galt—wife of Norman Galt, who owned one of the best known silver stores in the city—Mrs. Wilson herself had been part of the Washington business community. The store sent a polite invitation to the First Lady to come to see the American-made porcelain display. Mrs. Wilson came to the store unannounced and a Mr. Service from the Lenox headquarters in New Jersey showed her the china and told her of the efforts of the company to produce a porcelain which could compete with the European ware. Mrs. Wilson was very much interested in the story and was delighted with the china she was shown. It was only a few weeks later that Colonel Harts invited the Dulin, Martin Company to submit plans for a state dining service to be made at the Lenox potteries in Trenton, New Jersey.

The problem of design was turned over to Frank G. Holmes, chief artist for the factory at Trenton since 1905. Pattern after pattern was made and discarded. According to Mrs. Baker, President and Mrs. Wilson were following these developments of the design with great interest. Finally, Holmes produced a design that he described as "so simple and so unostentatious that it cannot but suit the most aesthetic taste and yet so rich in tone it commensurates with the dignity of the home of our Chief Executive. The motif is supremely patriotic—the stars and stripes and the Seal of the United States." [293] The design was approved by everyone—the Commission of Fine Arts as well as President and Mrs. Wilson. There was one change made; the president's seal was substituted for the coat of arms of the United States, and both Mrs. Baker and Mrs. Wilson herself attributed this change to a suggestion made by President Wilson personally.[294] The president may have made the suggestion to the Lenox firm, but the idea of using the president's seal must be credited to Dr. Kunz of Tiffany and Company who first asked about using it in his letter of the previous summer.

With the permission of Colonel Ridley, Mrs. Baker visited the Lenox pottery in August 1918 to get information about the new china. It was she who brought up the question of patent rights, and on September 19, 1918, Lenox made application through Mrs. Baker to the Library of Congress for a copyright for "The President Wilson Design." The application states that the design was made by Frank Graham Holmes for Lenox, and that Lenox would reassign the rights to Colonel Ridley as commissioner. The copyright patent covered the entire design of the service plate and the etched stars and stripes border on all of the other dishes.

The order for the state service was placed on March 30, 1918, and the pieces listed on the order were:[295]

10 doz.	Dinner Plates		10½″
10	"	Soup "	8″
10	"	Fish "	8″
10	"	Entree "	8″
10	"	Dessert "	6″
10	"	Salad "	7″
7	"	Bread & Butter Plates	5″
8	"	Oyster Plates (Soup)	9½″
8	"	Tea Cups & Saucers	
3	"	Bouillon Cups and Saucers	
10	"	After Dinner " " "	
2	"	Cream Soups & Saucers	
8	"	Cocktail Cups	
2	"	Ramekins & Plates	
2	"	Oatmeal	
6 only		Chop Dishes	14″
135½ dz.		Extra Raised Gold Crests	

This quantity of crests allows for a crest on every item

8 doz. Service Plates with Raised Gold Crests in center   11″

The order gives the total estimate for the service

as $11,251.60 and states that a sample of each piece would be submitted to the White House for approval before the remainder of the quantity was produced. The set was delivered piecemeal—some portions arriving in August, more in September and October, with the last in November. The bills were paid in several accounts, as the order stipulated that "it is understood that the time of delivery will probably extend over a period of several months, arrangements will be made to make you a payment each month for the quantities delivered and accepted during the preceeding month."[296]

The porcelain chosen was similar to the Irish Belleek with a rich but delicate, lustrous ivory tone. The decoration consisted of an outer and inner border of encrusted gold in a dull finish separated by a border of ivory slightly deeper than the body of the china. The outer border contains a conventional and unobtrusive motif of stars and stripes in gold, while the tinted band contains the seal of the president of the United States in raised gold. The only items which varied materially in decoration in the service of 1,700 pieces were the eight-dozen service plates. These were unusually large for the service plate of the period—eleven inches in diameter. They have a border of gold etched in a delicate Adams design, a still broader border of a deep rich lustrous blue, and the narrow inner border with the same motif of stars and stripes found on the rest of the service. The presidential seal on the service plate appears in raised gold in the center of the plate.

The teacups and dainty after-dinner coffee cups have golden handles, and all the serving pieces such as the flaring ramekins, the cereal bowls, the double-handled bouillon cups, and the sauce dishes are decorated with the same design as the plates. Though the china is so thin that it is transparent, yet Lenox had produced one of the strongest and most durable vitrified porcelains known in the ceramics industry.[297] The new china was hailed with delight in the press, both because of its beauty and because of the advance it heralded for the American ceramics industry.

The Wilson china is in the collections of the Smithsonian Institution and the White House.

80. *Group of china showing the shapes of various pieces in the Wilson service. The diameters of the pieces are: bouillon cup, 3½ inches, and saucer, 5½ inches; oatmeal bowl, 6½ inches. In rear, service plate and entrée plate, diameter of latter, 8 inches.*

81. *Mark in gold on the Wilson service: "The White House/ 1918 [Lenox trademark] Lenox/ Dulin & Martin Co./ Washington, D.C."*

80

81

There were also some additional pieces made for special exhibitions and for public relations activities of the Lenox firm.

Perhaps the most significant proof of the suitability of the design of the Wilson china is the fact that it remained in use as the state dinner service through the administrations of Presidents Harding, Coolidge, and Hoover, with additional pieces added as they were needed. It is still used occasionally for small luncheons and dinners at the White House.

The yearly inventory books which were kept by the National Capital Parks from 1925 on indicate that by the administration of President Herbert Hoover substantial replacements were made to the service. On December 9, 1929, probably in preparation for the Christmas entertaining, the following pieces of the Wilson design of china were purchased.

After dinner coffee cups	18
Cocktail Cups	18
Plates—5″	44
Chop plates	4
Salad plates	12
After dinner coffee saucers	18

The Hoover purchases of teacups and saucers in considerable quantity for the following three years indicates that the original Wilson state service had been depleted since its purchase in 1918.

Franklin D. Roosevelt

Harry S. Truman

Dwight D. Eisenhower

John F. Kennedy

Finally the table was set for formal, with service plates, napkins, and wineglasses, and all the silver, save for dessert, water glasses, the little colonial salt cellars of cut glass in the diamond design—and never any pepper shakers. For official affairs the nut dishes were decorative gold china; there were little silver ones for the family meals. The centerpiece for the family was always a bowl of flowers. A big silver ship in full sail was for teas. But for the formal affairs we [the Roosevelts] used the Monroe gold service. There was always a lot of to-do about this service, which was purchased by President Monroe in France, but to tell the truth it was brass, and plated, with the gold worn off. There was a big centerpiece and candelabra and I had them redipped, and they looked beautiful. . . .

Excerpt from *White House Diary* by Henrietta Nesbitt, pages 114-115. (Copyright 1948 by Henrietta Nesbitt. Used by permission of Doubleday & Company, Inc.)

By 1933 when President Franklin D. Roosevelt came to the White House, the Lenox china originally ordered during the Wilson administration was insufficient for formal entertaining. Before the inauguration on March 4, 1933, Mrs. Roosevelt had paid the usual visit to the White House to look at the house and the facilities which would be available to the incoming president. It was possibly at this time that the chief usher, Ike Hoover, told her that there was not enough state china on hand to set a formal dinner. The Lenox china originally ordered during the Wilson administration, was reordered by Mrs. Harding, Mrs. Coolidge, and Mrs. Hoover; but breakage had continued, and it was again time to order new china.

The announcement that the White House was to get a new state service was made on November 20, 1934. Two Washington newspapers carried articles about the set of 1,000 pieces which had been ordered by Mrs. Roosevelt. *The* (Washington) *Evening Star* stated that Mrs. Roosevelt had made the selection from various samples submitted to her by manufacturers of domestic china.[298]

Criticism of the extravagance of ordering a new service for $9,000 while the country was in the midst of a depression obviously prompted Mrs. Roosevelt to quickly justify the order for new china at her press conference on December 4.[299] She said that the high price of continuing to replace broken cups, saucers, and dish covers was the reason for ordering a new service, adding that it would have cost $15 for each piece needed as a replacement. The First Lady explained that she was making this statement because there had been no replacements of china since the family came to the White House in March 1933, and the supply was running so low that inexpensive cups, saucers, and other pieces had been bought to cope with official entertaining. As long as more china was necessary and the money had to be spent, she said that she felt that the order would give work to an American firm and that it would, on the whole, be more economical to order a full set.

The new porcelain was ordered from the New York firm of William H. Plummer, and the purchase order bears the date of October 13, 1934. In all, 1,722 pieces were ordered at a total cost of $9,301.20.[300] Plummer had the china made by the Lenox factory, and the media reported that the factory was working overtime to complete the set for use during the midwinter social season in Washington. The service consisted of the following pieces.

	Each	Dozen
Bowl, oatmeal	5.10	2
Cups, bouillon	4.90	3
Cups, coffee after dinner	4.50	10
Cups, cocktail	3.90	8
Cups, cream soup	5.80	2
Cups, ramekin	4.30	2
Cups, tea	4.60	8
Saucers, cream soup	4.90	2
Saucers, bouillon	4.30	3
Saucers, tea	4.30	8
Saucers, ramekin	4.30	2
Saucers, coffee after dinner	4.20	10
Plates, bread & butter 5"	4.70	7
Plates, chop	15.60	½
Plates, dessert, 6"	5.10	10
Plates, dinner, 10½"	6.50	10
Plates, entree, 8"	6.00	10
Plates, fish, 8"	6.00	10
Plates, oyster, 9½"	6.50	8
Plates, salad, 7"	5.50	10

| Plates, service | 8.20 | 8 |
| Plates, soup 8″ | 6.00 | 10 |

The set arrived at the White House in January 1935 and was first used at the annual state dinner given for the heads of foreign missions on January 24, the largest affair of its kind in the history of the White House. Ninety-nine men and women sat down to dine at the huge horseshoe table in the state dining room, and for the first time everyone dined off the same kind of china—from oysters on the half shell to the after-dinner coffee.

The press was very complimentary about the new service which was similar in style to the Wilson china. Made of the same Belleek-type porcelain, the basic ware was a pale cream color. It had a narrow, navy blue border around the edge which contained small gold stars. Inside the blue border was a narrow gold scroll made with the roses and three feathers taken from the Roosevelt family coat of arms. The presidential seal in color appeared on each piece.

The new china was marked on the back: "The White House/1934" with the script "L" for Lenox enclosed in a laurel wreath. Under the "L," the word "Lenox" is printed and "Made in U.S.A./Wm. H. Plummer & Co., Ltd./New York City." The entire inscription is in gold.

The public had been critical of the inclusion of a portion of the Roosevelt family crest, as well as its cost, when the announcement was made in October of the order for new china, so Mrs. Roosevelt also explained this at the December 4 press conference. The Dutch name "rose-veldt" or "field of roses" was taken from the name of the Dutch town from which the president's forebears had migrated to America, and the rose was included in the Roosevelt's coat of arms. The rose border had been used to distinguish the new china as belonging to the New Deal administration. Mrs. Roosevelt said that the president had chosen the design of the new china, but that she was personally responsible for the scroll of roses and feathers,[301] and she had done so to make the china more interesting historically.

With complete disregard for historical accuracy, *The Evening Star* excused the personal touch on the official china by saying that some of the Lincoln china had an ornate "L" and that the Harrison china bore the signature of the First Lady of that day, Caroline Scott Harrison—neither of which is true.[302]

The only other major change in design from that of the Wilson china was that the navy blue border of the service plate was three-eighths inches wide on the Roosevelt china in contrast to the wide cobalt-blue border of the Wilson service.

The china selected by President and Mrs. Roosevelt has a nautical feeling which is no doubt the result of the president's great affection for the navy fostered by his service as assistant secretary of the navy during the administration of President Wilson.

Examples of the Roosevelt china are in the collections of the White House and the Smithsonian Institution. There are also pieces in the history museum at the Franklin D. Roosevelt Library in Hyde Park, New York, and in the museum at the Lenox headquarters in Trenton, New Jersey.

In October 1940, at the end of the New York World's Fair, the White House was offered the tableware which had been purchased with public funds for use in the official dining room in the Federal Building on the fair grounds. This porcelain was delivered to the White House on November 1, 1940, with "Property Transfer Schedule 1026" and a letter which stated that it was being transferred on a loan basis as surplus property for official use without any exchange of funds. Mrs. Henrietta Nesbitt, the housekeeper of the Executive Mansion, signed the receipt for the china. It is listed on the transfer schedule as "Chinaware—Theodore Haviland & Co. Monogrammed/with the seal of the United States Government in gold." The list reads:

240	Dinner Plates—Size 10⅛″ actual size. Winchester (with seal)	$321.00
240	Salad & Dessert Plates 7″ actual size (with seal)	270.00
120	Bread & Butter Plates 6½″ actual size (with seal)	122.50
120	Soup Plates with rim 7¾″ actual size (with seal)	135.00
120	Tea Cups—footed (with seal)	145.00

In 1934, President Franklin D. Roosevelt purchased a porcelain state service which was made in the United States by Lenox, Inc., of Albany, New York. The service was ordered through W. H. Plummer and Company in New York City.

82. Dinner plate of cream-colored porcelain which has a narrow blue border encircled with 48 gold stars, gilt edge, and an inside border of roses and feathers in gold. The presidential seal in color is on the rim of the plate. Diameter, 10½ inches. The service plate is identical to the dinner plate, but is 11¼ inches in diameter.

83. *A group of china from the Franklin D. Roosevelt state service. Bouillon cup: height, 2¼ inches; diameter, 3½ inches; and the saucer diameter, 5½ inches. At rear, dinner plate as shown in figure 82 and dessert plate, diameter, 6¼ inches.*

84. *Mark in gold on the reverse of the Franklin D. Roosevelt service: "The White House/1934 [Lenox trademark] Lenox/Made in U.S.A./Wm. H. Plummer & Co., Ltd.,/New York City."*

83

84

120	Saucers for same (with seal)		61.50
120	Cream Soup Cups (no seal monogram)		140.00
120	Saucers for above item (no seal monogram)		74.50
240	Fruit Dishes 5" (with seal)		214.00
24	Caviars 12½" long (with seal)		85.00
24	Olive Dishes 9¾" long (with seal)		85.00

The Haviland china listing is followed by a list of "Chinaware—Lenox Monogrammed with the/ Seal of the United States Government (in Gold)."

84	Dinner Plates 11⅜" (with seal)		$513.00
120	After Dinner Coffee cup-footed (with seal)		218.00
120	After Dinner Coffee cup-Saucers (with seal)		161.00

The new china acquired at no cost to the White House was used during the remainder of the Roosevelt administration and that of President Harry S. Truman despite the fact that it seems more suited to a business establishment than to a private home.

In recent years, this World's Fair china has been called "Lenox" by the White House though Lenox made only the dinner plates and the after-dinner cups and saucers; the rest of the set is domestic Haviland porcelain.

The Lenox china with the Roosevelt crest was considered the state china from 1935 until 1951 when another large state service was purchased by President and Mrs. Truman. The Trumans selected china which would be appropriate in the newly redecorated state dining room of the White House after the major renovation of the house during the period 1948–1952. At that time, the carved natural oak paneling put in the dining room during the Theodore Roosevelt administration was painted a soft celadon green popularly called "Williamsburg green." The new china was banded with the same shade of green. Again, Lenox porcelain of the quality of the Wilson and Roosevelt china was chosen, but this time it was ordered through the decorating shop

of B. Altman and Company, the New York department store that had been awarded the contract for redecorating the White House after the renovation.

No doubt disturbed by the inconsistencies in the use of the president's seal over the years, President Truman by Executive Order of October 25, 1945, standardized its design. The eagle, which on the Woodrow Wilson and Franklin D. Roosevelt china faces the arrows, was reversed so that his head was toward the olive branch, and the banner with the motto "E Pluribus Unum" was grasped in his beak. The new seal, etched in gold, adorned each piece of the service. Each piece has a narrow band of green and etched gold with a 24-carat gold rim; the inner border is cream color. The service plates have a wide border of green with the president's seal embossed in gold in the center of the plate.[303]

The price of this new service reflected the inflated prices of the period after World War II, as the cost for almost the same number of pieces was three times that of the Franklin Roosevelt china. The following pieces were in the new service.[304]

Quantity	Item	Shape No.	Price per Doz.	Total Price
120	Service Plates	1326	$270.11	$2701.10
120	Dinner Plates	1830	202.86	2028.60
240	Entree Plates	2020	192.94	3858.80
120	Salad Plates	2021	177.50	1775.00
120	Tea Plates	2022	169.79	1697.90
120	Butter Plates	2023	162.07	1620.70
120	Teacups & Saucers	2904	222.26	2222.60
120	A.D. Cups & Saucers	3432	213.78	2137.80
120	Bouillon Cups & Stands	1305	266.57	2665.70
120	Cream Soups & Stands	1934	324.14	3241.40
120	Soup Plates	2024	177.50	1775.00
120	Oyster Plates	8"	192.94	1929.40
12	Chop Plates	14"	51.45 ea.	617.40
				$28,271.40

These prices include packing and transportation charges to Washington. The set was delivered to the White House on October 30, 1951, and was

China from a service sent to the White House
from the Federal Building at the New York
World's Fair, 1939.

85

86

85. *On the reverse of the dinner plate is the mark
"Theodore Haviland/New York/Made in America."
(Courtesy, Office of the Curator of the White House.)*

86. *The service plate with stars and the
after-dinner cup and saucer of the formal service
were made by Lenox. The serving dishes from the rest
of the service were made in the United States by
Haviland. (Courtesy, Office of the Curator of the
White House.)*

The porcelain state dinner service which was made in the
United States by Lenox, Inc., was purchased in 1951 by President
Truman from B. Altman and Company in New York City.

WHITE HOUSE SERVICE
BY LENOX
X-308
MADE IN U.S.A.
B. ALTMAN & CO.

*87. Mark in gold on the Truman
service which appears beneath the
Lenox trademark: "White House
Service/by Lenox/X308/Made
in U.S.A./B. Altman & Co."
The number on each piece is the
Lenox factory number assigned to
the various pieces of the service
for internal purposes, i.e., the
service plate is X307; dinner,
entrée, chop, salad, tea, and butter
plates, as well as teacups and
saucers, after-dinner coffee cups
and saucers, and bouillon cups and
saucers, are X308; oyster plates
are X300; cream soups and stands
are 1307; and the soup plates
are 2027.*

*88. Service plate of cream-colored porcelain which has a wide
celadon-green border edged with gold and the presidential
seal in raised gold in the center of the plate. Note that
the head of the eagle is turned toward the olive branch.*

89. *The cream-colored porcelain dinner plate has a narrow green border with a gold edge. The presidential seal on the rim of the plate is in raised gold. Diameter, 10½ inches.*

90. *A group of china from the Truman state service. Soup bowl: height, 3 inches; diameter, 5 inches; and the stand diameter, 7 inches. Teacup: height, 2 inches; diameter, 4 inches; and the saucer diameter, 6 inches. At rear, both service plate and dinner plate have diameters of 10½ inches.*

89

90

The porcelain service plates purchased by President
Eisenhower in 1955 were both ordered from and
made by Castleton China, Inc., of New Castle,
Pennsylvania.

91. *Mark in gold on the reverse
of the Eisenhower service plates.
The Castleton trademark is surrounded by the words: "Castleton/
Studios." Beneath is printed:
"The White House/November
1955."*

92. *Service plate of white porcelain with the
entire rim covered with pure coin gold in a raised-
gold medallion pattern. The presidential seal in
gold decorates the center of the plate.*

certified for payment by Howell G. Crim, the chief usher, on the following December 12.

The new china was first used on April 3, 1952, when President and Mrs. Truman entertained Queen Juliana and Prince Bernhard of The Netherlands at a small luncheon at the White House. The Trumans had moved back to the mansion just a few days before, on March 27, after a four-year residency across the street at Blair House during the renovation of the White House.[305]

The Truman china is marked on the reverse in gold with a script "L" in a wreath and the words "White House Service/by Lenox [factory number]/Made in U.S.A./B. Altman and Co." Aside from the White House and the Smithsonian Institution, there are pieces in the Harry S. Truman Library at Independence, Missouri, and at the Lenox headquarters in Trenton, New Jersey.

The large Truman service with the green border had only been in use one year when President Dwight D. Eisenhower was inaugurated in January 1953, so there was no valid reason for Mrs. Eisenhower to order another state dinner service. She was personally very much interested in beautiful chinaware, however, and wished to make her own contribution to the White House China Collection. She decided that gold service plates would look well with the gold flatware in use in the White House, so in 1955 a set of handsome service plates was selected by her and ordered from Castleton China at New Castle, Pennsylvania.[306] The 120 service plates, 11½ inches in diameter, cost $3,606.40. The entire rims of the porcelain plates are covered with pure coin gold in an embossed gold medallion pattern. The process of affixing the gold to the rims required eight separate firings to achieve the desired finish. In the center of the translucent white china is the president's seal in gold. The new service plates were delivered to the White House on October 25, 1955, and the bill was paid on November 29.

These service plates look very handsome with—and were usually used with—the Truman state china instead of the service plates which had been a part of the original Truman order. The

Eisenhower service plates are marked in gold "Castleton Studios/The White House/November 1955." The trademark of the studios includes "Made in U.S.A." There are pieces in the collections of the White House, the Smithsonian Institution, and in the museum at the Eisenhower Library at Abilene, Kansas.

Mrs. Eisenhower's interest in White House china resulted in a project, completed in 1957, to reclassify and reorganize the collection in the China Room. At this time, she lent her prestige and personal approval to efforts to secure pieces of china from administrations which had not ordered official china. Because of this, she sought personal china used by Presidents Andrew Johnson, William Howard Taft, Warren G. Harding, Calvin Coolidge, and Herbert Hoover to insure that each presidential administration was specifically represented in the collection.

President and Mrs. John F. Kennedy ordered no china for the White House and usually used the Truman china with the Eisenhower service plates for state dinners.

Whenever possible, Mrs. Kennedy, whose love and concern for the historical White House is now history, used the old china—Lincoln's purple china, the china designed by Mrs. Harrison, and pieces of the Hayes service—to represent the traditions of the past. Her preference for the Harrison china was shown in her selection of pieces from that service to decorate the breakfront which she had placed in the family dining room during the years that she and President Kennedy occupied the mansion.

Lyndon B. Johnson

Today was the occasion of the annual luncheon that the First Lady always gives for the Senate Ladies Red Cross unit. And how eagerly we wanted to make it different.

Bess [Abell] had the grand idea of having the twelve tables, seating 130 guests, set with china representing eighteen different Presidential Administrations, ranging from the George Washington porcelain with the emblem of the Order of Cincinnati on it to the Eisenhower china, with its elaborate gold medallion. There was a centerpiece on each table from a different Administration. Of course, not every one of the thirty-six Presidents had a special set of china. (When the supply gets so low that you can't seat a State Dinner of one hundred people, then it's time for the current Administration to buy more china.) These were just place settings, the most extraordinary of which, by all odds, was the Rutherford B. Hayes china, with its exotic patterns of wildlife. It is extremely rococo and Victorian, every piece different, decorated with a stag, a wild turkey, buffalos in the snow.

There were two tables set with the Lincoln china with its broad purple border. Mrs. Lincoln must have bought a lot of china, or else people into whose hands it has fallen through the years have been excessively kind in returning it to the White House.

The tables were overlaid with pale yellow organdy and had exquisite flower arrangements. . . .

At one o'clock I was in the Green Room to receive the Senate ladies, with Cabinet wives on hand to help as hostesses. As usual, there were many old-timers—about seventy-one wives of sitting members and about thirty-one wives of former members. . . .

We had a gourmet lunch, beginning with prosciutto and melon, but the conversation piece was the china! . . .

I went to bed thinking that this was enough of a day to have lasted a month—I hoped that my guests at noon had noticed the Andrew Jackson urn from the Hermitage, and the James Madison tureen, and, perhaps, the Franklin Roosevelt china with three feathers and roses that came from the Roosevelt family's coat of arms. And I hope they noticed Thomas Jefferson's Chinese export porcelain tureen with the heart-shaped escutcheon bearing the letter "J." There is such a wealth of history and meaning in this great house.

Excerpt from *A White House Diary* by Lady Bird Johnson (New York: Holt, Rinehart and Winston, Inc., 1970), pages 130–131, 133–134.

Although President and Mrs. Johnson moved into the White House late in 1963, it was not until early 1966 that there was a need for a new state service for the mansion. This would be the first full set of china ordered since the Truman china was purchased in 1951. From the very beginning the firm of Tiffany was involved in planning the design of the china. Tiffany was already producing many of the state gifts that the president presented to visiting dignitaries. It was during the delivery of such gifts that a new state service was first discussed.

This was also the first time that a state service would be purchased with other than a government appropriation. During the Kennedy administration, the White House Historical Association had been organized, and this private, nonprofit association could fund the state service. As a result, the White House did not have to ask for bids, a requirement which had previously been necessary when china was purchased with government funds.

Mrs. Johnson was especially interested in selecting the design and worked closely with Bess Abell, her social secretary, and the White House curator, James Ketchum, to guide the selection into something which would say "in an elegant and loving way 'this is from the 1960's.'"[307]

The work on the design for the service began in earnest in early 1967. J. Bernard West, the chief usher, in consultation with Mrs. Mary Kaltman, the housekeeper, and John W. Ficklin, maitrê d'hôtel, provided a list of pieces they considered necessary for a state china service. They presented the following list.

18 Dozen Service Plates
18 Dozen Dinner Plates
36 Dozen Entree or Fish Plates
18 Dozen Dessert Plates
18 Dozen Finger Bowl Plates
18 Dozen Cream Soups and Stands
18 Dozen Boullion Cups and Saucers
20 Dozen Demi Tasse Cups
18 Dozen Soup Plates
18 Dozen Small Sauce Cups
18 Dozen Oyster Plates

By May 1967, Mrs. Johnson had decided that the main decorative themes on the new china were to be the eagle which had been used on the Monroe china and wildflowers from all over the United States. In the words of Mrs. Johnson:

> We paid tribute to our heritage through the wildflower theme used on most of the pieces. Ours is a country whose people conquered the land, mile by mile from one ocean to another. To me, wildflowers will always portray not only the beauty of nature, but the life-giving qualities of our land as well.
> The wildflowers also reflect our contemporary concern for conservation and beautification.[308]

The designer selected by Tiffany and Company to carry out Mrs. Johnson's ideas was Van Day Truex, and the paintings for the floral reproduction were made by André Piette. It was even arranged for Piette to come to the White House at night to get the effect of china on the table in the dining room as it would look by candlelight.

Mrs. Johnson had asked that some of her favorite wildflowers be used in the design. In June she sent Tiffany's a book on *Roadside Flowers of Texas* with illustrations marked to indicate her favorites, specifically mentioning bluebonnets, Indian blanket, and coreopsis. She was doubtful if some of her favorites would be usable as china designs because she feared they might be "too stalky."[309]

After many conferences, the design selected utilized a warm cream-color porcelain as the basic china. The background of the wildflowers was to be a radiating pattern of gold dots, described in the press release as "gold dotted vaulting." There is a narrow apricot border around the rim of each piece. The eagle, shield, and motto which first appeared on the Monroe dessert service was incorporated into the design. The service plates would have wildflowers scattered on the swirling gold dots around the rim with the eagle across the center of each plate. On the dinner plates, the eagle would be smaller, placed amid the wildflowers on the border. All of the other pieces used wildflowers, radiating patterns of gold dots, and the eagle in their decoration.

More than forty different wildflowers were selected to appear on the various pieces of the service. The White House announcement stated that the dinner plates would include "the Poppy, Prickly Pear, Rain Lily, Bluebell, Eastern Dogwood, Indian Paintbrush, Black-eyed Susan, Wild White Rose and Fluttermill. The service plates feature the Bluebonnet, Indian Blanket, Goldenrod, Meadow Pink, Prairie Phlox, Bristle-leaved Aster, Prickly Poppy, Prairie Verbena, Evening Primrose, and Coreopsis. All demitasse cups illustrate the Wine-cup and Blue Gentian. The large and small bowls include (among others) the Crimson Clover, Scarlet Pea, Gold Star Grass, Periwinkle, Piriqueta, Vetchlings, Grape Hyacinth, Desert Marigold, Wide-leafed Spring Beauty, Desert Poppy, Tansy Aster, Blue Witch, Wild Geranium, Midland Lily, Blue-eyed Grass, and Toothwart."[310]

It was decided that each dessert plate would have in its center the state flower of one of the fifty states in the United States and the District of Columbia. As a result, each state was approached through its department of archives and history to furnish a picture of the flower which would be representative of it on the china. On the basis of this information, the following flowers were to be used on the dessert plates.[311]

State	Flower
Alabama	Camellia
Alaska	Forget-me-not
Arizona	Flower of saguaro cactus
Arkansas	Apple blossom
California	Golden poppy
Colorado	Rocky Mountain columbine
Connecticut	Mountain laurel
Delaware	Peach blossom
Florida	Orange blossom
Georgia	Cherokee rose
Hawaii	Hibiscus
Idaho	Syringa
Illinois	Violet
Indiana	Peony
Iowa	Wild rose
Kansas	Sunflower
Kentucky	Goldenrod
Louisiana	Magnolia
Maine	White pine cone and tassel
Maryland	Black-eyed susan
Massachusetts	Mayflower
Michigan	Apple blossom
Minnesota	Showy Lady's slipper
Mississippi	Magnolia
Missouri	Hawthorn
Montana	Bitterroot Lewisia

93. Mark on the reverse of the Johnson state service: "The White House/1968/The Smithsonian Institution/The White House China Collection/Designed by Tiffany and Company/Made by Castleton China, Inc./U.S.A."

The state china ordered for the White House in 1968 during the administration of President Johnson was designed by Tiffany and Company of New York City and was made by Castleton China, Inc., of New Castle, Pennsylvania. The service was an anonymous gift through the White House Historical Association.

94. Service plate of cream-colored porcelain has a border of wild flowers in natural colors set against a background of radiating gold dots with a narrow apricot line at the edge. The Arms of the United States are in color in the center of the plate. Diameter, 12 inches.

166

95. *The design of the dinner plate is the same as that of the service plate except that the Arms of the United States are in the top center of the border. Diameter, 11 inches.*

96. *Pieces from the Johnson state service. From left to right, the height of the two bowls is 5 inches and 4 inches, respectively. Dimensions of the after-dinner coffee cup are: height, 2½ inches; diameter, 2 inches; and the saucer diameter, 5 inches.*

95

96

State	Flower
Nebraska	Goldenrod
Nevada	Sagebrush
New Hampshire	Purple lilac
New Jersey	Purple violet
New Mexico	Yucca
New York	Rose
North Carolina	Dogwood
North Dakota	Wild Prairie rose
Ohio	Scarlet carnation
Oklahoma	Mistletoe
Oregon	Oregon grape
Pennsylvania	Mountain laurel
Rhode Island	Violet
South Carolina	Carolina yellow jessamine
South Dakota	American pasqueflower
Tennessee	Iris
Texas	Bluebonnet
Utah	Sego lily
Vermont	Red clover
Virginia	American dogwood
Washington	Coast Rhododendron
West Virginia	Rosebay Rhododendron
Wisconsin	Wood violet
Wyoming	Indian paintbrush
District of Columbia	American Beauty rose

Tiffany and Company contracted to have the service manufactured by Castleton China of New Castle, Pennsylvania, the same firm that had made the service plates purchased during the Eisenhower administration. During the final stages of production of the White House china service, the Castleton China firm was absorbed into the Shenango Products Division of Interpace Corporation.

An announcement of the new state service was released to the public on November 8, 1967,[312] after a meeting of the Committee for the Preservation of the White House. Mrs. Johnson told the members of the committee that there was a real and immediate need for a new set of china because the White House did not have enough china of any one set to serve a state dinner. With the increasing number of state visits, she told them that there was an increasing need for a full supply. The new china would make it possible to serve a state dinner of 140 or more from one set of china. The news release also mentioned that 24 large bowls and 24 smaller bowls had been included in the order to be used as centerpieces for fruits or flowers.

Details of the arrangement were confirmed in a letter from Tiffany and Company to the White House on December 7, 1967. The letter was intended to "put into writing, the decision and the details covering the purchase of the White House china from Tiffany & Co." The letter stated that "the following items will be delivered to the White House as near to May 1st, 1968, as possible. . . ." Prices for these items were included.[313]

Item	Quantity	Price Each	Total Price
Service Plates	216	$ 58.07	$12,543.12
Dinner Plates	216	50.80	10,972.80
Fish Plates	216	27.82	6,009.12
Dessert Plates	216	65.47	14,141.52
Salad Plates	216	23.39	5,052.24
Cream Soup Cups	216	16.93	3,656.88
Cream Soup Saucers	216	16.61	3,587.76
After Dinner Cups	216	17.29	3,734.64
After Dinner Saucers	216	14.51	3,134.16
Rim Soup Plates	216	19.22	4,151.52
Large Bowls	24	281.93	6,766.32
Small Bowls	24	261.59	6,278.16
		Total	$80,028.24

The contract with the White House specified that each piece of the service was to be identified on the back with the following text in gold: "The White House/1968/Designed by Tiffany and Company/Made by Castleton China, Inc./USA."

The White House also ordered six display sets, each consisting of one complete setting and one large and one small bowl, which were to be given to the following and identified on the back.

The Lyndon Baines Johnson Library—"The Lyndon Baines Johnson Library"

The Smithsonian Institution—"The Smithsonian Institution, The White House China Collection"

The White House Collection—"The White House China Collection"

Tiffany and Company—"Tiffany and Company Private Collection"

Castleton China, Inc.—"Castleton China, Inc. Private Collection"

Commercial Decal, Inc.—"Commercial Decal, Inc. Private Collection"

97. Border of the dessert plate is of radiating gold
dots, and there is an American Beauty rose in the
center of the plate. Diameter, 9 inches. This plate is
marked in gold on the reverse: "The White
House/1968/District of Columbia/America Beauty
Rose/"Rosa American Beauty"/Designed by
Tiffany and Co./Made by Castleton China, Inc./
U.S.A."

On the dessert plates, the wording was to be the same as on the other pieces of china, except that below "The White House/1968" was to appear the name of the state, the popular name of the state flower, and the scientific name. All marks on the reverse were to be in gold. There were other points specified in the contract.

> All designs must be approved by the White House before final production, and one sample of each item of the service must be approved before the full set is produced.
> Any use of the display sets, outside of the individual corporation's own showroom, must be approved by the White House in writing. This includes any use by the news media.
> All dishes which are not acceptable because of poor design or flaw in the production must be destroyed. This destruction must be accompanied by a witnessed statement.
> All drawings of designs will become the property of the White House. In the case of copyrighted material, the copyright will be assigned to the White House Historical Association.[314]

The work of producing the designs was a prodigious one. The flower and eagle paintings were done by André Piette of Tiffany and Company, and the gold dots and layout were by Van Day Truex. Piette's paintings were photoprocessed into full-color decalcomanias by Commercial Decal of Mount Vernon, New York, after which they were shipped to New Castle, Pennsylvania, where they were fired onto the dishes in production at Castleton China. Castleton made the huge, one-piece, gold-dot decals in its own plant. The Castleton work was under the direction of Paul W. Cook, the art director, and Albert G. Liversage, the director of design processes. Castleton officials estimated that it took nearly 12,000 castings of raw boltage clay to produce the 2,208 perfect pieces in the set. On average, imperfections somewhere along the line normally ruin two of every three pieces started, but the rate was five to one on the place-setting pieces and ten to one on the 48 fruit and flower bowls destined for the White House.

The china was presented to the public at the White House on May 9, 1968, at 4:30 P.M. when more than 150 guests, including craftsmen involved in the design and execution of the china, were present at the East Room ceremony and reception. It was announced at the ceremony that the new service had been made possible by a generous gift to the White House Historical Association from an anonymous donor.

The china was first used several weeks later on May 23 at the First Lady's luncheon for the senate wives at which Mrs. Eisenhower was the guest of honor. The first state dinner for which the new china was used was given on May 27 in honor of the Honorable John G. Gorton, prime minister of Australia.

Though most of the china was delivered and in use, the entire order had not yet been completed. In an effort to finish the whole service in the time agreed upon, Mrs. Johnson was not given the opportunity to see and approve the design of each dessert plate before it was produced. It was the opinion of both Mrs. Johnson and of Walter Hoving, chairman of the board of Tiffany and Company, that the dessert plates with the fifty different state flowers were not as "exact in coloring and proportion" as had been hoped; therefore, it would be necessary to remake the dessert plates. Hoving was of the opinion that the effect both Mrs. Johnson and he wished to achieve could not be done with the decalcomania process for it did not permit the intricate designs and colorings necessary for the dessert plates. These would have to be hand painted.

During the months of June and July, Mr. Ketchum and Mrs. Abell worked with Constance Carter, of the staff of the Library of Congress, selecting and assembling designs that would be more suitable for the dessert plates. Mrs. Johnson reviewed and approved the drawings and notes. Then, the staff from Tiffany's met with them and went over all the drawings and notes that had been assembled. On the basis of the meeting, a sample plate was hand painted and submitted to the White House in September 1968. Mrs. Johnson was pleased with the sample and gave her approval to the method used to produce the sample plate. The additional cost of hand painting the dessert plates was another problem, but this was resolved to the satisfaction both of Tiffany's and of the White House.

By November 1968, Tiffany and Company began sending the White House black-and-white renderings of the state flowers for Mrs. Johnson's approval of the composition of the design. From November on, three steps were to be necessary before production of the plates: the black-and-white renderings were to be submitted for approval of the composition; the drawing would be rendered in color for approval; and, finally, the hand-painted finished product was to be presented for approval.

Even if all went well, it was estimated that it would take another year before the dessert plates could be finished. Work was begun on the project and continued after Mrs. Johnson left the White House in 1969. It became increasingly hard to coordinate the project with Mrs. Johnson in Texas, Mrs. Abell and Mr. Ketchum in Washington, and the artist in New York City. Tiffany and Company are to be congratulated that they were able to complete the dessert plates and send them to the White House in the summer of 1972.

In retrospect, it might be said that the effort to achieve perfection involved the approval of so many people at so many stages of the production that it seemed at times that it would be impossible to produce the dessert plates at all. The quality of the plates fully repays all the time and care that went into their production.

The state china chosen by Mrs. Johnson was quite different in style from the more conventional formal services selected for the White House in the twentieth century, and it was received by the public with mixed emotions. Mrs. Johnson's idea was a most imaginative one, and it seems sad that the designers of Tiffany and Company did not respond to it in an equally imaginative way. The large and small bowls of the set give an idea of how delightful the design might have been for on these the effect is one of flowers scattered at random in a field of swirling golden raindrops. Placed in a formal arrangement around the edges of the plates, the wildflowers do not seem at home. The production of the Johnson service is a reminder of the trials and tribulations of producing the Hayes service, and it was fortunate that Theodore Davis and his friend, Theodore Haviland, did not have the assistance of a committee.

Notes

(NA-MTA used throughout stands for National Archives, Miscellaneous Treasury Account)

1. Catalogue of the Governor Caleb Lyon Collection of Oriental and Occidental Ceramics. Henry D. Miner, auctioneer, April 24, 1876. Alice Morse Earle in *China Collecting in America* writes that Governor Lyon was a frequent visitor to Mount Vernon and Arlington House (now known as the Custis-Lee Mansion) in the middle of the nineteenth century. She comments that "he was also collecting facts and details with a view to writing a 'History of the Ceramic Relics of the Revolution.' Unfortunately, he relied much on his memory and hence left few notes."

2. *The Ladies Home Journal,* May and July 1889.

3. Alice Morse Earle, *China Collecting in America.* New York: Scribner's, 1892.

4. Abby Gunn Baker, "The White House Collection of Presidential Ware," *The Century Magazine,* volume 76, number 6 (October 1908).

5. Abby Gunn Baker, "The China of the Presidents," *Munsey's Magazine,* volume 30, number 3 (December 1903).

6. *The Letters of Archie Butt,* edited by Lawrence F. Abbott (Doubleday, Page, 1924), pages 237–238. To date, no confirmation of any kind of an arrangement has been located either in the Smithsonian Institution archives or in the records of the commissioner of public buildings and grounds. Also, Butt's comment that some pieces were purchased by Mrs. Theodore Roosevelt is in contradiction to Mrs. Baker's statement that no pieces were to be bought.

7. Act of Congress, April 29, 1816. (3 Statute 324).

8. Ibid., March 3, 1849 (9 Statute 395).

9. Ibid., March 2, 1867 (14 Statute 466).

10. Ibid., February 26, 1925 (43 Statute 983).

11. Executive Order 6166, June 10, 1935.

12. Annals of Congress, 1st Congress, 1st session (March 4–September 29, 1789), Proceedings of the Senate of the United States, April 15, 1789.

13. Letter from Sarah Robinson, Samuel Osgood's niece, dated New York, April 30, 1789, quoted in *The Memorial History of the City of New York,* James Wilson, editor (New York, 1893), volume 3, pages 51–52.

14. Records of the Office of the Register of the Treasury, Record Group 53, volume 138, pages 316–324. The inventory is recorded in the book for the year 1796, but the list is the same as the one in the Osgood papers. As all the dealers listed are from New York City, there is no doubt that it is the record of the 1789 furnishings.

15. The firm of J. and N. Roosevelt was listed in New York City directories from 1789–1793, according to information provided by The New-York Historical Society.

16. Samuel Dunlap and Son is listed at 13 Queen Street in 1791. From Rita-Susswein Gottesman, *The Arts and Crafts of New York 1777–1799.* New York, 1954.

17. James Christie had a china and glass store at 37 Market Street from 1789–1792. From New York City directories, courtesy of The New-York Historical Society.

18. New York: Houghton, 1933.

19. The New York pound was worth $2.50 or 8 shillings to the dollar.

20. Manuscript Collection, Mount Vernon Ladies Association of the Union, Mount Vernon, Virginia.

21. George Washington to Tobias Lear, October 27, 1790. George Washington Papers, Library of Congress, Manuscript Division.

22. Tobias Lear to George Washington, New York, September 12, 1790. George Washington Papers, Library of Congress, Manuscript Division.

23. Ibid., Philadelphia, October 24, 1790.

24. *Mount Vernon China.* The Mount Vernon Ladies Association of the Union, Mount Vernon, Virginia.

25. Stephen Decatur, Jr., *Private Affairs of George Washington from the Records and Accounts of Tobias Lear, Esquire, his Secretary.* New York: Houghton, 1933.

26. List [made at Philadelphia] of Articles, Public and Private, 1797. George Washington Papers, Library of Congress, Manuscript Division.

27. Op. cit. (note 22), Philadelphia, March 15, 1797.

28. The Adams Papers, Massachusetts Historical Society. Quotations from the Adams Papers are from the microfilm edition by permission of the Massachusetts Historical Society. The notes on "delph" are from Ivor Noël Hume, *A Guide to Artifacts of Colonial America,* New York: Knopf, 1969.

29. Records of the 4th Congress, 2d session (1792–1793).

30. Op. cit. (note 22).

31. NA-MTA, Record Group 217, account 12175. Vouchers to support the expenditures are missing. The jacket of the account bears what appears to be a contemporary notation: "Vouchers in Box 34."

32. Thomas Claxton to John Adams, November 3, 1800. The Adams Papers, Massachusetts Historical Society.

33. Charles Francis Adams, *The Letters of Mrs. Adams* (Boston, 1848), page 384.

34. Op. cit. (note 28).

35. Letter from David Brooks to Maria Mallam Brooks dated June 9, 1797. Gift of Mabel Crane Walker to the Office of the Curator of the White House. Information on the blue and white export porcelain is from an article by J. Jefferson Miller, "The Porcelain Trade of America," *Discovering Antiques,* issue 43 (1971), pages 10019–10023.

36. National Archives, Papers of the Senate of the United States, Record Group 46-6A-65.

37. Ibid. This is one of the few official inventories of this early period which appeared in print in the official records of the Congress.

38. NA-MTA, Record Group 217, account 13460. Vouchers missing. The jacket of the account states: "Vouchers in Box 34."

39. Ibid., account 13907.

40. National Archives, Treasury Department Records, 1st Auditor's Report for 1805, account 17199.

41. Jacket of this account states: "Vouchers in Box 36."

42. NA-MTA, Record Group 217, account 20835.

43. Ibid., account 21304, voucher 2.

44. Letter of Thomas Jefferson to Thomas Claxton dated February 19, 1809. Thomas Jefferson Papers, volume 186, page 33058, Library of Congress, Manuscript Division.

45. Ibid., page 33064.

46. Talbot Hamlin, *Benjamin Henry Latrobe* (New York: Oxford University Press, 1955), page 353.

47. NA-MTA, Record Group 217, account 28634, voucher 12.

48. Ibid., voucher 14.

49. *Independent American,* volume 2, number 89 (October 20, 1810), page 3.

50. Long and Dixon were possibly operating a hotel or a boardinghouse as there was a Robert Long who was a hotelkeeper at various addresses in the city during the period from 1809 to 1815. The Madison inaugural ball in 1809 was held in Long's Hotel where the Library of Congress now stands. The "sett of china" may have been for Dixon's personal use.

51. NA-MTA, account 29494, record of purchases made by Lewis Deblois: voucher 9, Charles Moxley; vouchers 13, 14, and 55, Woodward and Cook; vouchers 6 and 7, John Thompson; and voucher 23, George Beale.

52. Ibid., see voucher 23 above.

53. Letter of Fulwar Skipwith to James Madison, dated September 3, 1806, documents the purchase of the Nast china while Madison was secretary of state. University of Virginia, Alderman Library 2988, Box 21.

54. George Boyd's name appears on NA-MTA, account 34714, but the vouchers for the expenditures he made during this period are to be found appended to account 28634 in three series marked vouchers 1, 2, and 3 with each bill numbered separately inside; i.e., voucher 1 contains bills from 1 to 34; voucher 2 contains bills from 1 to 49; and voucher 3 contains bills from 1 to 34—thus a double number appears on each individual transaction.

55. NA-MTA, account 28634: voucher 1, number 28, Mrs. Lear; voucher 2, numbers 17 and 29, A. L. Joncherez; voucher 2, number 46, J. Doyle; voucher 2, number 49, Harriet Campbell; voucher 3, number 22, Samuel McKenney; and voucher 3, number 23, A. L. Joncherez.

56. Ibid., voucher 2, number 49. Harriet was the wife of George W. Campbell, secretary of the treasury, who lived in one of The Seven Buildings.

57. Ibid., voucher 2, number 46. Perhaps this was a Mrs. Doyne who had a well-furnished boardinghouse on Pennsylvania Avenue near Sixth Street, N.W.

58. Ibid., voucher 3, number 22. Samuel McKenney was probably related to Mayor Thomas McKenney of Georgetown who was a lifelong friend and correspondent of both President and Mrs. Madison.

59. Ibid., voucher 2, numbers 17 and 29 and voucher 3, number 23. An advertisement in the *Daily National Intelligencer,* June 4, 1818, placed by Ann Joncherez states "just received from France, by the late arrivals, some very elegant *French China Tea setts.*"

60. The house which the Monroes occupied is at 2017 I (Eye) Street, N.W., and is designated an historic house. It is currently owned by the Arts Club of Washington.

61. No copy of this letter has been found, but Monroe refers to it in his report on the furniture fund published in the 18th Congress, 2d session (1824–1825), House Report 79, page 15.

62. Letter from William Lee to the Honorable B. Bassett et al., dated February 24, 1818, published in the 18th Congress, 2d session (1824–1825), House Report 79, pages 244–247.

63. NA-MTA, account 43754, voucher 86.

64. NA-MTA, account 37131, voucher 3. The list of the pieces in these two services translates from the French into:
one table service, in gilded porcelain for thirty people consisting of the following:
  2 soup tureens
32 oval dishes of various sizes
  8 square covered dishes
  3 dozen deep plates
12 dozen dinner plates
  4 stands for sauceboats
  4 sauceboats
36 custard cups
  4 fruit stands
  4 octagonal salad bowls
  4 mustard pots
36 egg cups
One porcelain dessert service for 30 people. Amaranth border with five vignettes representing Strength, Agriculture, Commerce, Arts, and Sciences and the arms of the United States in the center of the plate consisting of the following:
  3 dozen deep plates
  7 dozen flat plates
24 compotes of various shapes
  4 cheese dishes
  4   "   "   on feet
  2 chestnut bowls
  4 sugar bowls
  4 ice cream urns
  4 fruit baskets
It seems pertinent to list all pieces received as they provide an excellent checklist of items to be found in dinner and dessert services of the period.

65. Letter of May 25, 1818, published in the 18th Congress, 2d session (1824–1825), House Report 79, page 164.

66. M^{ture} = Manufacture; F. Honoré = Fils Honoré. Information on the Paris factories was taken from *A History and Description of French Porcelain* by E. S. Auscher and translated by William Burton (London, 1905).

67. Information about this china was supplied by Dwight P. Lanmon, curator of ceramics, The Henry Francis du Pont Winterthur Museum, Winterthur, Delaware. Design information is from *European Ceramic Art* by W. B. Honey. (London: Faber and Faber, 1949).

68. NA-MTA, account 43754, voucher 33.

69. Letter of James Brown to James Monroe, "Haver" (Le Havre), June 4, 1817. The James Monroe Papers, Library of Congress, Manuscript Division. Virginia-born James Brown had been a United States senator until he was defeated in 1817. Reelected in 1819, he served until 1823 when President Monroe appointed him United States minister to France.

70. Clock in the collection of The Henry Francis du Pont Winterthur Museum, catalog number 571037.

71. *Le Cannameliste Française* (1751) defines fruit as "that which comprises all the dessert."

72. Information about the dessert course is primarily from *Table Decoration: Yesterday, Today, and Tomorrow* by Georgiana Reynolds Smith, Rutland, Vermont: Charles E. Tuttle Company, 1968.

73. NA-MTA, account 43754, voucher 29.

74. H. Bertrand does not appear in the city directory of Baltimore for 1816, 1817, or 1818.

75. Records of the 18th Congress, 2d session (1824–1825), House Report 79, pages 1–286.

76. Lucius Wilmerding, Jr., *James Monroe: Public Claimant* (New Brunswick, New Jersey: Rutgers University Press, 1960).

77. NA-MTA, account 54100. Settling account of Samuel Lane, vouchers 12 and 19.

78. Ibid.

79. *Memoirs of John Quincy Adams,* edited by Charles Francis Adams (Philadelphia: J. B. Lippincott, 1874–1877). Entry for April 11, 1824 (volume 6, page 281).

80. Ibid., page 527.

81. This inventory is published in the Records of the 19th Congress, 1st session (1825–1826), House Document 2, series 131. It is worth noting the contemporary English translations of French terms: *saladiers* are called "celery dishes" and "marronniers" (chestnut baskets) are called "fruit baskets."

82. *New England Palladium and Commercial Advertiser.* Boston, Massachusetts, March 4, 1825.

83. NA-MTA, account 51873, voucher 10.

84. Ibid., voucher 103. The Philadelphia firm of Read and Gray is identified on the billhead as "Importers of China, Glass, Queen's Ware/No. 25 Market Street."

85. Letter of John Adams, Jr., dated February 8, 1826, in the National Archives, Record Group 233, House of Representatives 18-A-C20.4.

86. Op. cit., note 82.

87. *United States Statutes at Large* (Boston: Charles C. Little and James Brown, 1846), volume 4, page 194.

88. NA-MTA, account 51873, voucher 107. Information on ironstone china from Geoffrey Bemrose, *Nineteenth Century English Pottery and Porcelain.* London: Farber and Farber, 1952.

89. Ibid., voucher 143.

90. Ibid., account 52388.

91. *Congressional Register,* Act of Congress, March 2, 1827 (19th Congress, 2d session), pages 218–219.

92. NA-MTA, account 55314, voucher 51.

93. Ibid., voucher 83.

94. The Adams Papers, Massachusetts Historical Society. Quotations are from the microfilm edition of the John Quincy Adams diary, volume 39, by permission of The Adams Papers, Massachusetts Historical Society.

95. Guista came from Europe with John Quincy Adams in 1818 and served as his steward when Adams was secretary of state and later when he was president. Guista was retained at the President's House in the service of President Andrew Jackson until his dismissal in 1883 for excessive household expenditures. See Andrew Jackson account books, Library of Congress, Manuscript Division.

96. NA-MTA, account 61369, voucher 1.

97. Ibid., voucher 4. Robinson Tyndale appears in Philadelphia directories from 1813 to 1840. In 1831, his business was at 12 North Third Street. The "twiffling" or "twiffler" was a small plate for soft, breadlike spoon bread or batter bread. See Dennis G. Rice, *The Illustrated Guide to Rockingham Pottery and Porcelain* (London: Barrie and Jenkins, 1971), plate 16, for a set of similar price and number of pieces.

98. Ibid., voucher 13.

99. Ibid., list of estimates.

100. NA-MTA, account 70647. Letter from George W. South to Maj. William B. Lewis, dated July 26, 1833.

101. Ibid., voucher 4 only.

102. Ibid., account of sales at auction of old furniture.

103. Boulanger was steward until October 1836. James Cuthbert served from 1836 until the end of the administration. See Jackson account books, Library of Congress, Manuscript Division.

104. NA-MTA, account 71829, voucher 6.

105. Ibid., voucher 16.

106. Edwin Atlee Barber, *The Pottery and Porcelain of the United States* (New York: G. P. Putnam Sons, 1893), pages 131–132.

107. Arthur W. Clement, *Notes on Early American Porcelain, 1738–1838* (New York: The Court Press, 1946), page 34.

108. Correspondence between Susan Decatur (Mrs. Stephen Decatur) and Andrew Jackson on exhibition at The Hermitage, Nashville, Tennessee, courtesy of The Ladies Hermitage Association.

109. Records of the 18th Congress, 2d session (1824–1825), House Reports, volume 2.

110. The purchase of the Decatur china and silver coincides with the large purchase President Jackson made in Philadelphia for his home in Nashville. He personally ordered glass from Bakewell in Pittsburgh for The Hermitage at the time some was ordered for the President's House. Jackson's personal accounts in 1836 after the fire at The Hermitage show the same names as the official accounts, with most of the purchases made in Philadelphia through Henry Toland on such firms as L. Veron and Company, R. Tyndale, and G. W. South.

111. National Archives, letter book of the commissioner of public buildings (volume 30), June 12, 1840.

112. NA-MTA, account 75138, vouchers 1 and 2, and account of T. L. Smith, authorized purchasing agent for 1837–1838; and voucher 1, account of William Noland, commissioner of public buildings, purchasing agent for 1839.

113. Act of Congress of April 6, 1838, authorizing use of proceeds of sale of decayed furniture to be expended on other furniture.

114. Ogle's speech in full can be found in *Speech of Mr. Ogle of Pennsylvania on the Regal Splendor of the President's Palace. Delivered in the House of Representatives. April 14, 1840.* [Washington, D.C.? 1840?]

115. Levi Lincoln's speech in full can be found in *Speech of Mr. Lincoln, a Whig representative in Congress, in reply to Mr. Ogle, upon the proposition of the latter to strike out of the general appropriations bill a small item for alterations and repairs of the President's House, etc.* [Washington, D.C.? 1840?]

116. Records of the 27th Congress, 2d session, (1841–1842) House Report 552, volume 2, pages 1–58.

117. NA-MTA, account 96137, voucher 41.

118. National Archives, letter book of the commissioner of public buildings (volume 30), March 22 and 29, 1841.

119. NA-MTA, account 81944.

120. NA-MTA, account 29494, vouchers 8, 9, and 14.

121. NA-MTA, account 87086.

122. NA-MTA, account 87143, voucher 11.

123. Ibid., vouchers 2 and 12.

124. NA-MTA, account 96137, voucher 43.

125. NA-MTA, account 87086, voucher 2.

126. One voucher is in NA-MTA, account 87086, voucher 28. Another is in NA-MTA, account 93470, voucher 28, which was not paid until the Polk administration.

127. NA-MTA, account 81944, Hugh Smith and Company, entered June 23, 1841; account 87086, John Tyler, Jr., entered July 3, 1843; and account 87143, Seth Hyatt, entered July 11, 1843.

128. NA-MTA, account 90526.

129. NA-MTA, account 93470, voucher 2.

130. Ibid., voucher 10.

131. Ibid., voucher 39. Information on the factory from Régine de Plinval de Guillebon, author of *Porcelain of Paris, 1770–1850* (New York: Walker and Company, 1972).

132. NA-MTA, account 96137, voucher 41.

133. Ibid., voucher 43.

134. NA-MTA, account 100396, voucher 37.

135. Ibid., voucher 49.

136. Letter book of the commissioner of public buildings (volume 31), January 1, 1849, "Inventory of Furniture in the President's House."

137. NA-MTA, account 101316.

138. Ibid., voucher 2.

139. NA-MTA, account 102017.

140. NA-MTA, account 102509, fourth quarter, vouchers 3 and 26.

141. NA-MTA, account 103151; voucher 4, C. S. Fowler.

142. Ibid., account 103722.

143. Letter of December 31, 1849, to Col. W. W. Bliss. Letter book of the commissioner of public buildings, volume 31.

144. NA-MTA, account 105580, voucher 3.

145. NA-MTA, account 107778, voucher 66.

146. Op. cit. (notes 105, 112, 125).

147. Op. cit. (note 59).

148. James C. McGuire, related by marriage to the Madison family, handled the final disposition of the estate of Dolley Madison which was inherited by her son, Payne Todd. From 1850 on, McGuire ran the major auction house in the City of Washington, and he handled the sale of "decayed furniture" from the President's House until the end of the nineteenth century.

149. Letter from Commissioner Blake to the Honorable J. Glancey Jones, United States House of Representatives, dated December 17, 1856. National Archives, letter book of the commissioner of public buildings, letter 3448.

150. Information about the family life of President Pierce and about his law clerk and secretary, Sydney Webster, are found in Roy F. Nichols, *Franklin Pierce, Young Hickory of the Granite Hills* (Philadelphia: University of Pennsylvania Press, 1931).

151. *The World of Science, Art and Industry, Illustrated from Examples in the New York Exhibition 1853–1854,* edited by Professor Benjamin Silliman, Jr., and C. R. Goodrich, Esq. (New York: G. P. Putnam and Company, 1854), page 129.

152. This is explained by the fact that this was the first book in the United States to be illustrated with inserted photographs produced from negatives, and the printed page must have made a mirror image of the negative.

153. Horace Greeley, *Art and Industry as Represented in the Exhibition at the Crystal Palace New York 1853–1854 Showing the Progress and State of the Various Useful and Esthetic Pursuits.* (New York: Redfield, 1853).

154. Great Britain's Commissioners to the New York Industrial Exhibition, *General Report of the British Commissioners* (London, 1854), presented to the House of Commons in 1854.

155. NA-MTA, account 113810, voucher 4.

156. Op. cit. (note 151), page 147.

157. NA-MTA, account 113810, voucher 24. "Nappies" are small open bowls.

158. NA-MTA, account 125856. Letter of Sidney Webster, dated January 2, 1857.

159. NA-MTA, account 130243, voucher 12. The billhead identifies Tyndale and Mitchell as "Importers of all kind of Common and Fine China and Queenware" at 707 Chestnut Street, Philadelphia.

160. NA-MTA, account 134023, voucher 11.

161. Press release. Abby Gunn Baker papers, Office of the Curator of the White House.

162. Affidavit, dated March 20, 1962, accompanying the pieces of this service presented to the Governor's

Mansion in Richmond, Virginia, by Miss Sara W. Coe, Charles Town, West Virginia.

163. Theodore R. Davis, "Presidential Porcelain of a Century," *The Ladies Home Journal*, May 1889.

164. Letter, dated November 22 (ca. 1912), from May S. Kennedy to Mrs. Baker: "I remember quite well the conversation with my cousin Mrs. Johnson [Harriet Lane Johnston] about the China used by President Buchanan while in the White House. As she stated at the time, what was used there belonged to the Government and was left there. The china, plate, etc used by President Buchanan in his own house was left to his heirs." Abby Gunn Baker papers, Office of the Curator of the White House.

165. *Official catalog of the New York Exhibition of the Industry of all Nations, 1853*. New York: G. P. Putnam and Company, 1853.

166. Letter from William F. Dorflinger to Mrs. Baker, dated April 17, 1914, stating that "Solferino is a purplish-rose color invented by the French in the year 1859 and so named in honor of the victory of that year over the Austrians." Abby Gunn Baker papers, Office of the Curator of the White House.

167. Op. cit. (note 151), page 85.

168. *Lincoln Lore*. Bulletin of the Lincoln National Life Foundation, number 1492 (June 1962).

169. NA-MTA, account 141451, voucher 14.

170. Edwin Atlee Barber, "The Pioneer of China Painting in America," *The Ceramic Monthly*, volume 2, number 2 (September 1895), pages 15–20.

171. Letter from Charles Haviland, Limoges, France, to Theodore Haviland in the United States, dated March 4, 1869, in the archives of Haviland and Company: "It would certainly be a good thing to stamp all our china with our name if: 1st our china was better than any one else or at least as good and 2nd if we made enough for our trade. Without that it would turn against us and learn people that by ordering through Vogt or Nittal they could get Gibus or Julieus china which is better than ours. And if ours was the best but we did not make enough to fill orders there would be a complaint when we gave other manufacturer's china. So our first aim must be to manufacture as well or better than anybody else and to make all we sell. *Then & then only* it will be a capital thing to stamp all our make with our name." This was finally possible by the 1870s.

172. The city directory of Washington, D.C., lists "J. W. Boteler & Bro." from 1867 to 1881.

173. William Crump, who was steward of the White House under Presidents Hayes, Garfield, and Arthur,

personally collected White House china. Davis and Crump became friends when Davis designed the Hayes china. The Lincoln plate which Crump gave to Davis, now in the collections of the State Historical Society of Wisconsin, is broken at the edge so that it could be legally given away. It does not have a maker's mark, but by this time the pieces with the Haviland mark which had been ordered during the Grant administration were in the china cupboards. Thus, it is understandable why Davis in 1881 attributed all the Lincoln china to Haviland.

174. Elizabeth Todd Grimsley, "Six Months in the White House," *Journal, Illinois State Historical Society,* volume 19, numbers 3–4, pages 42–73. The "M.L." (Mary Lincoln) china has not been located but when last known, it was in the possession of Gov. Henry Horner of Illinois at the time of his death in 1940.

175. *The New York World*, September 26, 1864.

176. NA-MTA, account 157178, voucher 60.

177. Justin G. Turner and Linda Lovett Turner, *Mary Todd Lincoln: Her Life and Letters* (New York: Alfred A. Knopf, 1972), pages 198–199.

178. NA-MTA, account 157178, voucher 9.

179. Ibid., voucher 26.

180. Ibid., voucher 25.

181. George Fort Milton, *The Age of Hate: Andrew Johnson and The Radicals* (New York: Coward-McCann, 1930), page 229.

182. National Archives. Records of commissioner of public buildings and grounds, volume 38, entry 3713 (May 26, 1865).

183. NA-MTA, account 157178, voucher 18.

184. Edward Lycett was born at Newcastle, England, near the Staffordshire potteries, in 1833 and was apprenticed to Copeland and Garrett at Stoke-upon-Trent. From there, he went to London where he studied under masters of the art and had established a firm reputation before he came to this country in 1861. In New York City, he associated himself with the artists who followed Dailey of Haughwout and Dailey when that firm split in 1857. In 1884, Lycett joined the Faience Manufacturing Company at Greenport, Long Island, and assumed the direction of the factory; he severed his connection with that firm in 1890. His career in this country was identified with the development and expansion of the art of china painting from the beginning of the Civil War to the end of the century. He spent the last years of his life in Atlanta, Georgia, where he died in 1910.

185. Edwin Atlee Barber, op. cit. (note 170), and

"Then and Now," *China, Glass and Lamps,* volume 13, number 26 (June 7, 1897), page 15.

186. Article in the *Atlanta Journal and Constitution Magazine,* February 12, 1967, "Hand Painted China Treasures," by Wylly Folk St. John, furnished to this writer in 1970 by James L. Mitchell of Atlanta, Georgia.

187. National Archives, Letter book of the commissioner of public buildings and grounds. Letter from Orville H. Browning, secretary of the interior, to Benjamin B. French, docket 3800/1.

188. Ibid., docket 3813, 1867 inventory and relevant correspondence.

189. Ibid.

190. Ibid., docket 62/313. Office of Public Buildings and Grounds "Inventory of Public Property belonging to the United States submitted to the House of Representatives by letter dated January 24, 1871" for 41st Congress, 3d session (1870–1871).

191. Letter in the collection of the Office of the Curator of the White House. The letterhead identifies Covell and Company as "Designers and Manufacturers of Chandeliers, gas fixtures; Importers of French China, Glassware. . . ." at 554 Broadway, New York City.

192. Archives of Haviland and Company in Limoges, France, number 149.

193. If Walton was an American artist, he could be either William Walton (1843–1915) or William E. Walton (born 1824; in New York City until 1862) who painted during the period; but neither appears in New York City directories in 1869, and neither is known to have painted flowers.

194. NA-MTA, account 176596, voucher 15.

195. William H. Crook, *Memories of the White House.* Boston: Little, Brown, 1911.

196. NA-MTA, account 192686, voucher 29.

197. National Archives. Records of the commissioner of public buildings and grounds, "Catalog of White House China" (in manuscript) by Abby Gunn Baker.

198. NA-MTA, account 176596, voucher 15.

199. Crook, op. cit. (note 195).

200. "Presidential Porcelain of a Century," *The Ladies Home Journal.* Signed "Theo. R. Davis, May 1889."

201. NA-MTA, account 193617, voucher 102.

202. National Archives, Records of Office of Publc Buildings and Grounds, contract 1854 (February 20, 1879). This contract for the Hayes service seems to be the first time an official contract was entered into for the production of china for the Executive Mansion.

204. *Harper's Weekly,* November 25, 1876, page 950.

205. Theodore R. Davis, "The White House Porcelain Service for State Dinners," *The Ladies Home Journal,* July 1889, page 4.

206. *New York Tribune,* August 1, 1879.

207. Original letter from Theodore R. Davis to Webb Hayes, February 26, 1879, in the Webb C. Hayes, I, Papers, The Rutherford B. Hayes Library, Fremont, Ohio.

208. Original letter from Theodore Haviland to Theodore R. Davis, dated March 20, 1879. Privately owned.

209. National Archives, Records of Office of Public Buildings and Grounds, letter book (1879), entry 142.

210. Theodore R. Davis was born in Boston in 1841. He and his mother moved to Washington, D.C., when he was a young boy and he was graduated from Rittenhouse Academy in Washington. After his graduation he studied in Brooklyn under artists Herrick and Lumley. His first work was for *Frank Leslie's Magazine.* He was war artist and correspondent for *Harper's Weekly* during the Civil War and illustrated many important engagements including the battle for Fort Sumter, the battle of the *Monitor* and the *Merrimac,* the siege of Vicksburg, and Sherman's "March to the Sea" in Georgia. He was wounded at Shiloh and again at Antietam. The doctors threatend to amputate both legs, but the artist slept with pistols under his pillow and dared them to touch him. On another occasion, his sketchbook was shot from his hand as he worked on the battlefield. After the war, he accompanied Generals George Custer and Winfield Hancock in their campaigns against the Indians in the West. He moved to Asbury Park in 1880, where he lived until his death on November 10, 1894. During his last few years, he confined his activities to art work and writing occasional articles for magazines. It was during this period that he drew his plans for the Missionary Ridge panorama and a battle cyclorama which was exhibited in many parts of the United States. Information for this sketch was taken from Robert Taft, *Artists and Illustrators of the Old West* (New York: Charles Scribner's Sons, 1953) pages 59, 62–71, and from obituaries of Theodore Davis still in the possession of descendants.

211. Decalcomania is derived from the French "décalquer" meaning to transfer a painting, and "manie," a Late Latin word meaning rage or craze. It is the term applied to the art or process of transferring pictures and designs to objects of almost every description such as china, glass, or leather, from especially

prepared paper. The process began in a primitive form about 1863, but by the end of the nineteenth century such vast improvements had been made that it was almost universally adopted for commercial use. The Hayes china was the first china to be made by Haviland and Company using the decalcomania process. A large selection of the decals used in making the Hayes service were given to the Smithsonian Institution by Haviland and Company (accession 231180). None of the watercolor designs have survived either in the archives of Haviland and Company or in the ownership of Davis's descendants.

212. Op. cit. (note 205).

213. Original letter from Theodore Haviland to Theodore R. Davis dated January 1880. The following blank plates sent by Mr. Haviland have survived in the collections of the State Historical Society of Wisconsin: "Blank Soup plate/Blank Fish plate/Blank after dinner coffee cup and saucer/Butter chip (crude rendering of the final design)." This information was provided through the courtesy of Mrs. Joan Severa, curator of decorative arts, State Historical Society of Wisconsin.

214. National Archives, Letters of Office of Public Buildings and Grounds, 1879, entries 309, 325, 361, 391, and 400.

215. Ibid., 1880, entry 75.

216. Ibid., 1880, entries 151, 162, 199, 200, and 213.

217. NA-MTA, account 221176, voucher 1.

218. Op. cit. (note 213).

219. National Archives, Letters of Office of Public Buildings and Grounds, 1880, entries 250 and 272; NA-MTA 225211, voucher 56.

220. Op. cit. (note 213).

221. Original in the social affairs scrapbook, The Rutherford B. Hayes Library, Fremont, Ohio, in volume 116, page 97, under the heading "New York—1880."

222. Manuscript letter, privately owned.

223. Original letter of Theodore Davis to Mrs. Rutherford B. Hayes, dated July 24, 1880. The Rutherford B. Hayes Library.

224. *The White House Porcelain Service, 1879* (see Appendix I), page 88. Mrs. Hayes's original letter is privately owned. Another reference to the Hayes's feeling about the china is found in Archie Butt's *Taft and Roosevelt, The Intimate Letters of Archie Butt, Military Aide* (Garden City, New York: Doubleday, 1930), volume 1, page 113. In a letter to his sister, dated June 9, 1909, he writes: "The Hayes china is about as ugly as it is possible for china to be. Mrs. ——, who was Lucy Hayes called on Mrs. More [Mrs. Hayes's daughter was named Fannie, and Mrs. Louis More was Mrs. William Howard Taft's sister who often assisted her at the White House] at the White House the other day and remarked that when her mother had chosen this same china, they all thought it wonderful, but she would not be willing to purchase it for herself now. You have seen the same china about that time; I remember it. Every dish and plate covered with cheaply and badly painted fish, birds, flowers, all in colors which changed as a rule after burning." A newspaper article in the *New York Daily Graphic,* July 7, 1880, page 35, described Mrs. Hayes as "exhibiting her new treasure with all the zest of a child delighted with a rich Christmas present."

225. *New York Tribune,* August 1, 1879.

226. *New York Tribune,* November 6, 1880. This review in Davis's scrapbook bears this note in his handwriting: "Geo. W. Curtis has it that Clarence Cook né Thomas Tomahawk [wrote the review]. The above resulted in his being dropped from the New York Tribune." Davis also drew inspiration from the English, as a private collection has a teacup and saucer using the bamboo ring and tea leaves on the saucer and a stem and tea leaves as the cup handle making an almost identical cup to the one used in the White House service. This cup has an English registry mark with the date 1873.

227. *Harper's Weekly,* August 12, 1876, page 654.

228. "Ceramic Art at the Exhibition," *Lippincott's Magazine,* volume 18 (July to December 1876).

229. *Nation Magazine,* October 31, 1878.

230. *Louisville Courier Journal,* December 23, 1880. Copy in the social affairs scrapbook, The Rutherford B. Hayes Library, Fremont, Ohio, volume 116, page 113.

231. Op. cit. (note 205).

232. Abby Gunn Baker papers, Office of the Curator of the White House.

233. Newspaper clipping in the Frank G. Carpenter Collection, Smithsonian Institution's National Museum of History and Technology, Division of Political History, written on May 31 (1889?) by a special correspondent to the (Cleveland?) *Press.* The article is an interview with Mrs. Benjamin Harrison concerning housekeeping in the Executive Mansion.

234. Op. cit. (note 205).

235. NA-MTA, account 229124, voucher 83. R.W. stands for Royal Worcester, A.D./after dinner.

236. Report of the Chief of Engineers, U.S. Army, 1901; appendix DDD., page 3745, inventory of the

public property in the Executive Mansion, June 30, 1901.

237. NA-MTA, account 233637, voucher 45.

238. NA-MTA, account 245776, voucher 4.

239. NA-MTA, account 243322, voucher 16.

240. Op. cit. (note 238).

241. National Archives, Records of the Office of Public Buildings and Grounds, letter book 6, entry 171.

242. NA-MTA, account 255949, voucher 3.

243. When Theodore Davis took out the patent for marketing the Hayes china to the general public, he redesigned the seafood salad plate so that it was more like the other pieces in the set.

244. National Archives, Records of the Office of Public Buildings and Grounds, letters-sent book, volume 6, 1886, and letters-received entries 177, 180, 252, 264, 650, 651, 664, 672, 696, 738, 741, 913 contain accounts of the transaction between Colonel Wilson and Haviland and Company concerning the order.

245. NA-MTA, account 264544, voucher 30.

246. Paul Putzki was born March 9, 1858, in Germany near Breslau, close to the Polish border. While the name is of Polish origin, the immediate family was German. Putzki came to America as a young man of twenty-two to a job he had been promised as a decorator in a china factory in East Liverpool, Ohio. He stayed there a few years and then went to Chicago where he opened a studio. In one of his classes was a Mrs. P. B. Ware, a wealthy woman from Richmond, Indiana, who persuaded him to go once a week to Richmond and teach a class there. Among those in the class was Mrs. Benjamin Harrison. When her husband was elected president, Mrs. Harrison persuaded Putzki to come to Washington, where he located his studio in the old Metzerott Building at 1110 F Street, N.W. He died in Washington on February 25, 1936. This information was provided in a letter to this writer, dated April 27, 1971, from Dr. Paul Putzki, his son, who lives in the Washington, D.C., area.

247. *Carp's Washington,* edited by Frances Carpenter. New York: McGraw-Hill, 1960.

248. *China, Glass and Lamps,* volume 2, number 13 (September 9, 1891).

249. Margaret W. Brown (Klapthor). *The Dresses of the First Ladies of the White House in the United States National Museum.* Washington, D.C.: Smithsonian Institution, 1951.

250. Original letter of Mrs. William Schiffler, 1968, in the Office of the Curator of the White House.

251. *China, Glass and Lamps,* volume 3, number 2 (January 13, 1892).

252. National Archives, letter book of the Office of the Commissioner of Public Buildings and Grounds, entry 56, June–October 1891.

253. M. W. Beveridge first appears in the city directory of Washington, D.C. in 1879; the last entry appears in 1899.

254. NA-MTA, account 288960, voucher 18.

255. NA-MTA, account 293945, voucher 17.

256. National Archives, letter book of the commissioner of public buildings and grounds, entry 681, April 2–August 9, 1892.

257. NA-MTA, account 294899, voucher 14.

258. NA-MTA, account 300080, voucher 28.

259. NA-MTA, account 302209, voucher 20. The "F.C." referred to is probably the F. Cartlidge and Co. china which used the mark "F.C.," between 1889–1904. "R.W." stands for Royal Worcester.

260. National Archives, Records of the Office of Public Buildings and Grounds, letter book, volume 65, page 344.

261. Op. cit. (note 236).

262. Abby Gunn Baker papers, Office of the Curator of the White House.

263. Op. cit. (note 236), June 30, 1907.

264. National Archives, Records of the Office of Public Buildings and Grounds, "Itemized Expenditures for the Care, Repair and Furnishings of the Executive Mansion" for 1898, 1899, and 1900.

265. National Archives, Records of the Office of Public Buildings and Grounds; letters-sent book, entry 41/3.

266. Ibid., entry 844/1.

267. Op. cit. (note 264).

268. Op. cit. (note 236).

269. *China, Glass and Lamps,* volume 13, number 26 (June 7, 1897), pages 15 and 16.

270. Edwin Atlee Barber, *Pottery and Porcelain of the United States* (New York: G. P. Putnam's Sons, 1893), page 203.

271. National Archives, Records of the Office of Public Buildings and Grounds; letters sent, entry 426.

272. *Crockery and Glass Journal,* December 1, 1898, page 15.

273. Op. cit. (note 271); letters sent, entry 1059/1,2.

274. Ibid.; letters sent, entry 618.

275. Unidentified newspaper article of November 20, 1902. Copy in the Smithsonian Institution's National Museum of History and Technology, Division of Political History files.

276. *The Clay Record,* October 30, 1902, page 15.

277. Letter from William A. Billington, museum curator, Wedgwood, Barleston, Stoke-on-Trent, England, dated September 23, 1971, in the Smithsonian Institution's National Museum of History and Technology, Division of Political History files.

278. Copy of registry papers from The Patent Office, Designs Branch, 25, Southampton Buildings, Chancery Lane, London, W.C. England. Courtesy of William A. Billington.

279. Letter from William A. Billington (see note 277). Mr. Billington points out in this letter that the present-day Wedgwood production called "Colonnade" is based on the same design as the x5333 "Ulunda" pattern of 1902.

280. *China, Glass and Pottery Review,* volume 11, number 3 (October 1902), page 34.

281. National Archives, War Department Record, letter book of the commissioner of public buildings and grounds, entry 1059/4/5.

282. NA-MTA, account 32386, voucher 85.

283. The United States Patent Office, Design Files, design 36363, patented June 16, 1903.

284. NA-MTA, account 32386, voucher 4. The oyster plates ordered with this service were shallow bowls for oyster stew rather than plates molded to serve raw oysters.

285. National Archives, letter book of the commissioner of public buildings and grounds, entry 1059/9/.

286. Ibid., entry 1059/10. There is a note in red ink concerning payment.

287. Ibid., entry 1059/12/19.

288. NA-MTA, account 4767, voucher 36, April 21, 1908.

289. Report of the Chief of Engineers, U.S. Army, 1908 (Washington, D.C.: Government Printing Office, 1909), page 2482. The inventory gives the voucher number for the January order as 56, dated February 15, 1908. After the death of M. W. Beveridge in 1899, the firm of M. W. Beveridge was left to Beveridge's half-brother, Horace Dulin, and to William Martin who was an old and trusted employee. The firm was in business in Washington, D.C., at various addresses until the 1930s when the Great Depression forced the Dulin, Martin Company out of business. This information was kindly furnished in interviews in 1971 with Mrs. Horace Dulin and Wellstood White, former sales manager of the firm of Dulin, Martin.

290. Archie Butt, *Taft and Roosevelt, The Intimate Letters of Archie Butt, Military Aide* (Garden City, New York: Doubleday, 1930), volume 1, pages 8–9.

291. NA-MTA, account 16827, voucher 28, November 7, 1910.

292. National Archives, letter book of the commissioner of public buildings and grounds, volume 27. Copies of the correspondence between William Mitchell Kendell, Col. William W. Harts, Col. C. S. Ridley, and Tiffany and Company will be found under the following entry numbers: 192, 194–197, 199, 204, 213–217, 220, 226, 229, 230, 232, 234–238.

293. News release on the Wilson china prepared by Abby Gunn Baker for the White House for October 13, 1918. Abby Gunn Baker papers, Office of the Curator of the White House.

294. Mrs. Edith Bolling Wilson, *My Memoir* (Indianapolis and New York: Bobbs-Merrill, 1938), page 313.

295. National Archives, letter book of the commissioner of public buildings and grounds, volume 27, numbers 246–248.

296. NA-MTA, account 58310, voucher 106; and account 64106, voucher 84. The "oyster plate (soup)" is a more shallow bowl than the regular soup bowl. The cocktail cups are shaped like the ramekins, but are larger and were probably used for seafood cocktails.

297. Article in *The Washington Star,* October 20, 1918, "First American Made China for the White House" by Abby Gunn Baker.

298. *The Evening Star* and *The Washington Post,* Washington, D.C., of November 20, 1934.

299. *Washington Daily News,* December 4, 1934.

300. Department of the Interior, National Capital Parks, voucher 978388, bureau voucher 463, October 10, 1934.

301. Op. cit. (note 299).

302. *The Evening Star,* Washington, D.C., January 25, 1935.

303. J. K. Thomson, "The White House China Room," *The Antiques Journal,* volume 16, number 7 (July 1961), pages 8–11.

304. Department of the Interior, National Capital Parks, bureau voucher 28–267, December 13, 1951.

Note that this order did not include the oatmeal bowl found in the earlier state services made by Lenox.

305. *The Washington Post,* April 4, 1952.

306. Department of the Interior, National Capital Parks, voucher 138797, bureau voucher 28–287.

307. White House memo, dated January 11, 1966, from Mrs. Bess Abell to Mrs. Johnson. The Lyndon Baines Johnson Library.

308. Remarks of Mrs. Lyndon B. Johnson at the White House reception for the unveiling of the new White House china, May 9, 1968.

309. Letter from Mrs. Johnson to Mayor Anthony Holberton-Wood, associate manager, International Department of Tiffany and Company, June 28, 1967. Copy in the Lyndon Baines Johnson Library.

310. Press release, May 9, 1968, the White House, Office of the Press Secretary to Mrs. Johnson.

311. Ibid.

312. Ibid., November 8, 1967.

313. Letter from Mayor Anthony Holberton-Wood, Tiffany and Company, to Mrs. Bess Abell, the White House, December 4, 1967. Lyndon Baines Johnson Library.

314. Letter from Mrs. Bess Abell, the White House, to Mayor Anthony Holberton-Wood, Tiffany and Company, February 8, 1968.

Appendixes

Appendix I
The White House
Porcelain Service 1879.

*Reprint of the publication
by Haviland & Company
on the Rutherford B. Hayes
state dinner service*

Reproduced from a copy in the Office
of the Curator of the White House.

THE

WHITE HOUSE

PORCELAIN SERVICE.

✤

DESIGNS BY AN AMERICAN ARTIST,

ILLUSTRATING EXCLUSIVELY

AMERICAN FAUNA AND FLORA.

✤

1879.

The varied character of the subjects illustrated, and the novel features in the decoration of china that were introduced by the designer of the porcelain service for the Executive Mansion, rendered it necessary to provide this descriptive work to accompany the set.

The scientific names of the flora and fauna represented have been carefully revised by Profs. Spencer F. Baird, Elliott Coues, and Theo. Gill, of the Smithsonian Institute.

The formal delivery of the service at the White House was made by Haviland & Co., to Col. T. L. Casey, Commissioner of Public Buildings and Grounds, on June 30th, 1880.

The duplicate autograph sets will be precisely the same as the service made expressly for the White House, with the omission of the eagle and coat of arms, which is one of the decorations of the back of the first set.

HAVILAND & CO.

45 Barclay Street, New-York.

THE

WHITE HOUSE
PORCELAIN SERVICE.

1879.

———·:✳·:———

DESIGNS BY AN AMERICAN ARTIST,

ILLUSTRATING EXCLUSIVELY AMERICAN FAUNA AND FLORA.

———·:✳·:———

THE existence of kaoline, of superior quality, and in inexhaustible quantities, taken in connection with other advantages, induced David Haviland, an American merchant and founder of the house of Haviland & Co., to locate his potteries for the manufacture of hard china in Limoges, France.

At the Centennial Exhibition, Haviland & Co. made the most notable display of Porcelain and Faience, and later, at the Paris Exposition, received the Gold Medal and Cross of the Legion of Honor.

In the spring of 1879, an order was given to Haviland & Co. to furnish the Executive Mansion at Washington with a dinner service, which, as it was to be used only for state occasions, the President's wife desired should combine elegance and appropriate American decoration. The time specified for the completion of the set was limited, and the obstacles to be overcome unprecedented, and its successful production would involve innumerable trials of color; added to this, no European artist was known who was conversant with a wide range of American subjects, and their appropriate use for the decoration of porcelain.

Mr. Theodore Haviland requested the aid of his friend Theodore R. Davis, who undertook the invention of shapes and the production of water-color studies, which Haviland & Co. have reproduced in china.

Mr. Davis possessed the artistic skill, and a knowledge as essential as it was remarkable. Professional duty, and a love of adventure, had led him to study the native flora and fauna in every part of the country. He had fished in the rivers of the East and West and in the sea, hunted fowl and wild game in the forests, the swamps and the mountains; shot the buffalo on the plains, and visited the historic haunts of the Indians in the East; met the Indians in their wigwams, and studied their habits on the prairies of the far West.

The artist selected a unique atelier. The novelty of the studio induced Haviland & Co. to request him to furnish a water-color drawing of the place, which we introduce with the fruit series, where it is quite fully described. The location was chosen because of its convenience to subjects both from sea, field and forest, and its isolation prevented the intrusion of visitors.

In presenting the service to the public, we desire to make some statements which seem to be important to enable a just criticism of it. The designs were made in water-color, and although in nearly every instance they were bold and striking, they were difficult to reproduce perfectly upon porcelain, with hard mineral color. And to successfully accomplish this, it was necessary to invent new methods, and to have recourse to peculiar mechanical appliances.

We coincided with the artist in the opinion that a high degree of finish should not be attempted in every plate, fearing the sacrifice of breadth and tone which he deemed necessary to the general effect of the series, when arranged upon the table. This was undoubtedly correct, for some of the plates, when examined singly, lose a part of their attractiveness, but the same plates, when placed upon the table, will not seem inferior to others, which may have been separately examined to more advantage. Another result thus obtained is the absence of the feeling of timidity noticeable in most examples of fine porcelain, where a high degree of finish is the principle feature of the decoration. It must not be inferred that we believe that coarse, inartistic drawing and design could ever compete with refined work, but we do insist that a plate, when decorated with a strong, firm drawing, closely studied from nature, which tells clearly the story of the subject, will attract more attention and be productive of more enjoyment than the plate which has great beauty of finish, but lacks the qualities noted above.

The artists engaged in the production of this set, and the special work performed by each, were:

THEODORE R. DAVIS	*New York*	Designer.
BRACQUEMOND	*Auteuil*	Etcher.
TOCHUM	*Auteuil*	Chromiste.
VALENTINE	*Paris*	Engraver.
LISSAC	*Limoges*	Painter.
CHADAL	*Limoges*	Manufacturer.
GOURMAULT	*Paris*	Modeler.
VALETTE	*Limoges*	Modeler.
CHARLES RICROCH	*Limoges*	Decorator.
LAMBERT	*Sevres*	Painter.
BARBARIN	*Limoges*	Painter.
LAFOREST	*Limoges*	Painter.
HAYON	*Limoges*	Painter.
DUCLAIR	*Limoges*	Painter.
DOMINIQUE	*Limoges*	Painter.
MLLE. ANNA DARDAUD	*Limoges*	Gilder.

The composition of the set is as follows:

A SPECIAL OYSTER PLATE.

SOUP.

A plate designed for this course, and decorated with twelve subjects:

MOUNTAIN LAUREL *(Kalmia)*.	TOMATO.
THE BLUE CRAB.	GREEN TURTLE.
AMERICAN SOUP OF THE XV. CENTURY.	SOUTHWARD FLIGHT OF DUCKS.
	CLAM BAKE.
PALMETTO CABBAGE.	FROG ("SONG OF SPRING").
HARVEST MOON, MAIZE.	1776.
	OKRA.

THE FISH SERIES

Is composed of twelve subjects, which decorate plates shaped expressly for this course, and a platter which exhibits a careful study of

THE SHAD.

RED SNAPPER.	STRIPED BASS.
SPANISH MACKEREL.	FRESH-WATER LOBSTER.
SMELT.	POMPANO.
TERRAPIN.	BROOK PIKE (TROUT PIKE).
SPECKLED TROUT.	BLUE-FISH.
BLACK BASS.	SHEEP'S-HEAD.

THE DINNER SERIES

Embraces twelve illustrations, beside the Platter: the subjects are

THE WILD TURKEY.

THE MAY-FLOWER (TRAILING ARBUTUS).	PECCARIES.
	BIG HORN (ROCKY MOUNTAIN SHEEP).
BEAR IN A BEE TREE.	
MULE DEER.	ANTELOPE, PRONG HORN.
BUFFALO *(Bison)*.	FLOATING FOR DEER.
COON IN A PERSIMMON TREE.	CRANES' WALK 'ROUND.
CHICKENS IN A GARDEN.	ON THE PLAINS AT NIGHT.

THE GAME COURSE

Is supplied with a novel Platter.   The series consists of twelve subjects.

"ON CHESAPEAKE BAY."

THE CANVAS-BACK DUCK.	WILD PIGEON.
RAIL, "SORA."	TEAL DUCK.
PTARMIGAN'S BATH.	YELLOW-LEGGED SNIPE.
RUFFED GROUSE.	RICE, OR REED BIRD.
BOB WHITE.	THE WOODCOCK.
CALIFORNIA QUAIL.	PINNATED GROUSE.

THE DESSERT OR FRUIT PLATE

Is of special design, and the twelve illustrations are :

CHINCAPIN NUT.	HUCKLEBERRY.
PECAN NUT.	PERSIMMON.
PAPAW.	OHIO GOLDEN-ROD.
LOCUST.	BALTIMORE ORIOLE, AND VIRGINIA CREEPER.
MOCKING BIRD.	
MAPLE SUGAR.	STUDIO.
CONCORD GRAPE.	

AN AFTER-DINNER COFFEE CUP,

Of novel form.

A TEA-CUP

Expressly designed for this set.

AN INDEPENDENT BUTTER PLATE.

The account appended contains an interesting and detailed description of each plate.   It is compiled from letters that were received with each design, and from note-books used by Mr. Davis during years of a most eventful life.   The wide range of subjects, and the acute knowledge evinced, will indicate the amount of study which the designs for the Presidential service necessitated.

THE OYSTER PLATE

(Ostrea Virginica)

Will be an acceptable innovation. The rich effect of the design is enhanced by the method adopted in its manufacture. The colors are laid upon the china clay under the glaze. China, color and glaze are fired at the same time, producing an effect and integrity of color which is pleasant to the eye and as durable as the porcelain itself.

Five Blue-Point oyster shells cover the principal surface of the plate; beyond these is portrayed a cluster of the raccoon oysters, which are so well known in the Southern Atlantic States. Sprays of sea-weed cluster about these, and serve for decoration about the Blue-Point shells. The background offers a glimpse of the ocean.

The plate is not so large as the one ordinarily used for this course.

SOUP.—MOUNTAIN LAUREL.

(Kalmia Latifolia.)

The soup plate is modeled from the Kalmia flower, the mountain laurel, so well known and admired throughout the Atlantic States.

The shape is more that of a ten-sided angular bowl than of a plate, since the contour conforms to the natural base and edges of the laurel flower. The outside surface is delicately enriched with gold. The rays which compose the base are decorated with a light green color. *Each plate of this series has a separate design for the interior.* The Kalmia flower is selected as one of the subjects, a cluster of these flowers being the principal feature of the picture.

CRAB.

(Collinectes postatus.)

The richly tinted blue crab, so abundant along the Atlantic coast of the United States, is peculiar to America, and valued for table use. The European or green crab, a distinct species, is of different form, and though common along the coast of New England, it is seldom used for food, even by fishermen. The blue crab undergoes a curious change when seeking sequestered waters. It sheds its shell and becomes the soft-shell crab, so well known and appreciated by epicures in the United States.

The design is rich in color,—a picturesque coast scene, into which a magnificent blue crab is introduced as the principal feature of the foreground.

AMERICAN SOUP OF THE XVth CENTURY.

The design represents an Indian reclining upon a ledge of rocks, his calumet convenient to his hand, and his bow-case, which is made from the skin of a spotted fawn, is thrown carelessly beside him. To the right, the deer which he has slain indicates the material of which the soup is to be composed; from the circular opening of a cavity in the rock steam arises; near the pot-hole lie blackened stones used to heat the water. Beyond the ledge is seen the edge of a fall, the mist arising from which is tinged with a delicate rainbow. Spruce and hemlock trees form the background. The top of the design is clouded with the smoke from the fire used to heat the stones. These pot-holes are to be seen in the ledge rocks of the coast, and in similar formations in the interior of the United States.

Sabbattus, an old Iroquois Indian, said that it was a legend that his ancestors used these holes to boil their meat, make medicine, and grind their corn. A fire was built to heat stones, which made the water in the pot-holes boil.

PALMETTO CABBAGE.

(Chamærops palmetto.)

The palmetto cabbage-tree is the only known wood of which wharves in the Southern States can be built in salt water to withstand the destructive work of the "teredo," the sea-worm, which bores away a ship's bottom in a few months, if unprotected by copper.

The terminal bud of the young tree resembles the stalky part of a cabbage-head, and is cooked and eaten in the same way. The removal of the cabbage involves the destruction of the tree. The palmetto cabbage-tree grows near the sea-coast, south of Cape Fear.

The scene represents Charleston Harbor, Fort Sumter, Charleston and Fort Moultrie, which, originally constructed of palmetto logs, successfully withstood the British fleet in the Revolutionary war. The tree is on Morris Island, a short distance in front of the old Swamp Angel Battery.

THE HARVEST MOON.

One of Mr. Davis's peculiarly American subjects introduces maize, or Indian corn *(Zea mays)*. Pumpkin-vines twine among the hills of corn, and the chief material for that favorite American tart or *pie*, the pumpkin, is scattered about the ground. The scene is illumined by the autumnal moon that is known in nearly all countries within the temperate zone as the "harvest moon." Farmers noted the peculiarities of the September moon before scientists.

The moon usually rises about fifty minutes later on each succeeding night. The harvest moon, when full, rises for several nights with but twenty minutes difference in time. The days and nights are then of nearly equal length, and the sunset tinge has not faded from the western sky before the harvest moon gives light to the husbandman.

The October moon is known as the "hunters' moon."

TOMATO.

(Solanum lycopersicum.)

There is little doubt of the indigenous character of this accept-able vegetable, which had been cultivated in Peru, upon the table-lands of Mexico, and undoubtedly within the present limits of the United States, previous to the arrival of Europeans upon the American continent. In common with other vegetables and fruits, the tomato has been greatly improved by intelligent culture, both in Europe and America. The Aztec name was *jic* tomato.

Illustrating this subject, the artist shows a log-house situated in a mountain country, where the summer is too short to ripen the tomatoes upon the vine, from which they are culled in season to prevent their destruction by the early frost. An incident which took place in the sea-side studio involves an interesting description of this plate. Among the welcome visitors to the studio was a naval officer, whose life from boyhood had been spent either by the sea-shore or upon the ocean, and his knowledge of all things pertaining thereto was greatly appreciated by the artist. On this particular morning, among other subjects that Mr. Davis had upon his drawing-boards were the pictures of the American soup of the fifteenth century and "The Tomato." "The XVth Century" was warmly commended, "for," remarked the captain, "you can have no idea of the interest which this subject will attract; it carries me back to the days when we youngsters filled the pot-holes in the rocks at Stony Point, on the Connecticut shore, with the salt water from the ocean, and heating it with hot stones, we boiled mussels and had an Indian dance; in fact, we were playing Indian. But this other design, 'The Tomato,' although it pleases me as a picture, seems so absolutely impossible that I am tempted to ask that it should not be included in the designs for the White House." At this moment another visitor entered; it was Professor H———, who, after a hasty glance at the drawings, pointed to that of the tomato, and turning to the artist, said: "I must shake hands with you on this most successful design. I was born in a house like that, and the scene is so familiar that I can almost see myself, a barefooted boy, hastening to take those unripe tomatoes from that old slab, upon which they had been sunning, among the milk-pans; even the old spruce-trees seem familiar friends."

A hearty laugh from the captain answered the professor's commendation, and the naval officer insisted that this particular design should not be omitted from the package to be sent to Europe the following day. "For," said he, "my lore is salt water. The professor has taught astronomical facts of such importance that I must defer to him. His delight in the design renders it more acceptable than the novel 'XVth Century.'"

GREEN TURTLE.

(Chelonia Mydas.)

The green turtle is unknown in European waters, but this cannot be said of turtle soup, which is popularly supposed to be the normal diet of London aldermen.   The turtles are taken from the West Indies and Florida alive to Europe, and to the northern cities of the United States.   Although the West Indies and Florida reefs are their true homes, occasional specimens of the green turtle are captured as far north as Sandy Hook, at the entrance of New-York harbor.   The turtle visits the shore of the Florida reefs for the purpose of depositing its eggs in the sand, usually selecting moonlight nights.   It is at this time that hundreds of them are captured by simply turning them on their backs, leaving them to be removed at the convenience of the hunter.   Turtles are taken weighing five hundred pounds.

We take from the London *Times* the following concise description of the design: "The green turtle is on a Florida reef, crawling between the ribs of an old wreck, which is stranded. The moon is shedding a mellow light which tinges the waves, and the moss on the wreck and the phosphorescence of the waves give life to the drawing."

SOUTHWARD FLIGHT.

During the month of October, the flight of ducks to the south is a familiar sight along the sea-board States, north of the capes of the Delaware. A flight composed of Canvas-back, Red-heads and Widgeon pass ; next a group of Sheldrake, all of these flying close to the surface of the ocean, and just beyond gun-shot from the beach. At a great height above, the "honk" of geese is heard. Not only by day, but by the light of the "hunters' moon," this same procession wings toward the south, leaving the chilly north for a more congenial climate.

CLAM-BAKE AND CHOWDER.

A scene on the Connecticut shore of Long Island Sound. An excursion steamer appears in the distance. Smoke curls from the fire in the foreground, where a chowder party has under way a clam-bake and a kettle of chowder. It is said of Daniel Webster that he was as clever in making chowder as in fulminating oratorical thunder. His method was as follows: Put your slices of clear pork into the pot and fry brown; remove the meat, leaving the fat; in this put a thin layer of broken pilot-bread crackers; then a layer of sliced potatoes; then thin-sliced onions and a few slices of tomatoes, covering all with a layer of chopped clams; season with ground cloves, mace, thyme, red and black pepper and salt. Begin again with the crackers, and proceed in the same manner until the material is used up or the chowder is large enough to answer the requirements of the com-

pany. Pour over all the liquor of the clams. Increase the heat slowly until the kettle boils, leaving it in that state for forty minutes or an hour; before serving add a few slices of lemon and two glasses of sherry.

The process of the clam-bake is more primitive : Hollow out a place in the sand and pave the bottom and sides with stones; build a hot hard-wood fire thereon, which should burn down to coals and ashes; if the hot enough to convert water into steam, begin a layer of sea-weed on the ashes; next make a layer of the shell, placed with the mouth down; then layer of sea-weed; on this may be placed a layer of green corn, spring chickens, or any other delicacy which it is desired to add. Cover all thickly with sea-moss and pack closely; then leave the whole to bake, with no fear of the viands being overdone.

In the early history of the Plymouth colony, the clam *(Venus mercenaria)* was more than once the sole source of sustenance to the people. The Indian name for the hard-shell is quahaug, and from the shell was made the wampum, a specie currency of the aborigines. The clam-bake is usually attended by gentlemen only, although ladies in the cities of Boston, Mass., and Providence, R. I., occasionally arrange clam-bakes and invite gentlemen to participate.

THE FROG.

(Rana fontinalis.)

This merry amphibian of North America is represented in as happy a situation as he could ask, for he is seen seated on the broad leaf of a pond-lily, croaking his *"song of spring"* in the midst of an April shower.   His first appearance in soup in this country, if the story is to be relied upon, was on the occasion of Count D'Estaing's visit to Boston.   The commander of the French fleet and his officers were entertained at dinner by a generous patriot, who, having learned that Frenchmen were very fond of frogs, prepared a surprise for them.   He sent boys into the neighboring marshes to get the biggest bull-frogs they could catch, and the enterprising boys brought back more than one for each guest. Not many minutes after the soup was served, each horrified guest was holding up an enormous bull-frog by his hind leg, and begging to be excused from further acquaintance with the soup.

The original of this novel subject was captured from a spring near the Sunset Lake, in Asbury Park, and became so tame that the artist's children would call him to lunch upon flies caught for that purpose.

1776.

This interesting design presents the hearth-stone of a New England home, with its capacious fire-place and swinging crane, the Dutch oven and old-time clock. Some "willow" plates ornament the shelf, and above is suspended a flint-lock rifle, powder-horn and bullet-pouch. A few potatoes, which have been roasted in the ashes, are seen upon the hearth.

It is not generally known that the potato is native to America, but of this there is no doubt. It is still found in its wild state in the Peruvian island San Lorenzo, and in the mountains near Quito, the capital of Ecuador, from which country it was brought to Spain, and later it was also carried to Ireland, from Virginia, by colonists sent out by Sir Walter Raleigh, in the latter part of the sixteenth century. Raleigh cultivated the potato on his estate near Cork,

and it was from this source that it was distributed throughout
Ireland and England, with the express purpose of preventing
famine, especially among the inhabitants of the first-named country.
The introduction of the potato into France was due to the persist-
ence of one of the medical staff of the army, who noted, while a
prisoner of war, its valuable qualities.   He was ridiculed, but
obtained the patronage of Louis XVI., who set apart a tract of
crown land for experimental purpose; blossoms from the potato
vine were worn by the King in his button-hole, thus attracting
attention, which made it necessary to set guards about the field.
These being withdrawn at night afforded an opportunity for the
theft of the potatoes when ripe—a performance that afforded Antoine
Parmentier great delight, being convinced that a thorough distri-
bution of the seed had been accomplished.

OKRA.

The origin of the okra plant *(Abelmoschus esculentus)*, so well known throughout the United States, cannot be definitely stated. It is credited to the East as well as to the West Indies, but the evidence is strong that it originated in the latter, and that it was certainly known in America at a very early date. The pod is used in the composition of the favorite American soup known as gumbo. Chicken is the usual base of this delicious soup.

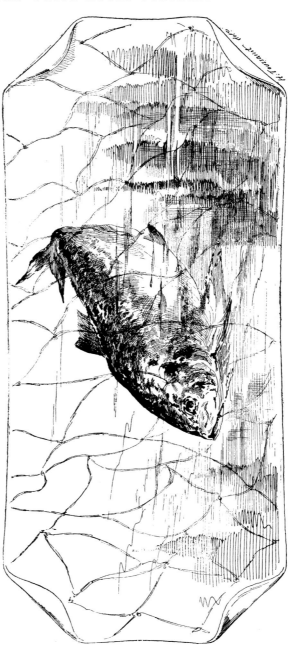

FISH.—THE SHAD.

(Alosa sapidissima.)

The platter which accompanies the fish series is novel in form, being rectangular, with the corners rolled and enriched with gold. The decoration of the plate is bold and original. A magnificent shad is struggling to free itself from the meshes of a net in which it has become entangled. The cords of the net are in gold, and cover the entire surface of the dish.

The American shad is highly prized as food. It makes its appearance in the southern rivers flowing into the Atlantic Ocean as early as January, and as the vast schools journey northward the fish improve both in size and flavor. The shad taken in the Hudson and Connecticut rivers are considered superior to all others. The shad proceed as far north as the British Provinces, ascending the rivers for the purpose of depositing their spawn in fresh water, returning to the ocean during the months of July and August. It has been for years the custom to send to the President of the United States the first shad taken from the waters of the Potomac river. It is quite unusual to take shad in the vicinity of New-York during the winter months. A number of fine specimens have, however, been taken this winter by the fishermen, in nets which they had set for other fish in New-York bay.

The female shad usually commands a higher price than a male fish of equal weight, although the flesh of the male is superior to that of the roe, or female shad. Species of shad, differing from and inferior to the American shad, are found in some of the rivers of Europe.

The form of the service plate for fish is derived from the scallop shell, two of which are combined to form the plate, the larger shell being designed for the dish, and the smaller receiving the decoration. By this arrangement, the painted surface is not hidden from view when the plate is in use. The tone color of the principal shell varies to correspond with that of the decorated shell.

RED SNAPPER.

(Lutjanus Blackfordii.)

A popular sea fish found along the south Atlantic coast of the United States; and although it has been for years an acceptable table fish, it was not until 1878 that it was classified, when Professor G. Brown Goode, of the Smithsonian Institute, Washington, D. C., named the fish Blackfordii, in honor of Eugene Blackford, Esq., one of the Fish Commissioners of New-York State. In color it is a brilliant crimson, and in the clear southern waters it can be seen to a considerable depth pursuing small fish. A favorite food of the Blackfordii is the young of the flying-fish. This fry is frequently designated the Butterfly.

Some authorities confound this fish with the grouper—both fish being of the same genus.

SPANISH MACKEREL.

(*Cybium maculatum.*)

This favorite American fish, now abundant during the warm summer months as far north as the coast of Long Island, was not known, a few years ago, north of the mouth of the Delaware river. The design represents the mackerel lying upon the beach near the surf. The footprints of children are seen in the sand, accounting for the writing thereon.

SMELT.

(Osmerus mordax.)

A choice breakfast fish, which enters the rivers of the Northern and Middle States during the winter, and is taken in great numbers through the ice. The fish seldom exceed six ounces in weight.

The smelt from the Raritan river, New Jersey, is very small in size, and seldom found in market. The Raritan smelt is regarded as unequaled. Fishermen will point out a resemblance to Washington's portrait in the markings which are visible in the nearly transparent head of this fish.

Two distinct varieties of the smelt are believed to exist in American waters. These differ from the European specimens.

TERRAPIN.

The diamond back or salt-water terrapin *(Malaclemmys palustris)* is abundant in the salt marshes of the Atlantic coast, where it is found along the shores of the Middle and Southern States. It is an expert swimmer, and captures its food with surprising rapidity. The States of Delaware and Maryland furnish the principal supply. Terrapin is most appreciated during the winter months, at which season it is in its most perfect condition. It hibernates during this season of the year, burying itself in the soft bottoms of the marshes.

The terrapin is so highly prized as a delicacy that efforts have been made to introduce it in European waters.

SPECKLED TROUT.

This is the epicure's own, the speckled beauty of the spring brooks, the *Salodinus fontinalis.*   They vary in size, usually from half a pound to three pounds, though speckled trout weighing four and a half pounds have been caught in the Adirondack waters.   The attempt to naturalize this trout in Europe met with indifferent success.   In the picture, one of the sprightly tribe has come with a rush to the surface of a pond, and is jumping for a fly.   The color of a speckled trout, as well as its contour, depends greatly upon the character of the water in which it is found ; and partly with a view of exhibiting this fact, Fish Commissioner Blackford, of New-York State, arranged an exhibition which comprised specimens from various streams of the Rocky Mountains, from the waters of the Alleghanies, from the Adirondacks, from Maine, and from the British Provinces ; beside these were trout from many other States, and a large aquarium, containing trout of considerable size, which had been hatched artificially and regularly fed.   These tame trout, as they are called, become so familiar with the persons feeding them that they rush to the feeding point at a recognized signal.

BLACK BASS.

(Microfterus Salmoides.)

This vigorous fish, a favorite with sportsmen, originated in the waters west of the Alleghanies and Adirondack ranges of mountains. It has from these native waters been introduced into rivers and lakes of the States east of these ranges. It affords capital sport to the angler, and is an appreciated fish. The rapidity with which it multiplies and its rapid growth are astonishing. The Potomac river, which, above Washington, abounds with black bass, was stocked but a few years ago by a locomotive engineer, who brought a few specimens in the water-tank of his tender from a tributary of the Ohio river.

The upper shell is decorated with a fine bass swimming in the swift current of a clear stream. The bud of a pond-lily, which falls gracefully to the surface of the principal shell, characterizes it as a fresh-water fish.

STRIPED BASS.

(Roccus lineatus.)

Striped bass is taken in salt as well as fresh water. In the waters of the Potomac and Delaware rivers it is known as the "rock fish." The favorite fishing ground for the striped bass is along the coast of Rhode Island, where fish weighing as much as seventy-five pounds are taken with rod and reel. It makes its appearance in the rivers about the same time as the shad, but, unlike the shad, remains until early winter.

FRESH-WATER LOBSTER.

(*Cambarrus Bartonii.*)

Found in the water of sluices and tail-races of mills, and beneath stones in swift-running streams. In some parts of the United States it is regarded as a great delicacy—in other localities it finds no favor as food; it is, however, quite as acceptable for the table as its European namesake. In the picture, two of them are having a pitched battle, pugnacity being the fresh-water lobster's main characteristic. It is the cause of a new variety of school-boy mischief, the boys frequently catching two of these lobsters for the sake of seeing them fight.

Upon the occasion of a visit to Mr. Davis's studio, Mr. Theodore Haviland discovered the artist busily transferring this scene to his paper, and his models, as he explained, could not be kept from fighting; and, as he proposed to represent nature, he did not see how a picture of them could be made without showing them as gladiators. Their habit is nocturnal, and the tone of the design would indicate the twilight hour as the one selected for the duel.

POMPANO.

(Trachynotus Carolinus.)

This is a choice southern fish that is seldom caught north of the Delaware capes, where they were unknown a few years since. The full-grown fish weighs between five and six pounds. The design shows a fish-hawk hovering over the surf, watching a pompano on the sand, where the hawk has dropped its prey, having fastened its terrible claws into heavier booty than it could carry away. The fishermen at Asbury Park relate an incident of avenged rapacity that is probably not an unfrequent occurrence. A fish-hawk was seen to rise from the water with a good-sized blue-fish, which proved too great a burden; but owing to the peculiar fish-hook form of the hawk's talons, and since they were firmly set in the fish's flesh, the hawk could not let go, and was borne, as by a plummet, to the water and drowned. The fishermen manned a boat and captured the double prize.

THE PIKE.

The pike family, of which so many varieties are known in America, has comparatively few representatives in Europe. The brook pike *(Esox Americanus)*, which is the subject of this design, is known also as the grass or trout pike and Long Island pickerel. It rarely attains a size of more than eight inches in length. The color of the fish is the richest of any of the pike family. Its back is of dark green, the sides banded, and the fins are of orange-yellow, nearly approaching red. It is quick in its movements, and, lurking beneath the broad leaves of water plants, darts with surprising rapidity in pursuit of its food.

BLUE-FISH.

(Pomatomus saltatrix.)

The blue-fish is chasing the porgee *(Stenotomus argyrops)*, which he has bitten and purposes to eat.

This is the only fish that will turn on one when captured, and attempt to bite. During the summer months, blue-fish are taken in great numbers along the New Jersey, Long Island and New England coast. They seem to follow the northward journey of the ducks, but precede them in their return to southern waters. They frequently attain the weight of ten or twelve pounds, and occasional specimens are captured which weigh more than twenty pounds. In the early history of Massachusetts, mention is made of a large fish—the blue-fish—twenty of which would fill a barrel.

The porgee is known along the coast of New England as the scup, a name derived from the Indian name *miscup.*

SHEEP'S-HEAD.

The favorite resort of the sheep's-head *(Archosargus probatocephalus)* is the vicinity of wrecks and wharves which have become covered with barnacles and other shell-fish that abound in the waters of the South Atlantic States.   The teeth of the fish are of sufficient strength to crush shells of considerable thickness; even the roof of the mouth is paved, as it were, with great flat teeth. For the table, the sheep's-head is considered by some persons superior to the turbot of Europe.

It is one of the most timid fish known, and it is to the hook of the most quiet angler that the greatest number of fish will come.

The design shows the fish in the vicinity of a barnacle-covered palmetto log, and numerous small fish that await the fragments which they may obtain when the sheep's-head crushes the shell-fish.

A spray of sea-weed falls from the decorated shell to the shell beneath.

The exquisite drawing and delicate color to be noted in this very simple design show a close study of nature and admirable artistic appreciation of the laws of decoration.

DINNER.—WILD TURKEY,

(Meleagris gallopavo)

Which is the largest, and in plumage the most gorgeous of American game birds, is the decoration for a platter.　Upon the surface of the dish is painted a magnificent wild turkey, who struts through the light snow, upon which are seen delicate reflections from his rich-colored plumage.

A sunset sky, against which are sharply defined the forms of distant trees, composes the background for this most perfectly American dish.

The turkey is erroneously supposed by some persons to be a native of the East Indies.　It was not, however, known in Europe until the sixteenth century, when it was taken to England from America by one of Sebastian Cabot's officers; and so distinctively American was the wild turkey considered, that Benjamin Franklin urged its adoption as the national bird of the United States.　The tame turkey differs considerably from its wild progenitor; less brilliant in plumage, it has white mottles upon its feathers, and legs and beak of rusty color instead of the nearly crimson tint of the wild turkey, with which it mates readily and produces superior birds.

The form of the dinner plate is coupe, surrounded by a narrow rim, and will be found a convenient dish for service, and also for decorative purposes.　*The shape of the plate is unusual, and was made expressly for this series.*

The twelve illustrations are vigorous in subject, drawing and color, presenting in themselves a very unique and interesting collection.

THE MAY-FLOWER.

(Epigæa repens.)

The May-flower plate shows a cluster of trailing arbutus, the much-loved flower of New England.

It grows near the ocean as well as in the woods, perfuming the mossy banks and pine woods.

The leaves blemish at the time of flowering, and the surface of the leaf is peculiar.

The design is completed by the introduction of a spray of the wild American lady-slipper.

We quote the following from Emerson, who says: " Often from beneath the edge of a snow-bank are seen rising the fragrant, pearly white or rose-colored, crowded flowers of this early harbinger of spring. It abounds in the edge of the woods about Plymouth, as elsewhere, and must have been the first flower to salute the storm-beaten crew, on the conclusion of their first terrible winter. Their descendants have thence piously derived its name, although its bloom is often passed before the coming of the month of May."

BEAR.

(Ursus Americanus.)

The black bear's fondness for honey frequently leads him into painful situations. This picture is called "A Bear in a Bee Tree." Bruin has disturbed a hive of wild bees, and been so violently assailed by what the Indian terms "the white man's fly" that he needs one paw to protect his face, while he hangs by the other from a friendly branch. It is maintained that the bear has the sense of the ridiculous. To all appearance, the bear that watches his companion's discomfiture from the mossy bank of the opposite side of a brook is indulging in mirth. The scene is located in a wild mountain gorge, through which are seen the dark clouds of a distant thunder-storm.

THE MULE DEER,

(Cariacus macrotis)

Which is so named by reason of the shape of its head and length of its ears. The study of the deer in this design was made from sketches in the artist's note-book, and from the head of a noble buck killed and set up by Mrs. Maxwell, the famous lady hunter and taxidermist of Colorado. The drawing represents the deer descending a snow-covered slope of the Rocky Mountains at sunrise.

BUFFALO.

Vast herds of buffalo *(Bison Americanus)*, or American bison, roam over the plains, led invariably by a splendid bull known among the hunters as the herd-leader. When the herd-leader becomes decrepit, he is driven out by the younger bulls to wander alone over the plains, and soon falls a prey to wolves *(Canis occidentalis)* and coyotes *(Canis latrans)*, which do not directly attack, but surround and harass until the bull falls from exhaustion.

The design pictures an old bull, with blood-shot eyes, in the last moments of defense. He stands knee-deep in the snow, which is still falling, surrounded by howling coyotes and gray wolves, who wait their prey.

The gray wolf is quite as powerful as its European cousin, but the American wolf is believed to be a distinct species, and seldom attacks man unless driven to do so by hunger. The coyote, a considerably smaller specimen, and the noisiest of all the wolf tribe, is very difficult to tame. Mr. Davis vainly attempted to establish friendly relations with some single member of a litter of eight, which he captured when they were no larger than small kittens. The artist believes all coyotes to be possessed of bad character and worse temper.

The antelope captured by the artist he tamed with but little difficulty; also numerous other animals which he secured upon the western plains.

RACCOON.

(*Procyon lotor.*)

Roasted 'coon is a dish not to be despised, and is a delicacy with the negroes of the South. Before the rebellion, when they were seldom allowed to carry fire-arms, they could hunt the 'coon with success. Their dogs would strike the trail of a 'coon in the corn-field, and, since the hunting was done in the night, the negroes followed with a pine-knot torch. The picture shows a 'coon in a persimmon-tree, on the edge of a corn-field. The glow of the torch and the bright eyes of the 'coon contrast strongly with the shadows of the night. The following is from a favorite negro song:

> " De 'coon he am above us,
> His meat am in de tree,
> We know he do not lub us,
> But fon' of him is we."

The raccoon is found throughout North America, but is more frequently met with in the Southern than in the Northern States. The flavor of its flesh somewhat resembles that of the pig. The food of the raccoon covers a wide range: oysters, birds, green-corn, frogs, rabbits and fish are alike acceptable to his palate. And the exceeding care of the animal to wash his food before eating it, and the pains that he takes to cleanse his paws after the repast, afford great amusement to the little folks, who delight to watch the movements of the pet 'coon which is usually to be found in the vicinity of " Uncle Tom's Cabin."

CHICKENS IN THE GARDEN.

This plate is appropriately called "dinner." The young Shanghai chicken is feasting upon ripe tomatoes that are quite out of the reach of two game chickens near him. The drawing is richly colored, and seems to be a study made in sunlight, and the design has so many features that interest and attract the beholder that it will certainly prove to be not the least pleasing of the dinner series.

COLLARED PECCARY.

(Dicotyles torquatus.)

The flesh of this wild pig of America is more delicate than that of the domestic hog, but it is necessary, after killing it, to immediately remove the dorsal gland, which contains a fluid that quickly permeates the flesh and renders it unpalatable. The peccary does not attain the size of the domestic hog. It is a dangerous adversary, defending itself successfully against wild beasts, and frequently forcing hunters to take refuge among the branches of trees.

Mr. Davis had once a narrow escape from a band of these brave little animals, and, in referring to this design, says that it is made from a sketch found in a note-book used by him during 1861.

It is in the States of Texas and Arkansas that the peccary chiefly abounds.

BIG-HORN.

The Rocky Mountain sheep or big-horn *(Ovis Montana)*, a name derived from the great horns which would be burdensome but for the compact form of the animal, that is known upon the eastern and western slopes of the Rocky Mountains, ranging farther to the north upon the Pacific than upon the Atlantic side. The color of the big-horn is a rich brown. That it will breed with domestic sheep and improve the quality of the wool is certain. This fact is not generally known. If space permitted, an interesting account substantiating the fact could be given.

The hunter has no more difficult game to pursue than the big-horn, which is not easy of approach and capable of accomplishing surprising leaps without injury to itself. It is unusual to obtain a shot at less than one hundred and fifty yards' distance, though instances are known where accident has afforded a close observation of the animal, without apparent timidity on its part at the presence of an *unarmed man*.

THE ANTELOPE, OR PRONG-HORN,

(*Antilocapra Americana*)

Somewhat resembles the chamois of the Alps. It has peculiarities which mark it as a distinct species. The hair, during the
winter, seems to be rather of a vegetable fiber that stands out
almost like quills. Antelopes are found in herds numbering
thousands. Each herd has its attendant band of coyotes, or
prairie wolves, waiting for the sick or maimed that may become
separated from the herd. The antelope is difficult of approach.

In the artist's note-book we find the following memorandum,
that seems of more than ordinary interest: " Spent two days with
Colonel Boone, a grandson of Daniel Boone, the pioneer of
Kentucky. My purpose being to study the form and habit of the

antelope, on the second day succeeded in approaching within fifty yards of a considerable herd, and, after nearly an hour's study of their movements, killed two at one shot with my rifle." Another interesting memorandum is the account of his capture and taming of a young antelope. Mounting upon his pony, he forced the fawn to run in a circle, until the little antelope was completely exhausted. He carried it to camp and placed it securely in his blankets. After a few days of gentle treatment, the young antelope was allowed his freedom, and became a pet with General Custer's command, and on one occasion made its appearance at an Indian council, where it nibbled the beads upon the Indians' robes, and astonished the wearers by its perfect familiarity with the officers present.

Hundreds of square miles of western plains of the United States are so thickly covered with cactus plant that the surface of the ground presents the appearance of a richly colored carpet. This is the "*Cactus bad land*." Beautiful to the eye, they are the *mauvaise terre* of the American plains to those journeying through them. Dogs cannot endure the suffering occasioned by the sharp points of the cactus, and are usually placed in the wagons during the march through the cactus lands. The doe antelope, aware of the safety of this harbor from the wolves, frequently seeks refuge there for her young.

FLOATING FOR DEER.

The American, or, as it is best known, the Virginia deer *(Cariacus Virginianus)*, is, next to the bison, the most valuable game of America.

The Indians met by early settlers were chiefly indebted to this beautiful animal for food, raiment, sinews for bow-strings, and the bottom of their snow-shoes, while the horns served for various implements.

The deer is still found in considerable numbers in the sea-board States of the Atlantic, and also throughout many of the Western and Southern States. In autumn its flesh is in the best condition for food.

The mode of hunting it depends upon the season of the year. During early summer months, floating is practiced.   The deer is then in his red coat, that is so thin as to afford but little protection from the swarms of black flies and mosquitoes; to escape these the deer resorts to the lakes, which abound in lily-pads and other food.

The hunters, usually two in number, occupy a light boat, in the bow of which is placed a short staff, surmounted by a semicircle of hemlock bark, arranged to reflect the light of two candles placed therein. This contrivance is known as a "jack"; by means of it a considerable space directly in front of the boat is illuminated, and the occupants of the boat are rendered invisible. The hunter in the stern paddles noiselessly toward the sound of splashing water, caused by the deer, which stands with head erect, knee-deep among the lily-pads or leaves, gazing intently at the fast-approaching light, the reflection of which sparkles upon the water, and tinges the floating leaves with gold. The hunter seated in the bow, with his rifle in readiness, is frequently brought within twenty or thirty yards of the deer. It is almost unnecessary to say that the following description of an illustration, "Floating for Deer," published in *Harper's Weekly* in 1868, is from the pen of the artist. It will enhance the interest in this excellent plate.

Max is Maximo Treado, a well-known hunter in the Adirondack Mountains.

"Some time after nightfall, we lit the two candles in the jack and left the shanty, taking the trail for the lake, a few rods distant. Finding the light skiff we quickly blew out the candles, and set the jack-staff in its position in the bow. Max took his usual place in the stern. Shoving off, I located in the forward seat, with face toward the bow. Now all was quiet. Presently a slight rustle against the side of the boat, as she was urged with noiseless paddle among and through the broad lily leaves that girdle the shore. Some moments elapsed, during which time I had made some astronomical observations, and Max had made a considerable distance with our little craft; now we were only floating, for the paddle, though still in the water, was motionless. It is almost indescribable—this stillness, which was only broken by the occasional splash of a trout jumping for a miller, or the hoot of an owl far up the mountain-side. Splash! splash! far down by the marsh at the lower end of the lake. I stop my musing. Max's paddle is moving silently as ever, but each push is stronger. Splash! splash! again. The paddle-stroke is stronger, but no noise.

I feel for my matches and the rough pebble that is to be used for lighting them. The paddle-stroke now is longer and slower. The boat is being headed directly toward the spot from which the occasional sound of the splashes seems to come. Again the paddle is still; match and pebble are ready. I am only awaiting Max's signal—a slight jerk of the boat. The match is lit, and hidden in the hands until it burns freely; now up to the candles, which are lit in an instant, and the jack is turned fair to the front. The paddle is already sending the boat forward. Max is no longer guided by the splash; two bright sparks of light glow through the darkness in front of us; these are the eyes of the deer. In a moment more there is a light spot discernible. Gradually this takes shape. The boat is just moving; my rifle is slung forward and cocked; now we are within fifty yards of a handsome buck. The motion of the boat has ceased. The slight jerk that comes from Max is answered by a stream of fire which flames from the long, black rifle-barrel; this for a single instant lights up the scene. The crack of the rifle echoes and re-echoes across the lake and amid the forest-clad hills. 'Only jumpt twice,' quoth Max. 'Bustin' about over the plains after buffaler an' the like aint took none of the shoot off you, that's sure. The deer that was, venison that be, will now take a ride on the lake,' remarked Max, as we proceeded to haul the dead deer into the boat, and shove off for the shanty, on the way to which we laughed over the scenes that we had both witnessed while paddling green ones up to deer. 'Many's the buck-shot-gun I've seen emptied by fellers close up to the wild cattle that climbs over these mountains without doing worse than getting up a scare for them,' said Max, as his now noisy paddle splashed and splashed again.''

THE CRANES' WALK 'ROUND.

The sand-hill crane *(Grus Canadensis)* is familiar to the people of the Western States, who do not hesitate to serve up his craneship as they would a turkey, and pronounce the roast delicious. The uninitiated sometimes show a squeamish reflection on this point. The design represents a flock of cranes dancing and going through their usual antics at sunset. General Custer has told how he has lain prone on the buffalo grass and watched the cranes dance. It is a "walk 'round." An old patriarch stands in the center and the flock walk around in a circle, flopping their wings and performing the strangest gyrations. The drawing and motion of each particular bird give to the composition interest which is enhanced by the rich coloring of quaint design.

"ON THE PLAINS AT NIGHT."

This design has only a pictorial significance. It is from a sketch made by the artist while with General Custer, and it is from his note-book that the following description is taken: "The buffalo are heading away from the fire and are making for the river for safety. The buttes are on the other side, and the river itself glowed with reflected light, the moon struggling through the clouds of smoke, giving to the whole scene one of the most weird effects imaginable. The wolves that night were, if possible, more noisy than ever. The coyotes were our picket guard about the bivouac." It would seem impossible for the artist to devise a more difficult combination of color and general effect than that presented in this magnificent plate. The reproduction upon porcelain involved difficulties that experts alone will comprehend or appreciate, though all admirers of ceramics will enjoy the result obtained.

THE GAME PLATTER.

The game plate is in form of a coupe or plaque, less in size than the dinner plate, but equally serviceable for decoration. The treatment is intentionally less massive than the dinner series, and the designs, both in composition and color, are of a different character than those which decorate the dinner series. They, however, maintain the interesting features which will be noted throughout the entire service.

GAME.—THE CANVAS-BACK DUCK.

(Fuligula vallisneria.)

The delicacy of the flavor that gives the canvas-back duck preference for the table is due to its favorite food, the wild celery of the Chesapeake Bay and its estuaries, in the State of Maryland. The canvas-back, notably the choicest American sea duck, is, until after its autumnal arrival at these feeding-grounds, inferior to ducks which are to be found in its company in the waters of Long Island and New Jersey.

The canvas-back is a strong diver, brings up celery roots from a considerable depth, rising to the surface of the water to eat the choice morsel which it must frequently defend from ducks less expert as divers.

The feeding-ground is limited in extent, and good ducking-points along the shore are in great request by gentlemen, who organize clubs and construct comfortable houses in the vicinity, and arrange "blinds" or screens of branches and sedge along the shore.

The canvas-back is bold, and easily decoyed within gun-shot of the sportsman concealed behind these blinds, ingenious devices being resorted to for this purpose. Wing-shooting only is deemed sportsman-like. The rapid flight of the duck and heavy coat of feathers upon its breast, which is almost shot-proof, make canvas-back shooting difficult for novices. The duck derives its name from the color of the feathers upon its back.

The cranberry *(O. palustris)* found in European countries is inferior to the American fruit of the same name, which will explain the partiality of foreigners for the cranberry *(Oxycoccus macrocarpus)* brought from the United States, to which country it is indigenous, and where it was used by the Indians to heal the wounds inflicted by poisoned arrows. The fruit is believed to possess valuable medicinal qualities, and is acceptable upon the table.

It is introduced with the canvas-back duck, not only as a point of color in design, but to locate the scene in a State adjacent to the feeding-grounds of the duck.

RAIL. "SORA."

(Ortygometra Carolina.)

Numerous representatives of the rail family are distributed throughout the temperate zone of the world. One of the largest of the species, the sora, is peculiar to the United States; and the marshes of the Delaware river are noted shooting-grounds during the autumn months. Flat-bottomed boats are used by the sportsmen, and the long pole, by means of which the boat is propelled, is also serviceable for beating the sedge to dislodge the birds. The eggs of the sora are considered a delicacy, and are gathered in large numbers by persons residing in the vicinity of the breeding-grounds. The sora is one of the most esteemed of American game birds.

PTARMIGAN'S BATH.

(Lagopus albus.)

The ptarmigan is found in the Rocky Mountains, also in some of the British possessions.

The American bird, of which there are several varieties, differs materially from the European, being without the collar of the Norway bird. Its plumage in the winter is perfectly white, but during the summer months becomes mottled reddish brown, tinged with black.

The bird is enjoying a bath. Overhanging him is a budding sprig of a pine-tree.

RUFFED GROUSE.

(Bonasa umbellus.)

Known by various names. In Virginia, Maryland and Pennsylvania it is the pheasant. Its flesh is white and very palatable. It is one of the choicest of American game birds. During the spring months the cock bird makes a peculiar noise known as drumming. This sound can be heard at a considerable distance, and is produced by beating the wings rapidly against his inflated crop. During the mating season the cock birds fight deadly battles, and when so engaged may be frequently captured with the hand.

Some authorities state that the true partridge does not occur in America, although the name is given indiscriminately to quail, ruffed and spruce grouse.

The wintergreen berry, which is a favorite food of this grouse, is introduced, together with stems of the ferns, that are intended to indicate the season of the year; this peculiar formation of the fern is noticeable in the spring-time.

BOB-WHITE.

(*Ortyx Virginiana.*)

No game is so well known in America as the quail or Bob-White—a name given to the bird on account of its peculiar call. Its flesh is white, and, in the fall of the year, quite juicy. The color of its feathers resembles that of the ruffed grouse. In size it is smaller than the grouse; and the Bob-White of the Northern States is usually larger than that found in the South. These birds do not migrate, and, during severe winters, perish in large numbers when deprived of their food by protracted snow-storms. The design illustrates a cock and a hen quail comfortably sheltered in a depression that has been formed in the snow beneath a pine bough. The wind which produced this retreat has scattered autumn leaves in the foreground.

CALIFORNIA QUAIL

(Lophortyx Californicas)

Is quite different from the Bob-White. The color of its plumage is nearly black, a distinct collar of white feathers surrounds its throat, and a plume composed of two feathers surmounts the head, the plume of the male being considerably larger than that of the female bird.

The design is characteristic of the Golden State, and very rich in color. Grapes and wheat are introduced, and form an acceptable feature in the treatment of this subject.

WILD PIGEON.

The passenger or wild pigeon *(Ectopistes migratorius)* is known throughout North America, where such vast flocks frequent certain localities as to become a scourge. Competent authorities have estimated the number in a single flock to be more than a billion. The color of the bird is very beautiful, and the flesh of the young or squab is much esteemed for the table. This bird is peculiar to North America.

TEAL.

Blue-winged teal *(Querquedula discors)*, a small fresh-water duck, is found throughout the United States; it is particularly abundant in the vicinity of Chicago, where it is highly prized by sportsmen and epicures.

The drawing upon this plate is particularly noticeable for its aerial perspective. The ducks seem to swing through the air toward the foreground, where a little drake teal is watching the approaching flights, evidently disturbed by the intrusion. A hen teal swims near the drake, and a few stalks of sedge-grass complete the design, which will be remarked as one of the simplest in treatment of the entire service.

THE YELLOW-LEGGED SNIPE.

(Totanus melanoleucus.)

One of the many American varieties believed to be unknown in Europe, where many species of snipe are to be met with; in fact, the snipe family is scattered throughout the world, and embraces more species than any other representative of feathered game.

The design is effective; the bird is in full flight along the sea-shore.

RICE OR REED BIRD.

The rice *(Dolichonyx oryzivoras)* bird of the South, the reed bird of the Middle States, and the bobolink of the North, are the names by which this bird is known in America. His joyous note is heard during the early months of summer in the apple orchards of New England. The male bird is then in full color, and his mate is in her dress of quiet brown. Later in the season the male bird's coat becomes changed to nearly the same color as that of the female, and in great flocks they visit the vicinity of the Delaware, tarrying for a short time on their way to the southern rice fields, where they are regarded as a scourge, and become so fat that their bodies are like a lump of butter, and, when shot, sometimes burst on falling to the ground.

THE WOODCOCK,

Which is well known in Europe *(Scolopax rusticola)*, where it is prized as a game bird, is larger than the American species *(Philohela minor)*, and differs from it in many respects. The decoration of this plate gives an interesting picture of two young birds on the border of a marsh. One is vainly trying to capture a May-fly that is just beyond its reach, and the other is dozing in the sunshine. A prominent feature of the picture is the Indian pipe, a marsh plant, which is graceful in form and delicate in color, and is a lighter shade of pink than the apple blossom.

THE PRAIRIE-HEN,

(Cupidonia cupido)

In full flight, to escape one of those terrible fires of the western prairies, is a striking subject that will be interesting to the casual observer; and to those persons conversant with the history of this bird this drawing will have a significance which will hardly escape attention, for the bird, which is really the "pinnated grouse," was once plentiful (as was the bison) in some of the northern Atlantic States, where it was known as the "heath hen." Its western movement was coincident with that of the Indian. A few years since, the prairie-hen was abundant in Illinois, where the Prince of Wales enjoyed a few days' shooting. This is not the case to-day. The plains of Kansas, where until a few years since the bird was quite unknown, abound with this game. Unlike the ruffed grouse, it has dark meat, and is a larger bird, and more clumsy in form as well as in movement.

THE FRUIT PLATE.

Modeled from the leaf of the American wild apple. The artist refers to the early history of the apple in the Garden of Eden, and also to the fact that the apple may be regarded as the best known and most generally used fruit of the temperate zone.

This plate is very beautiful and most convenient for use. The exquisite modeling of the form gives to it an art value which will afford great pleasure to all lovers of the beautiful. The twelve designs of the series are appropriately drawn to decorate the frame that the outline of the leaf form presents.

THE CHINCAPIN.

(Castanea pumila.)

A small nut of the chestnut species. The tree, if such it can be designated, seldom attains a height of more than twenty-five feet; the bur contains a single nut, that has a delicate flavor. It is more distinctly American than the chestnut, a species of which tree is peculiar to America. The European variety of chestnut is also known in the United States, as it was introduced into Virginia by Thomas Jefferson nearly a century ago.

PECAN.

(Carya olivæformis.)

It is from the state of Texas that the chief supply of the pecan nut is obtained. Thousands of bushels are annually shipped to Europe, where it is more appreciated than in the United States. The tree is known as far north as Pennsylvania, but there only by cultivation. The Texas red or fox squirrel *(Sciurus ludovicianus),* which is introduced in the design, gives additional interest to the subject which decorates this plate.

PAPAW.

(Uvaria triloba.)

The papaw somewhat resembles in form the fig banana, but differs from it in size, and contains large seeds. It is known throughout many States, but flourishes best in the alluvial soil in the vicinity of western rivers. The purple blossom is one of the most beautiful of the American flora. The color of the fruit, when ripe, is yellow tinged with brown. The fruit is sweet in flavor, and appreciated for its healthful properties. A variety of papaw *(Carica papaya)* known in South America has peculiar value: the juice or sap from the tree, or a decoction made from the leaves, will, if placed in water, render tough meat immersed therein tender, and the flesh of animals fed on the fruit or leaves becomes noticeably improved.

LOCUST.

The locust-tree *(Robinia pseudacacia)* was sent to Europe in the seventeenth century, during the reign of Henry IV. of France, and received the name of Robinia, in honor of the person who introduced it. The tree, although of rapid growth, produces timber of great durability.

The picture shows a cluster of locust blossoms, the perfume of which attracts the bees and June-bugs. An apple orchard in full bloom reflects itself in the waters of the clear stream, on the banks of which it is located.

THE MOCKING-BIRD.

(Mimus polyglottus.)

The Spanish moss, that drapes so gracefully the gnarled limbs of the live-oaks in the southern States, is, to the close observer of nature, indicative of the haunt of that remarkable songster, the mocking-bird, and the picture which decorates the plate was suggested by the fact. " The Evening Song" would seem to be an appropriate title for this design.

MAPLE SUGAR,

So well known and appreciated in the United States, is made from the sap of the rock or sugar maple *(Acer saccharinum)*.   The design shows a sugar camp in the woods.   In the foreground is a maple-tree, into which a spout has been introduced, and the sap trough that is to receive the sweet water, which flows drop by drop from the wounded tree.   The sap is reduced to the consistency of thick syrup by boiling it several hours in a cauldron, which is suspended over a great log fire, near the shanty that affords the sugar-makers shelter, and protects them from the driving snow-storms, that accelerate rather than retard the flow of the sap.

Two peculiarly American festivities suggest themselves here— the " corn-husking bee " of the autumn and the " sugaring off " at early spring-time.   When the season of sugar-making is nearly at an end, the young people assemble at the camp ; when the boiling sap has been reduced nearly to the granulating point, it is thrown in small quantities over the surface of the clean snow, and immediately candies ; then commences the feast, which usually ends with a dance.

More than thirty million pounds of maple sugar is annually produced in the United States.

THE CONCORD GRAPE.

The grapes indigenous to the United States, although the vines were hardy, did not produce acceptable table fruit. The Scuppernong of North Carolina, and the wild fox grape, were the chief native vines. Other varieties have been produced by cultivation. The Concord grape, discovered in 1854, by Mr. Bull, of Concord, Massachusetts, was not at first appreciated in the Eastern States, but quickly accepted in the West. It is to-day the choice table grape of the States east of the Rocky Mountains, and five or six million gallons of wine are annually made from it.

A green-coated Katy-did *(Platyphyllum concavum)*, whose nocturnal strain is so familiar during the autumn, has located itself upon the stem of the bunch of purple grapes,—"To sing, so the farmers say, of early frosts not far away."

HUCKLEBERRY.

(*Vaccinium Pennsylvanicum.*)

Huckleberry-picking in the United States furnishes employment to many hundreds of persons, who gather thousands of bushels from mountain-sides and wild pasture lands, where camps are sometimes made by the pickers. Women and children roam over the mountains in search of the finest fruit. There is another expert huckleberry-picker, that carries no pail and eats as he culls. This is the common black bear, whose fondness for sweet food is noted in the "Bee Tree," one of the designs of the dinner series.

The scene is a rough mountain-side; an overturned tin pail, from which the berries are scattered. The cover of the pail, the picking-cup and a well-worn palm-leaf hat seem to have been abandoned by the owner. The reason for this is explained by the presence of a trio of bears—an old one, keeping watch, and two cubs or young bears, enjoying a feast upon berries, the picking of which has occasioned them no trouble. Huckleberry bushes and a stalk of the wild blackberry, relieved by a sunset sky, complete the picture.

A noted American jurist remarked, when he saw the drawing illustrating huckleberry-picking: "That design may have fun in it for you, Mr. Artist, but when a boy I abandoned my huckleberries under similar circumstances, and did not enjoy the situation."

The huckleberry is common to many States, and, while kindred to European varieties, is quite distinct and a far more palatable and valuable fruit.

THE CEDAR BIRD, OR CHERRY BIRD AND PERSIMMON.

(Ampelis cedrorum.)

Known throughout many States of the Union. Its fondness for fruit, and the rapidity with which flocks of the birds deplete the trees, render the cedar bird an object of distrust on the part of the fruit-grower, who usually refuses to believe that the insects destroyed by the birds more than recompense the loss of fruit.

The Persimmon *(Diospyros Virginiana)* is well known throughout the Middle and Southern States. Its fruit is the size of a large plum, but it is not edible until a strong frost has occurred, when it must be quickly gathered to secure it from the birds and tree-climbing animals, like the raccoon and opossum. The difficulty of transporting the ripe persimmon will account for its rare appearance where fruit is offered for sale. It is one of the few fruits which may not be gathered before it is perfectly ripe. One bite of an unripe persimmon would suffice to attest this fact.

OHIO GOLDEN-ROD.

(Solidago Ohioensis.)

The swallow is introduced with the Ohio golden-rod as indicative of home. The name swallow is applied to so many birds having the same characteristics, and so many species occur throughout the world, that it is difficult to distinguish the difference between the American bird and that so well known in European countries. The bird is known throughout the American continent, but it does not remain in the northern States during the winter months. The Ohio golden-rod is the most beautiful of the wild plants of this family. This design is intended as a compliment to the wife of President Hayes.

BALTIMORE ORIOLE.

The Virginia creeper *(Ampelopsis quinquefolia)* and Baltimore oriole are peculiar to the United States. Other names are applied to the vine. In some States it is called woodbine, in others the American ivy. It is of rapid growth, the foliage is dense, and its leaf-forms very beautiful. The autumnal tints of the leaves vie with those of the maple in brilliancy.

The Baltimore oriole *(Icterus Baltimore)* is greatly admired for its song and beautiful plumage. The bird has various names, one of which, the " hang-bird," it derives from the peculiar construction of its nest. It is also known as the " fire-bird " and " golden robin." The range of the oriole extends from South America to the British Provinces. They are migratory, spending the summer months in the North, returning to the South for the winter.

THE STUDIO.

The studio selected by "our artist" was novel, as the picture of it which decorates one of the fruit plates will show. It was located on the sea-beach at Asbury Park, a quiet resort six miles below Long Branch, New Jersey, where General Grant makes his summer home.

In this diminutive atélier, from May to October, the original designs for the President's set were made. The studio proper was composed of three small dressing-rooms thrown into one; but the collection of birds, animals, fish, plants and other objects, from which the artist made his drawings, grew gradually to such proportions that he required no less than six of the adjoining dressing-rooms. In one, suspended by numerous cords, hung a great fish-hawk (for the possession of which he was liable to a fine of twenty-five dollars). A raccoon occupied a separate apartment. In a tank of water, in another dressing-room, swam fish of various kinds, which fishermen frequently brought. A green turtle enjoyed a bed of sea-weed in the same apartment. Fish were here that had been sent from the Gulf of Mexico. Objects in the collection were from States many hundred miles distant.

Mr. C. C. Buel, of the editorial staff of the *New-York Tribune*, gives this interesting account of the studio :

"First take a peep into the studio. When Mr. Davis came down here for recuperation and work, his eye settled on a somewhat isolated bathing-house containing several dressing-rooms. Mr. Bradley, the founder of Asbury Park, gave him plenary powers. He appropriated three of the dressing-rooms on the end facing the sea, knocked out the partitions, cut out a large space for a window, affording a view of the ocean, and imported his artist's kit. The corner from which he draws his inspiration contains a box covered with a gorgeous American Indian woven blanket, of great value. Here the artist sits in his working hours, with a water-color board on his knee, his colors at his hand, and the ever-changing sea before his eye. Sea-tints and sea-scenes enter largely into his designs, for which reason the studio could not be better located. The studio is in the shape of a letter L, and in size about eight by four feet in either arm of the L. In one corner is a basin of water-lilies. In the box is a big frog, which, when there are no visitors, sits on the bench and looks with a quizzical eye at the artist, who once kept him for a model, but now boards him for his company. Unfriendly pins hold beautiful insects and shining bugs to the walls, and a piece of dried fungus makes a delicately tinted background for a gorgeous beetle. Bold water-color drawings and engravings ornament the sides of the nook which contains the artist's throne, and over his head are shelves holding a few pieces of choice Haviland ware. A shelf holds brushes, glasses and other artist's utensils, and at one side are numerous bottles containing colors. Upon a high shelf is a large photograph of the conservatory of the White House, with Mrs. Hayes in the foreground, surrounded by her two youngest children and Mr. Davis's little girl, who makes pies in the sand outside while her father lays in the water-color."

The artist was occasionally mistaken for a bathing-master, and invited to furnish suits and bring pails of water from the ocean. The fishermen were his constant and welcome visitors, for the value of their criticism was appreciated.

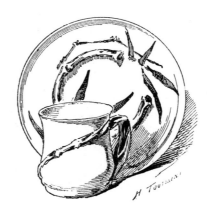

COFFEE CUP.

The form of the after-dinner coffee cup is derived from a joint of the bamboo stalk; a sprout which springs from the eye of a joint serves, successfully, for the handle. The decoration, though simple, is exceedingly rich. The saucer will be an acceptable innovation. In color the cup simulates that of the bamboo.

THE TEA-CUP.

In shape like a Mandarin's hat (inverted), the handle being formed by the stem of a tea-plant, the leaves of which are used as decoration on the exterior of the cup. The interior of the cup is tinted a delicate green, the saucer and outside of the cup being further enriched with dead gold. All the colors are applied under the glaze. The saucer of the tea-cup is provided with a device similar to that of the coffee.

INDEPENDENT BUTTER PLATE

Is a close copy of the leaf of the white water-lily *(Nymphœa odorata)*, a flower highly prized for its delicate perfume. The surface of the leaf is a tender green color; the curled stem is arranged as a base. Drops of water are represented on the leaf.

We append the following letter from Mr. Davis:

ASBURY PARK, N. J., October 2d, 1879.

MY DEAR MR. HAVILAND:

These designs complete the different series for the state dinner service for the Executive Mansion, at Washington, and with the drawings you will find the usual notes for the description of the subject.

I believe that you appreciate fully my intention to make the set thoroughly American in subject, and to represent the flora and fauna peculiar to nearly every State; and while I have drawn largely from my own sketch-books, I wish to tell you of the cordial interest manifested by gentlemen who, from education and position, could furnish information and specimens from which to study.

To Prof. Spencer F. Baird, of the Smithsonian Institute, Gen. William G. Le Duc, Commissioner of Agriculture, Mr. Eugene Blackford, Fish Commissioner of New-York, Hon. Jacob R. Shotwell, Fish Commissioner in New Jersey, and Mr. Jas. A. Bradley, of this place, I am particularly indebted. Friends, who are citizens of far-off States, forwarded specimens of plants, etc., which were peculiar to their locality. Even the fishermen and farmers in the vicinity have been so interested in the work that their contributions of material have at times overcrowded my diminutive studio.

As regards the general effect of the various series, you, with all the drawings, can judge better than I can. My original intention was a simple oyster plate, that should be rich and quite different from any now in use. The soup series to be novel, both as regards form of plate and design, and in color strong. The fish subjects to be treated with more delicacy and a suitable form for the plate. The dinner series the strongest in color of the whole service. Game to comprise a collection of our birds, and the dessert series, such fruit, nuts and other subjects as would be decorative for a plate of some pleasing shape. Your excellent modelers have interpreted my drawings for form admirably, and to all of the artists engaged upon the work please say that they have the hearty thanks of yours,

THEO. R. DAVIS.

EXECUTIVE MANSION

Mr Theodore R Davis
  Asbury Park
    New Jersey

EXECUTIVE MANSION.
WASHINGTON.

Mr Theo R Davis
    Dear Sir

        My absence
from home when the beautiful
porcelain Set arrived is my
apology for the delay in sending
you my thanks. The exquisite
State dinner service executed
by Haviland & Co from original
designs by you is universally
admired by all competent judges
of such works of art who have
seen it. It is a delight to
study the beautiful forms and
paintings. One almost feels
as if such ceramic Art
should be used for no other
purpose except to gratify the
eye. I congratulate you
on the accomplishment of the task
which you so kindly imposed upon
yourself in the production of the
beautiful designs which have added
fresh laurels to American Art.
With best wishes for yourself and my
little friend.   Truly
Aug 2nd 1880,   Truly RB Hayes.

*Appendix II
Guide to marks on china
of the administration
of Rutherford B. Hayes*

a

Eagle under rim

b

FABRIQUE PAR
HAVILAND & C?
d'après les dessins
DE
(signature)

b¹

FABRIQUE PAR
HAVILAND & C?
d'après les dessins
DE
THEODORE R. DAVIS (initial "D.")

c

LIMOGES
HAVILAND & C?
(monogram)

c¹

DESIGN PATENTED
AUGUST 10 ᵀᴴ 1880
Nº 11935

d

$\underline{\underline{\text{H \& C?}}}$

d¹

$\dfrac{\text{H \& C?}}{\text{L}}$

The original White House order of 1879 and the portions of the service delivered in December 1880 were marked as shown in *a, b, c,* and either *d* or *d¹*.

Pieces of the Hayes design ordered during the Arthur and Cleveland administrations were marked as illustrated in *a, b, c¹* and either *d* or *d¹*.

In order to ascertain if pieces marked as shown in *c¹* could ever have been in the White House, it is necessary to check the list of pieces actually ordered in those administrations and then consider the provenance of the piece being considered.

There were only two dinner platters ordered by the White House and two each of the platters for game, fish, and dessert. All of these were marked as shown in *a, b, c,* and *d*. These are all accounted for today with the exception of one fish platter which was missing by the time of the itemized inventory taken in 1904.

Appendix III
Guide to marks on
china of the administration
of Benjamin Harrison

a

T.V.
[across front of bell]
FRANCE
DÉCORÉ POUR
M.W. BEVERIDGE
WASHINGTON, D.C.

b

HARRISON 1892

c

T & V
FRANCE

d

LIMOGES
FRANCE

e

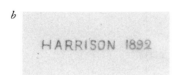

T & V
LIMOGES
FRANCE

f

DÉCORÉ
PAR
LIMOGES
T.V.
[across front of bell]
POUR
Dulin, Martin Co.
WASHINGTON

From pieces of the Benjamin Harrison china which have survived in the White House collection, it can be conjectured that the original order consisted of 9½-inch dinner plates, 9-inch soup plates with the wide blue border, 8½-inch breakfast plates, and 7¼-inch tea plates with the narrow borders of blue and white. These pieces were marked as illustrated in *a, b,* and *c.*

There are also 8½-inch plates in the collection which have a wide blue border and also have the marks illustrated in *a, b,* and *c.* These are probably the Harrison design ordered early in the McKinley administration. The marks shown in *a, b,* and *d* on the 8½-inch plates with the wide blue border and the 8½-inch plates with the double border would have been ordered later in the McKinley administration.

The china of this same design made for the Dulin, Martin Company which this writer has examined bear the marks shown in *f, d,* and *b.*

The marks illustrated in *a, b,* and *f* are in gilt; those in *c, d,* and *e* are in green.

98. China of the same design as that purchased for the White House which bears this mark seems to have been produced for sale to the general public as souvenirs, possibly as early as 1876.

99. There is also reason to doubt the authenticity of the Polk dessert plates with the flat rim which are found occasionally. These may have been produced for sale to the general public in the late nineteenth century or they may have been painted to use with the plates of the original service.

100. Note that there was no order for teacups and saucers of the Benjamin Harrison china, so they must have been made for sale as souvenirs.

101. This design of a seafood salad plate was made by
Theodore Davis *after* the Hayes china was delivered
to the White House. Plates of this kind were never
used in the White House; in fact, three of them were
returned by the White House because they did not
match the ones in the state service. The only
platter missing from the Hayes state service is a fish
platter. It was probably broken, but if it was sold at
one of the auction sales it should be damaged and
have a mark as is shown in either *a, b, c,* or *d* in Appendix II.

Acknowledgments

The people who have contributed to this book are almost too numerous to list. I mention only the major contributors with the hope that my thanks to them will be accepted by all who have contributed to my knowledge and enthusiasm for this subject.

Special acknowledgment is made to my husband, Frank E. Klapthor, who willingly has shared with me his professional knowledge of the decorative arts and to our children who have lived in the shadow of this manuscript for the last two years. To my mother and my father, Mr. and Mrs. Paul D. Brown, I owe an appreciation for American history that brought this manuscript into being. Perhaps the greatest contribution of my family has been their encouragement to keep at the task that at times seemed beyond endurance.

I also wish to express my gratitude to my friend Robert J. McNeil, Jr., and The Barra Foundation, Inc., who assisted this publication materially with funds for a research assistant during my year of sabbatical and with assistance to the Smithsonian Institution Press for the publication of this book.

The administration of the National Museum of History and Technology, especially Silvio A. Bedini, the deputy director, has been most cooperative during the production of this book.

My research assistant and Barra Foundation Fellow, Mrs. Edith P. Mayo, provided intelligent and dedicated assistance in locating many of the details to be found in this text. I wish to especially acknowledge her research on the service of Wedgwood china purchased during the administration of President Theodore Roosevelt.

I am tremendously indebted to Louise Heskett, editor, Smithsonian Institution Press, for her careful editing of this book and for its readability.

When I acknowledge the assistance of those closest to me, I am especially grateful to members of the staff of the Division of Political History—my colleagues Herbert R. Collins, associate curator; my assistant, Miss Barbara Coffee, who assumed most of my personal responsibilities at the National Museum of History and Technology during 1971–1972 when I was on sabbatical leave; to William Costley who has helped in so many ways, especially in taking care of the White House china collection at the Smithsonian Institution; to the secretaries who have cheerfully typed and retyped the manuscript for me, among whom Mrs. Sherrill Berger, Mrs. Marilyn Lee, and the Misses Undine Johnson, Flora Murray, and Wendy Obert deserve special thanks.

I wish to express my gratitude to Rebecca Bean and Alice Reno for assistance in proofreading and indexing this book.

To the readers of my manuscript, I owe a debt of gratitude. Only I am aware of how much they have improved the basic text. My thanks go to Jay Jefferson Miller II, Division of Ceramics and Glass, Smithsonian Institution; Miss Betty Monkman, Office of the Curator of the White House; Mrs. Susan Detwiler, Barra Foundation Fellow; Robert J. McNeil, Jr., of The Barra Foundation, Inc.; Miss Christine Meadows, Mount Vernon Ladies Association for the chapter on Washington china; Watt P. Marchman, for the chapter on the Hayes china; and James Ketchum for the chapter on the Lyndon B. Johnson china.

Clement E. Conger and the staff of the Office of the Curator of the White House, especially Miss Betty Monkman, have been unfailingly courteous and generous in sharing with me information from the files they maintain and about the china which has survived in the White House. I must admit that if that office had been in existence fifteen years ago when I started on this project, there would have been no reason for me to assume responsibility for research on White House furnishings. I only hope that their task will be made easier as the result of our cooperation.

Members of the White House staff, beginning in the Eisenhower administration with Mrs.

Mary Jane McCaffree, and which have included James West, William Elder, James Ketchum, and Rex Scouten, have all been generous with their assistance.

Special thanks go to Stanley McClure of the National Capital Parks, National Park Service, whose pioneer work in the White House records in the National Archives gave me a trail to follow.

Mrs. Dorothy Waterhouse and Stanley Wohl, two collectors of White House china who have graciously shared their knowledge with me, also deserve special recognition.

Others especially interested and knowledgeable about White House china who have helped are the following.

The Adams Papers editorial staff, Massachusetts Historical Society, Boston, Massachusetts

James Arnold, director, The Ladies Hermitage Association, Hermitage, Tennessee

Mrs. William T. Bartlett, Greensville, Tennessee

James A. Bear, Jr., curator, Thomas Jefferson Memorial Foundation, Charlottesville, Virginia

William A. Billington, museum curator, Josiah Wedgwood and Sons, Ltd., England

Mrs. Caroline H. Bivins and William Moore, Greensboro, North Carolina

Mrs. Julie Corallo, Los Angeles, California

Charles Dorman, Independence Hall, National Historic Site, Philadelphia, Pennsylvania

Mrs. Elton Dulin

Miss Barbara Edgerton, Tiffany and Company, New York City

Mrs. Robert Fletcher, Leesburg, Virginia

Douglas Green, research assistant, The Ladies Hermitage Association, Nashville, Tennessee

Richard Hagen, Pensacola, Florida

Mrs. Wilhelmina Harris, director, The Adams Mansion National Historic Site, Quincy, Massachusetts

Richard P. Hartung, Rocky County Historical Society, Janesville, Wisconsin

Frederick Haviland, vice president, Haviland and Company, Inc., New York City

Lawrence G. Hoes and The Board of Trustees of the James Monroe Museum and Memorial Library, Fredericksburg, Virginia

Miss Conover Hunt, Association for the Preservation of Virginia Antiquities, Richmond, Virginia

Mrs. Ernestine C. Jackson

Dwight Lanmon, curator of European glass, The Corning Museum of Glass, Corning, New York

Watt P. Marchman, director, The Rutherford B. Hayes Library, Fremont, Ohio

Miss Christine Meadows, curator, Mount Vernon Ladies Association, Mount Vernon, Virginia

James F. Mitchell

The New-York Historical Society, James J. Hestin, director

Mr. and Mrs. C. E. Parmelee, Upper Montclair, New Jersey

James K. Polk Memorial, Columbia, Tennessee

Dr. Paul S. Putzki

Mrs. Helen S. T. Reed, collections division, Virginia Museum of Fine Arts, Richmond

Miss Joan Severa, curator of decorative arts, The State Historical Society of Wisconsin

Cecil B. Wall, director, Mount Vernon Ladies Association, Mount Vernon, Virginia

Wellstood White

Index